The Greatest Book of the BIGGEST and Best

Brian Williams

TED SMART

Author
Brian Williams

Designed, Edited and Project Managed by
Starry Dog Books

Editor
Belinda Gallagher

Assistant Editor
Mark Darling

Artwork Commissioning
Lesley Cartlidge

Indexer
Janet De Saulles

Colour Reproduction
DPI Colour, Saffron Walden, Essex

Art Director
Clare Sleven

Editorial Director
Paula Borton

This edition produced for
The Book People Ltd, Hall Wood Avenue,
Haydock, St Helens
WA11 9UL

Produced by Miles Kelly Publishing Ltd
Bardfield Centre, Great Bardfield, Essex CM7 4SL

24681097531

A British Library Cataloguing-in-Publication Data.
A catalogue record for this book is available from the British Library

ISBN 1-902947-81-9

Printed in China

www.mileskelly.net
info@mileskelly.net

The Greatest
Book of the
BIGGEST
and Best

CONTENTS

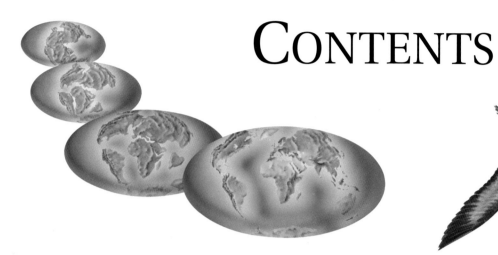

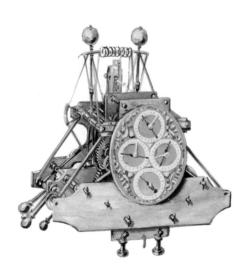

Sport and Entertainment

The Way We Live

Science and Technology

The Natural World

Wonders of the World

The Greatest Book of the Biggest and Best

Planet Earth

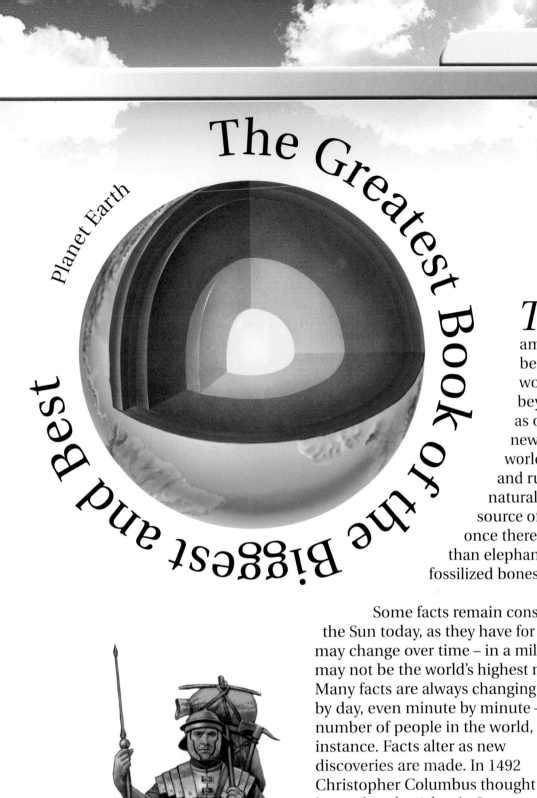

*T*he *Greatest Book of the Biggest and Best* is full of amazing facts and mind-bending marvels about our world, the Universe and beyond. Many facts change, as old records are broken and new ones are set. The human world alters too, as countries and rulers come and go. The natural world has always been a source of wonder – we know that once there were dinosaurs bigger than elephants, but now only their fossilized bones remain.

Some facts remain constant – the planets orbit the Sun today, as they have for billions of years. Others may change over time – in a million years Mount Everest may not be the world's highest mountain. Many facts are always changing, day by day, even minute by minute – the number of people in the world, for instance. Facts alter as new discoveries are made. In 1492 Christopher Columbus thought he knew that the Atlantic Ocean was quite narrow, and that Asia was on the other side. Two mistakes, which he never quite accepted, in spite of sailing across the ocean four times!

In this book you can discover a mind-blowing world of information. There are big, serious facts – for reference – and for fun, a number of less serious ones too. Packed into these pages are some of the biggest and best, oddest and strangest, smallest and funniest facts around!

History

Universe

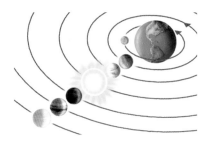

UNIVERSE

The Universe is a pretty difficult subject to comprehend. It is so vast that scientists simply do not know its full extent. The easiest way to describe it is as everything that exists – from the Earth to the Solar System and whatever lies beyond.

Here are thousands of mind-boggling Universe facts that will really fry your brain. For instance, if the Sun was reduced to the size of a football pitch, the Earth would be the size of a pea. And did you know that Jupiter is the biggest planet? In fact Jupiter is so big, that 1,000 Earths would fit inside it.

Explore the biggest and best facts of the *Universe* and unravel some totally cosmic statistics. There are the big, serious facts – for reference – and less serious ones, too, for fun. These pages are packed with some of the biggest and best, oddest and strangest, smallest and funniest, facts around!

BIGGER AND BIGGER

The Universe is the biggest thing there is. Scientists think that it began with an incredible Big Bang – an unimaginably enormous explosion of energy – between 12 and 15 billion years ago. Light from the edge of the Universe takes this long to reach us on Earth. The explosion sent matter flying through space. From this matter the galaxies were formed. Galaxies are great whirling masses of stars. One of those billions of stars is our Sun.

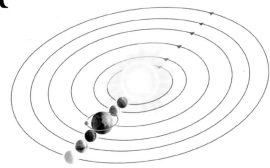

▲ *In 1543 Nicolaus Copernicus proposed a revolutionary theory – that Earth and other planets move around the Sun. Before this people had believed that the Sun and planets moved around the stationary Earth.*

▶ *When the Big Bang happened, it released all the energy in the Universe. As the energy spread out across space, galaxies were formed. The galaxies are still speeding away from each other as the Universe expands.*

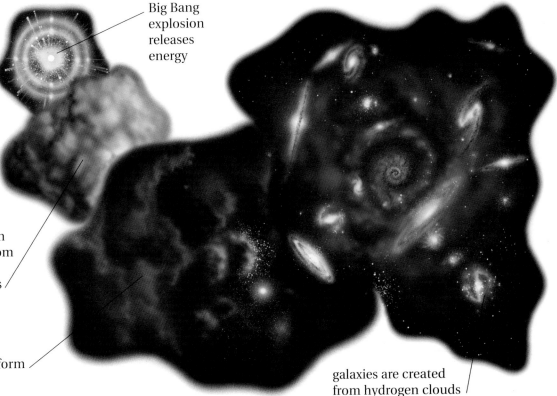

Big Bang explosion releases energy

atoms of hydrogen form as energy from the Big Bang expands outwards

over millions of years massive hydrogen clouds form

galaxies are created from hydrogen clouds

GALAXIES

● The Universe is made up of many millions of galaxies with empty space between them.

● Some galaxies contain as many as 100 billion stars.

● A new star is born in the Milky Way about every 18 days.

▶▶	LIGHT TAKES THIS LONG TO REACH EARTH	
	ORIGIN	**TRAVEL TIME**
1	**From the Moon**	**1.26 seconds**
2	**From the Sun**	**8 minutes, 17 seconds**
3	**From Pluto**	**5 hours, 20 minutes**
4	**From the nearest star**	**4.22 years**
5	**From the nearest galaxy**	**150,000 years**

spiral galaxy

elliptical galaxy

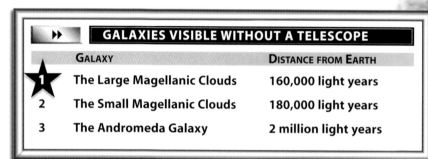

◀ *Some galaxies are elliptical or egg-shaped. Unlike the spiral galaxies, which contain dark, trailing lanes of dust and clouds of gas, elliptical galaxies are huge collections of stars with very little dust or gases. Some elliptical galaxies are much flatter than others when viewed side on.*

▲ *This is a typical spiral galaxy. Shaped like a catherine wheel, its arms form a thin disc that spiral out from a central bulge. Another type of galaxy is the barred spiral galaxy. Its spiral arms curve away from a bar that crosses the central bulge. Both spiral and barred spiral galaxies contain large amounts of gas and dust as well as stars.*

	GALAXIES VISIBLE WITHOUT A TELESCOPE	
	GALAXY	**DISTANCE FROM EARTH**
⭐1	The Large Magellanic Clouds	160,000 light years
2	The Small Magellanic Clouds	180,000 light years
3	The Andromeda Galaxy	2 million light years

◀ *The Milky Way is a spiral galaxy, and our Sun is one star among many millions on one of its arms, known as the Orion arm. The biggest galaxy, which is in the Abell 2029 cluster, is 80 times bigger than the Milky Way.*

▶ *A black hole is all that remains of a collapsed star. You cannot see a black hole. It has such a powerful gravitational pull that not even light can escape from it – so it is invisible. The black hole sucks huge amounts of space matter into a tiny space, making it unbelievably dense – a bit like if Earth was squeezed to the size of a marble.*

IT'S A FACT
Stars give out light. Earth's light comes from the Sun. Nothing travels faster than light. A ray of light travels 300,000 km in one second.

THE BRIGHT STARS

There are millions and millions of galaxies, or star-clusters. Each galaxy contains millions of stars. A star is a blazing hot mass of gas, giving off heat and light. The stars are so far away that their light takes years to reach us. The light from the brightest star in the night sky, Sirius, takes almost nine years to reach Earth. Each star is 'born' from a cloud of gas. It grows bigger and hotter, and finally either cools and fades away or explodes like an enormous firework display.

STARS
- Some giant stars give out 50,000 times as much light as the Sun!
- Red stars are the most common stars, but are fairly dim and hard to spot.
- Neutron stars may be only 15 km across.

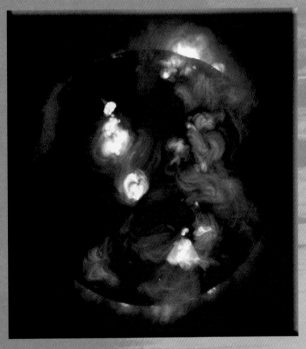

▶ *Our Sun is a star. It is 150 million km from Earth, and is the closest star to us. The next closest star, Proxima Centauri, is 40 million million km away. The distance between stars is measured in 'light years' – the time it takes for light to travel in one year. Proxima Centauri is 4.22 light years away.*

	HOTTEST STARS	
	STAR TYPE	TEMPERATURE
1	Blue	up to 40,000°C
2	Blue-white	11,000°C
3	White	7,500°C
4	Yellow	6,000°C
5	Orange	5,000°C
6	Red	3,500°C

	BRIGHTEST STARS	
	STAR	CONSTELLATION
1	Sirius	Canis Majoris
2	Canopus	Carina
3	Alpha Centauri	Centaurus
4	Arcturus	Bootes
5	Vega	Lyra

▶ *A dramatic way for a star to end its life after shining for millions of years is to explode. This is called a supernova, and is billions of times brighter than the Sun. All that is left is a tiny pulsar, or neutron star.*

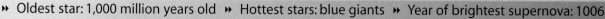
» Oldest star: 1,000 million years old » Hottest stars: blue giants » Year of brightest supernova: 1006

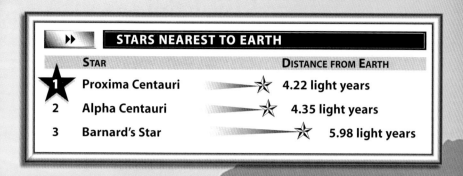

	STARS NEAREST TO EARTH		
STAR			**DISTANCE FROM EARTH**
1	**Proxima Centauri**		**4.22 light years**
2	**Alpha Centauri**		**4.35 light years**
3	**Barnard's Star**		**5.98 light years**

▶ *Stars are being born and they die all the time. Not all die in a supernova explosion. Small stars fade away. But before a small star goes out, it expands like a balloon and becomes an enormous red giant one hundred times bigger than the Sun.*

▶ *A red giant lasts for a few million years. Then the centre of the star begins to shrink and its outer layers are blown away. Finally it becomes a tiny white dwarf like this one, and gradually cools, fades and dies.*

▶ *Thousands of years ago in ancient Greece, astronomers identified patterns in the groups of stars, called constellations. They gave these patterns the names of heroes or animals, such as Ursa Major, the Great Bear. Scientists have since identified 88 constellations altogether.*

Shown here are:
1) Ursa Major
2) Pegasus
3) Hercules
4) Orion
5) Hydra

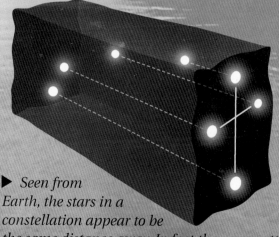

same star pattern. seen side on

arrow indicates view seen from Earth

▶ *Seen from Earth, the stars in a constellation appear to be the same distance away. In fact they are scattered in space. This diagram shows the relative distances of stars in the Southern Cross constellation.*

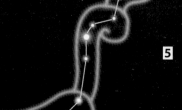

THE FIERY SUN

The Sun is one of more than 100 billion stars in the Milky Way galaxy. With other stars, it moves around the centre of the Milky Way galaxy at enormous speed – about 900,000 km/h. It is about 4.6 billion years old, and probably about halfway through its life. The hottest part of the Sun is its core, where temperatures can reach 15 million °C. The Sun is much bigger than Earth, but it is only a middleweight in star terms. The giant star Betelgeuse is 500 times bigger than the Sun!

A LONG WAY TO THE SUN

● The Sun is about 150 million km from Earth. The distance varies as Earth travels around the Sun.
● A spacecraft travelling at the speed of a jet airliner (about 900 km/h) would take nearly 20 years to get to the Sun.
● A spacecraft travelling at 40,000 km/h – the speed needed to escape the pull of Earth's gravity – would take 5 months to reach the Sun.

▲ *A total solar eclipse is a spectacular sight as the Moon covers the face of the Sun. Light from the Sun streams out around the Moon, and on Earth the sky is made dark by the Moon's shadow.*

▶ *Sunspots are cooler, dark patches on the Sun's surface. They are caused by changes in the magnetic field within the Sun. Sunspots can be 30,000 km across. The biggest group ever seen, in 1947, was ten times that size! Sunspots increase during an 11-year cycle.*

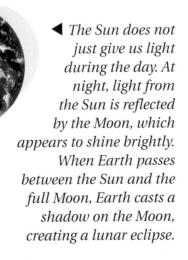

◀ *The Sun does not just give us light during the day. At night, light from the Sun is reflected by the Moon, which appears to shine brightly. When Earth passes between the Sun and the full Moon, Earth casts a shadow on the Moon, creating a lunar eclipse.*

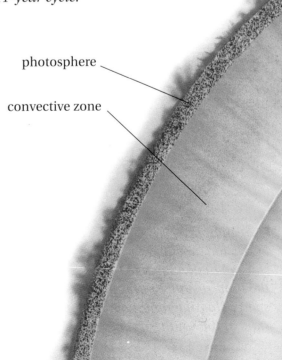

photosphere

convective zone

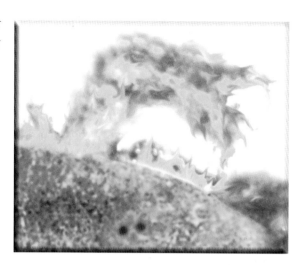
→ Worst year for sunspots: 947 → Most impressive event: total eclipse → Biggest benefit to Earth: makes life possible!

DID YOU KNOW?

All life on Earth depends on energy from the Sun. People in ancient times worshipped the Sun and told stories to explain the rising and setting of the Sun. The Egyptians thought the Sun-god Ra sailed a boat from east to west.

▶ *The Sun sends out long, arching plumes of gas that flare for thousands of kilometres into space. The Sun also gives off strong bursts of radiation that can knock out radio and TV signals and sometimes even power supplies to cities on Earth.*

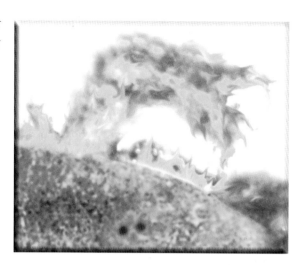

▼ *Earth appears tiny next to the massive Sun. If the Sun were reduced to the size of a football, the relative size of Earth would be no bigger than a pea!*

▼ *The surface of the Sun is called the photosphere. It is about 5,500°C and 300–500 km thick. Beneath lies the turbulent convective zone, at about 1 million °C. Below this active zone is the even hotter radiative zone, at about 2.5 million °C. The core is about 15 million °C.*

core

radiative zone

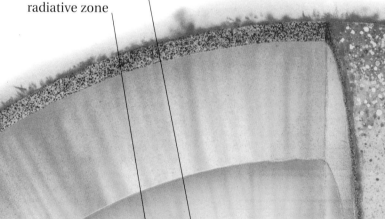

SUN FACTS

● The Sun measures 1,392,500 km across. That is 109 times the diameter of Earth and ten times bigger than Jupiter.

● The Sun is 330,000 times heavier than Earth. Its volume, the amount of matter in it, is roughly 1.3 million times bigger than Earth's.

● The Sun is 400 times farther away from us than the Moon.

OUR SOLAR SYSTEM

After the Sun was formed from a great cloud of gas, lots of matter was left over. This whirled around the new star, in time forming a system of nine planets, which we call the Solar System. The four planets closest to the Sun are small and rocky. The four much larger outer planets are made of liquid gas and ice. The outermost planet, Pluto, is the smallest. There may be another small planet beyond Pluto.

▸▸ PLANET EXTREMES

Hottest	Venus	462°C
Coldest	Pluto	About -235°C
Fastest	Mercury	172,000 km/h
Faintest	Pluto	Visible only by telescope
Densest	Earth	5x water

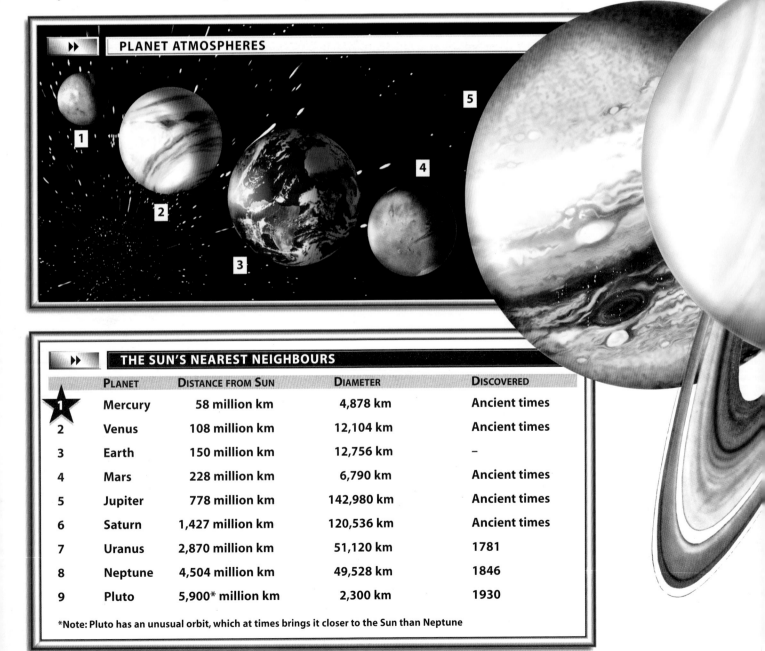

▸▸ PLANET ATMOSPHERES

▸▸ THE SUN'S NEAREST NEIGHBOURS

	PLANET	DISTANCE FROM SUN	DIAMETER	DISCOVERED
★ 1	Mercury	58 million km	4,878 km	Ancient times
2	Venus	108 million km	12,104 km	Ancient times
3	Earth	150 million km	12,756 km	–
4	Mars	228 million km	6,790 km	Ancient times
5	Jupiter	778 million km	142,980 km	Ancient times
6	Saturn	1,427 million km	120,536 km	Ancient times
7	Uranus	2,870 million km	51,120 km	1781
8	Neptune	4,504 million km	49,528 km	1846
9	Pluto	5,900* million km	2,300 km	1930

*Note: Pluto has an unusual orbit, which at times brings it closer to the Sun than Neptune

» Smallest planet: Pluto » Other known solar systems: the star Upsilon Andromedae is circled by three planets

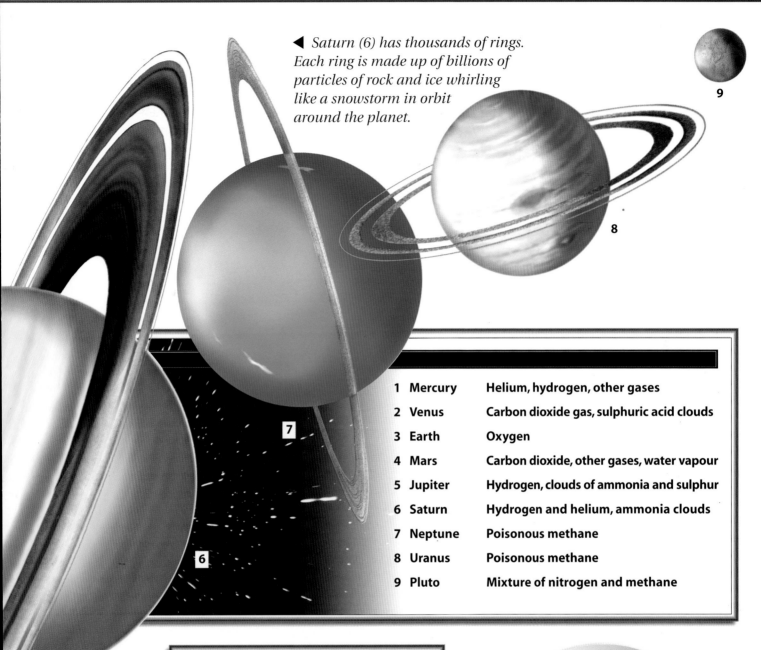

◀ *Saturn (6) has thousands of rings. Each ring is made up of billions of particles of rock and ice whirling like a snowstorm in orbit around the planet.*

1	Mercury	Helium, hydrogen, other gases
2	Venus	Carbon dioxide gas, sulphuric acid clouds
3	Earth	Oxygen
4	Mars	Carbon dioxide, other gases, water vapour
5	Jupiter	Hydrogen, clouds of ammonia and sulphur
6	Saturn	Hydrogen and helium, ammonia clouds
7	Neptune	Poisonous methane
8	Uranus	Poisonous methane
9	Pluto	Mixture of nitrogen and methane

▲ *All the planets are held in their orbits around the Sun by the Sun's gravitational force. Planets also have their own gravity. The bigger the planet, the bigger its gravitational pull. This means that an astronaut on Jupiter would weigh 2.5 times as much as a person on Earth.*

»» ORBIT ROUND THE SUN

	PLANET	YEARS	DAYS
1	Pluto	248	0
2	Neptune	164	298
3	Uranus	84	4
4	Saturn	29	168
5	Jupiter	11	314
6	Mars	0	687
7	Earth	0	365
8	Venus	0	225
9	Mercury	0	88

Note: Years = Earth years, days = Earth days

OTHER SOLAR SYSTEMS?

● The distant star Upsilon Andromedae is 44 light years away from Earth. It has three planets circling it.

● One of Upsilon Andromedae's three planets is four times bigger than Jupiter.

● About 20 planets have been found orbiting other stars. But the Upsilon Andromedae solar system is the only other solar system spotted so far.

EARTH AND ITS NEIGHBOURS

Earth and its three nearest neighbours, Mercury, Venus and Mars, are all rocky planets. All three are smaller than Earth. There are also at least 5,000 known 'minor planets' or asteroids that orbit the Sun between Mars and Jupiter. Most asteroids are very small. The biggest, named Ceres, is only 930 km in diameter. It is unlikely that Earth's neighbouring planets have life on them, but there is evidence that water once flowed on Mars.

▼ Asteroids are huge lumps of rock that orbit between Mars and Jupiter. The biggest is Ceres at 1,000 km in diameter. Astronomers think there may be millions of asteroids in space.

VENUS AND MERCURY

● Although Venus is the brightest of Earth's neighbours, its surface is hidden by clouds.

● Venus is the hottest planet, but Mercury is closer to the Sun.

● Mercury is only slightly bigger than the Moon. In Mercury's sky the Sun looks twice as big as it does from Earth.

▶▶ PLANET STATISTICS

	PLANET	MASS	DIAMETER
★1	Earth	1	1
2	Venus	0.8	0.9
3	Mars	0.1	0.5
4	Mercury	0.05	0.3

Note: Figures are comparisons with Earth. Earth = 1

Planet with biggest canyon: Mars ▸ Brightest neighbouring planet: Venus ▸ Biggest asteroid: Ceres

▲ Asteroids crossing Earth's path hit the surface as meteorites. Thousands of meteorites hit each year, but giants are very rare.

DID YOU KNOW?

The mass (weight) of Earth is about 6 x 21 zeros. Written out it looks like this: 6,000,000,000,000,000,000,000 tonnes. It's quicker to say Earth weighs about 6 sextillion tonnes.

▲ Mountains rise over Venus, where temperatures can reach almost 500°C. Sulphuric acid rains down and the surface pressure is similar in strength to the water pressure on Earth's ocean beds.

◀ Mars is known as the red planet because of its red-brown soil. At 27 km high, its highest mountain, an extinct volcano called Olympus Mons, is three times higher than Mount Everest.

4   2   1   3

GIANT PLANETS

The four biggest planets in the Solar System are the ringed 'gas giants': Jupiter, Saturn, Uranus and Neptune. These are the four planets farthest from the Sun, apart from Pluto. The orbits that they make around the Sun are not perfect circles, but are 'elliptical'. This means that each planet's distance from the Sun varies during one orbit. The best time to see the outer planets is when they are closest to Earth and opposite the Sun.

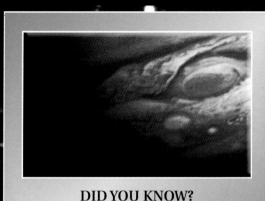

DID YOU KNOW?
The Great Red Spot visible on the surface of Jupiter is a huge storm – a giant gas hurricane as big as two Earths.

Jupiter

Saturn

▲ *Jupiter is a ball of gases, mostly hydrogen and helium. Spinning faster than any other planet, the clouds in its atmosphere are whipped up into vast, swirling storms with winds of up to 500 km/h. Jupiter has the shortest day of all the planets. A day on Jupiter lasts just under 10 hours (9 hours 55 minutes).*

▲ *Saturn is the second biggest gas giant. This planet's rings are one of the most spectacular sights in the Solar System. Measuring 270,000 km from edge to edge, they are made up of millions of whirling blocks of ice. Saturn spins almost as fast as Jupiter, and is colder and even windier, with storm winds ten times faster than a hurricane on Earth.*

▶ *In 1995 the little* Galileo *space probe reached Jupiter on its mission to photograph the planet. The probe was named after Galileo Galilei, who in 1609 was the first person to see Jupiter's moons (he spotted four). After entering Jupiter's atmosphere, the* Galileo *probe survived an hour in the stormy, freezing clouds before it was crushed and vaporized.*

▼ *Uranus is a blue-green world of freezing chemical slush shrouded in clouds of methane gas and tilted on its side. It was discovered in 1781 by William Herschel – the first person in recorded history to find a new planet. In 1986* Voyager *discovered that Uranus had 17 moons in all.*

▼ *Neptune is almost four times larger than Earth. Scientists believe that, like Uranus, it is a sea of liquid methane surrounding a core of rock. The Great Dark Spot on its surface is a huge, rotating storm bigger than Earth. Neptune is 30 times farther than Earth is from the Sun.*

Uranus

Neptune

JUPITER AND THE SUN

● Jupiter is so big that 1,000 Earths would fit inside it.
● The Sun is so much bigger than Jupiter that 900 Jupiters would fit inside the Sun.
● There are stars 2,000 times bigger than the Sun. Mind-boggling!

»	THE FOUR GIANT PLANETS	
	PLANET	**VOLUME**
1	**Jupiter**	1,300
2	**Saturn**	766
3	**Uranus**	63
4	**Neptune**	58

Note: Volumes are compared with Earth. Earth = 1

MOONS

Moons are satellites that are held in orbit around planets. Earth has one satellite, the Moon, which is a lump of rock about as wide as Australia. Earth weighs as much as 81 Moons! An astronaut can jump six times higher on the Moon than on Earth, but because the Moon has no air, a human cannot walk there without a spacesuit and life-support system. There are many other moons in the Solar System, some of them much bigger than our Moon.

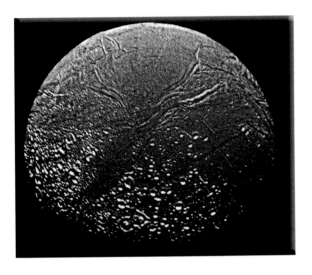

▲ *Saturn, with its 18 moons, has more moons than any other planet. One of them is the small, 500-km-wide moon called Enceladus, shown here. It glistens as light reflects off beads of ice on the surface. Enceladus is unusual in having deep valleys, which indicate geological activity.*

▲ *The Moon spins on its axis in 27.3 days – the same amount of time it takes to complete one orbit of Earth.*

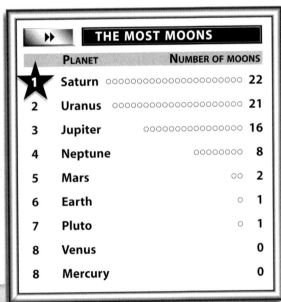

▸▸ THE MOST MOONS	
PLANET	NUMBER OF MOONS
1 Saturn	○○○○○○○○○○○○○○○○○○○○○○ 22
2 Uranus	○○○○○○○○○○○○○○○○○○○○○ 21
3 Jupiter	○○○○○○○○○○○○○○○○ 16
4 Neptune	○○○○○○○○ 8
5 Mars	○○ 2
6 Earth	○ 1
7 Pluto	○ 1
8 Venus	0
8 Mercury	0

▼ *From samples brought back by astronauts, scientists learned that the top soil of the Moon is just dust, firm enough to support a spacecraft. They think the rocks may contain water, which would be useful for a future Moon base. Astronauts in the 1970s used a Lunar Rover, or Moon buggy, to explore the Moon's surface.*

Callisto
4,820 km in diameter

Ganymede
5,276 km in diameter

Europa
3,126 km in diameter

Io
3,632 km in diameter

▲ *The four biggest of Jupiter's 16 moons are all bigger than Pluto. Ganymede is the biggest in the Solar System, Callisto has the most craters, Io has the most volcanoes and Europa is encased in ice.*

▶▶ FACTS ABOUT THE MOON

Distance from Earth	**384,399 km (average)**
Diameter	**3,476 km**
Biggest crater (far side)	**South Pole-Aitken: 2,500 km across, 12,000 m deep**
Biggest crater (visible from Earth)	**Bailly: 295 km across, 4,250 m deep**
Highest mountains	**8,000 m, near the Korolev Basin on the far side**
Length of day/night	**Roughly 15 Earth days each**
Coldest time	**Night: temperatures fall to -163°C**

▲ *Triton, the biggest of Neptune's eight moons, is gradually spiralling towards Neptune and in 10 million to 100 million years time will break up and form rings round the planet. Triton's geysers shoot out frozen nitrogen gas.*

IT'S A FACT
There is no wind or rain on the Moon, so any mark made in the powdery dust stays intact. Footprints left by the Apollo *astronauts will last for thousands of years – unless a meteorite hits them!*

SHOOTING STARS

Millions of meteors whizz through space all the time. Meteors are pieces of dust or lumps of rock from the tails of comets. When they hit Earth's thick atmosphere they heat up and for a second or two trail glowing tails before burning up. These brief flashes, like brilliant fireworks, are called shooting stars. A large meteor sometimes hurtles through Earth's atmosphere and smashes into the ground. The charred rock that remains is called a meteorite.

▲ *The Hoba meteorite was found in Namibia, southern Africa, in 1920. It is big enough for a football team to sit on.*

▲ *A meteor shower is a dramatic display of shooting stars. For a short period more than a thousand a second may flash across the sky. August is the best month to see one.*

▶▶	BIGGEST METEORITES TO HIT EARTH		
	NAME	**COUNTRY**	**WEIGHT**
★1	Hoba	Namibia	54 tonnes
2	Ahnighito	Greenland	31 tonnes
3	Bacuberito	Mexico	27 tonnes

DID YOU KNOW?
A comet that appeared in 1064 – probably Halley's – is shown in the Bayeux Tapestry, which records William of Normandy's successful invasion of England in 1066.

▼ *The most famous hole made by a meteorite is Meteor Crater in Arizona, USA, shown here. It measures more than 1,700 m across and nearly 200 m deep. An even bigger impact crater, partly beneath the sea, is the Chixulub Basin in Mexico, which is 300 km across. This hole was probably made by an asteroid hitting Earth about 65 million years ago – the impact may have wiped out the dinosaurs.*

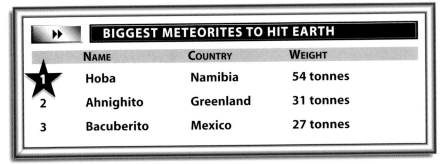

◄ *In medieval times people thought the fiery tail of a comet was a bad omen, foretelling disaster. Now we know that comets orbit the Sun just like planets, and return on schedule. Halley's Comet comes close to Earth roughly every 77 years.*

THE TALE OF HALLEY'S COMET

1066	The comet was recorded in the Bayeux Tapestry.
1705	Edmund Halley calculated the orbit took 76 to 77 years
1758	Great excitement: the comet returned as Halley predicted
1835	The comet was seen, but it was not as bright as before
1910	Many people feared the world would end
1986	Several spacecraft flew close to the comet
2062	This is the next time Halley's Comet will return

▶ *Some comets travel much farther out into space than the planets, and take thousands of years to make one orbit of the Sun. The nucleus or core of a comet is a small chunk of rock, dust and ice. As it comes nearer the Sun's heat, the ice core warms up and gives off glowing tails of gas and dust that can be millions of kilometres long.*

▲ *The Hale-Bopp Comet was spotted by two astronomers hundreds of kilometres apart on the same night in 1995, so it was named after both of them. It made a spectacular display in March 1997, and will come close to Earth again in about 2,380 years time!*

SPOT THE COMET

- You don't have to wait 77 years for Halley's Comet to see a comet. Others are visible from Earth much more frequently.
- Comet Encke returns every 3 years.
- Comet Grigg-Skjellerup returns every 4 years. In 1992 the *Giotto* space probe flew within 200 km of its nucleus.
- Biela's Comet can be seen every 6.7 years.

STAR GAZING

About 1,900 years ago the Greek astronomer Ptolemy counted 1,080 stars. Like all astronomers of the ancient world, he had no telescope. The Egyptians, Babylonians, Chinese and Greeks all studied the night sky. They named the six planets they could see, and also gave names to the stars. People in ancient times believed gods lived among the stars. They built temples to line up with the positions of bright stars or with the Sun and Moon, and set up stone circles to mark sunrise and sunset on the longest and shortest days in the year.

▲ *In ancient times people believed the view of the great classical thinker, Ptolemy, that Earth was at the centre of the Universe and that the heavens moved around Earth. This view was widely accepted for 2,000 years, until Copernicus dared to disagree.*

▶ *The first simple telescope – two lenses held in line – was invented in 1608. The following year, Galileo Galilei became the first person to use a telescope to study the Sun, Moon and planets. He observed that the Sun was not perfect, as people believed, but that it had spots! By the 1700s astronomers were building huge telescopes.*

▶▶	EARLIEST ASTRONOMERS	
	WHO	**WHEN**
1	Chinese	1300s BC
2	Pythagoras	569–475 BC
3	Aristarchus	310–230 BC
4	Eratosthenes	c.270–190 BC
5	Copernicus	AD 1473–1543

▶ *The world's biggest optical telescope is the Keck Telescope in Hawaii. It has 36 mirrors, each 1.8 m wide. Using lasers, the mirrors are adjusted to act as one giant mirror, four times more powerful than the Mount Palomar telescope in California, USA.*

▲ *Radio waves from space were discovered by Karl Jansky in 1931. The biggest radio telescope is in New Mexico, USA. Called the Very Large Array (VLA), it has 27 dishes, each measuring 25 m across.*

▼ *The Hubble Space Telescope, which was launched in 1990, weighs 11 tonnes and has a 240-cm mirror. Orbiting above Earth's polluted atmosphere, it gives astronomers a clear view of the stars.*

ACHIEVEMENT

Drew maps of the stars and constellations

Declared that Earth was round

Proved the Sun was farther away from Earth than the Moon

Calculated the size of Earth using geometry

Explained how the planets move around the Sun

◀ *Stonehenge is the most famous ancient monument in Britain. It was built between about 2950 and 1500 BC. The huge stones were put up in stages, in three circles that made a giant calendar. This was used to fix the days for religious ceremonies, which were linked to the Sun's movement.*

SPACE RACE

French writer Jules Verne wrote about a voyage to the Moon in 1873, and in the 1920s Robert Goddard of the USA launched small home-made rockets. These dreamers were the pioneers of space travel. The space race began in earnest in the 1950s with a contest to put people into orbit around Earth. The Russians won this race. They had the biggest rockets and were able to launch much heavier spacecraft than the Americans. The first big Soviet rocket sent Yuri Gagarin into space in 1961.

▸ SATELLITE LAUNCHES		
	COUNTRY	YEAR
1	USSR	1957
2	USA	1958
3	France	1965
4	Japan	1970
5	China	1970
6	UK	1971

▸ *Soviet cosmonaut Yuri Gagarin was the first person in space. On April 12, 1961, in the 5 tonne spaceship* Vostok 1, *he made a complete circuit of Earth in just 1 hour and 29 minutes.*

◀ *In 1957 the Russians took the lead in the space race with the first artificial satellite,* Sputnik 1. *Not much bigger than a beach ball, it contained a radio transmitter.*

▼ *The two* Pioneer *space probes launched by the USA in 1972 and 1973 were the first space probes to head for the outer planets. They flew past Jupiter and Saturn.*

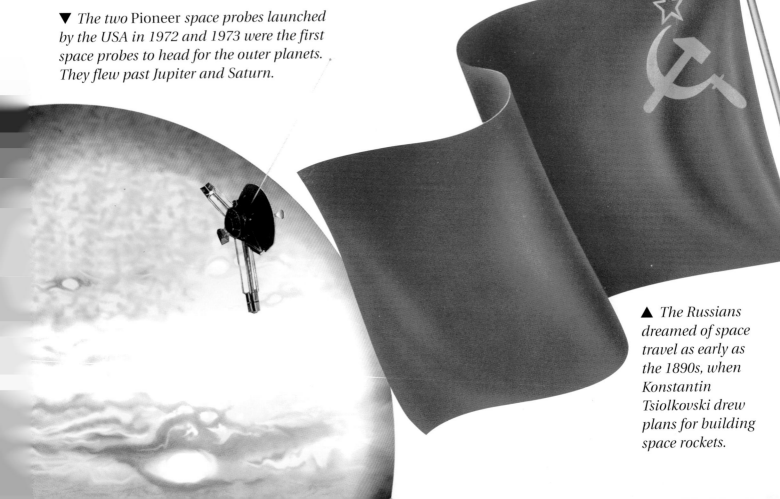

▲ *The Russians dreamed of space travel as early as the 1890s, when Konstantin Tsiolkovski drew plans for building space rockets.*

THE FIRST SATELLITES

	SATELLITE	COUNTRY	LAUNCH DATE
★1	*Sputnik 1*	USSR	October 1957
2	*Sputnik 2*	USSR	November 1957
3	*Explorer 1*	USA	February 1958
4	*Vanguard 1*	USA	March 1958

▼ *Laika, a fox terrier dog, was the first animal to travel in space. In 1957 she spent a week in orbit aboard the Russian craft Sputnik 2. The Russians knew that they would not be able to bring Laika back, and she died when her oxygen ran out.*

FAST AS LIGHT

● If you could travel at light-speed, like the Millennium Falcon in the film *Star Wars*, you would reach the Moon in under 2 seconds, Pluto in 6 hours, and you would cross the Milky Way in 100,000 years.

▲ *American Neil Armstrong (left) was the first person on the Moon. He took his "giant leap for mankind" on July 20, 1969. Apollo 11's other crew were Edwin 'Buzz' Aldrin (right) and Michael Collins (centre).*

◀ *In 1972 Pioneer 10 was the fastest craft ever launched into space. It left Earth at more than 51,000 km/h on its mission to the outer planets. In 1983 it became the first human-made object to leave the Solar System, and it is now about 11 billion km away!*

▼ *Space races of the future are likely to focus on trying to colonize other planets. This artist's impression is of a futuristic settlement on Mars, where buildings would need their own air supply.*

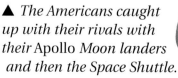

▲ *The Americans caught up with their rivals with their* Apollo *Moon landers and then the Space Shuttle. Today Russians, Americans and other nations are working together in space.*

GREAT JOURNEYS

Rocket building became a very expensive contest between the Russians and the Americans in the 1960s. Space scientists from both countries borrowed ideas from the Germans, whose V2 rocket of World War II was the first big, long-range rocket. The first big Soviet rocket, *Vostok 1*, put Yuri Gagarin into space. But this was followed by an even bigger rocket, *Saturn 5*, from the Americans. This sent astronauts to the Moon. In the 1980s probes travelled across the Solar System to send back the first close-up pictures of Jupiter and Saturn, and explore the even more distant planets, Uranus and Neptune.

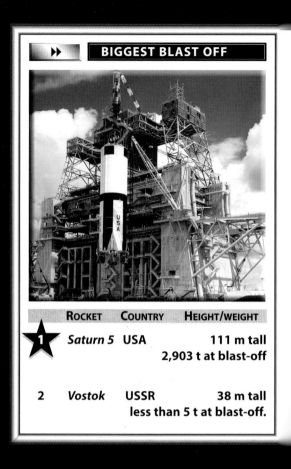

» BIGGEST BLAST OFF

	ROCKET	COUNTRY	HEIGHT/WEIGHT
★ 1	*Saturn 5*	USA	111 m tall 2,903 t at blast-off
2	*Vostok*	USSR	38 m tall less than 5 t at blast-off.

DID YOU KNOW?
Voyager 1 was launched by the Americans in 1977 to explore Jupiter and its moons. It revealed a faint ring that astronomers had never seen before from Earth.

▶ *In July 1969 the three-module* Apollo *spacecraft, shown here, was launched into the atmosphere by a* Saturn 5 *rocket. The three astronauts travelled in the Command Module. Once in lunar orbit, the Lunar Module took two of them to the Moon.*

four rockets

▶ *The view of Earth from space has only been seen by humans for just over 40 years!*

▲ *The astronauts were able to guide the* Apollo *spacecraft in any direction using its four thrusters, each with fou rockets pointing in different directions.*

▶▶ MISSION FIRSTS

Luna 9, Surveyor 1	1966	**First Moon landing by unmanned spacecraft**
Apollo 11	1969	**First Moon landing by astronauts**
Lunokhod	1970	**First Moon robot rover**
Galileo craft	1995	**First probe to explore Jupiter's atmosphere**
Sojourner	1997	**First rover to move about another planet**

▶ Apollo 11's *mission to the Moon covered 1.5 million km and lasted 195 hours.*

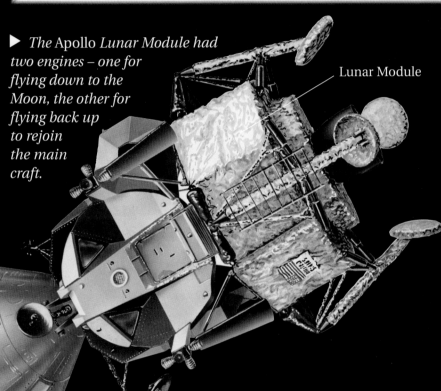

▶ The Apollo *Lunar Module had two engines – one for flying down to the Moon, the other for flying back up to rejoin the main craft.*

Lunar Module

Command Module

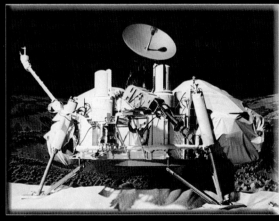

▲ *Deep space probes such as* Voyager 2 *travel millions of kilometres from Earth without the use of engines. They send back pictures and other information by radio.*

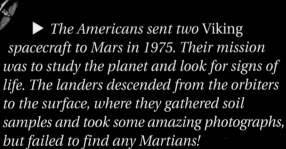

▶ *The Americans sent two* Viking *spacecraft to Mars in 1975. Their mission was to study the planet and look for signs of life. The landers descended from the orbiters to the surface, where they gathered soil samples and took some amazing photographs, but failed to find any Martians!*

▲ *The* Apollo *Command Module was the only part of* Apollo *to return to Earth. The Lunar Module was set adrift once the two astronauts who had taken it to the Moon had returned to the Command Module.*

▶▶ SPACE PROBE FIRSTS

Luna 2	USSR	1959	**First to hit the Moon**
Luna 3	USSR	1959	**First to photograph the Moon's far side**
Venera 4	USSR	1967	**First to hit Venus**
Mars 2 and 3	USSR	1971	**First to hit Mars**
Viking 1 and 2	USA	1976	**First long-stay Mars landing**
Pioneer 10	USA	1983	**First to leave the Solar System**

▼ Apollo 15 *was launched by a* Saturn 5 *rocket from Cape Canaveral, Florida, USA, at 9:34 am on July 26, 1971, just 187 milliseconds behind schedule! The 111-m-high* Saturn 5 *is seen here on the launch pad just before lift-off.*

SPACE MISSIONS

The first astronauts were pilots, trained to fly fast jet planes. An early exception was Valentina Tereshkova, the first woman in space. She was a textile technologist, but also an expert parachutist. Later astronauts included scientists and doctors, as well as a geologist on *Apollo 17*. By the 1980s astronauts had proved people could stay in space for up to a year without harming their bodies or going mad. There have been some tragedies, however, and at least one near-disaster. Space can be a dangerous and hostile place.

▲ Apollo 15's *Lunar Module*, Falcon, *took two astronauts to the Moon's surface. There, for the first time, they used the Lunar Rover or Moon buggy to travel about. The crew proudly left the US flag standing in the Moon's dust before they left for home.*

»	ASTRONAUT FIRSTS		
Gherman Titov	USSR	1961	First day in space
Andrian Nikolayev	USSR	1962	First 3-day flight
Valentina Tereshkova	USSR	1963	First woman in space
Voskhod 1	USSR	1964	First 3-person crew
Aleksei Leonov	USSR	1965	First space walk

IT'S A FACT
In 1971 US astronauts David Scott and James Irwin were the first people to drive on the Moon. They rode around in a battery-powered, four-wheeled Moon buggy.

▶▶	FIRST FIVE PEOPLE IN ORBIT		
	NAME	**COUNTRY**	**DATE**
★ 1	Yuri Gagarin	USSR	April 12, 1961
2	Gherman Titov	USSR	August 6–7, 1961
3	John Glenn	USA	February 20, 1962
4	M. Scott Carpenter	USA	May 24, 1962
5	Andrian Nikolayev	USSR	August 11–15, 1962

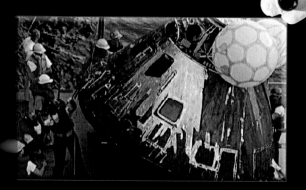

▲ *Apollo 13 limped back to Earth low on power and air after an explosion damaged the main part of the craft. Millions of television viewers held their breath awaiting the return of the three crew.*

▶ *Astronauts do spacewalks to make repairs to their craft or to satellites or space telescopes.*

▶▶	US MOON MISSIONS AND MOON WALKERS	Note: *Apollo 9* orbited Earth
Apollo 8	December 1968	Three astronauts flew around the Moon
Apollo 10	May 1969	Flew to within 14 km of the Moon's surface
Apollo 11	July 1969	Neil Armstrong and Edwin Aldrin landed
Apollo 12	November 1969	Pete Conrad and Alan Bean landed
Apollo 13	April 1970	Flew around the Moon
Apollo 14	January 1971	Alan Shepard and Edgar Mitchell landed
Apollo 15	July 1971	David Scott and James Irwin landed
Apollo 16	April 1972	John Young and Charles Duke landed
Apollo 17	December 1972	Harrison Schmitt and Gene Cernan landed

▸▸ Most valuable cargo: space telescope ▸▸ Best way to sleep: tied to the wall ▸▸ Hygiene luxury: vacuum toilet

SPACE SHUTTLES

The American Space Shuttle was the world's first reusable spacecraft. It can carry eight astronauts into space, stay in orbit for up to 10 days, and then fly back to land on an airstrip. It can launch satellites from its cargo bay, and bring back faulty ones for repair. Other satellite launchers, such as the European *Ariane* rocket, can be used only once. The Shuttle first flew in 1981, and will be used many times to carry equipment to and from the new International Space Station.

SHUTTLE FACTS

- The Shuttle weighs 2 million kg at lift-off.
- From nose to tail it measures 56 m.
- It orbits at a height of between 200 and 600 km above Earth.
- The four original Shuttles were named *Columbia*, *Challenger*, *Discovery* and *Atlantis*.
- In 1991 *Endeavour* replaced *Challenger*, lost in 1986.

▶ *In orbit, circling Earth at a speed of about 28,000 km/h, the Shuttle can launch satellites from its 18-m-long cargo bay, which can carry a load of more than 35 tonnes. The crew use a 'remote manipulator arm' to catch satellites for repair.*

DID YOU KNOW?
Rocket engines burn fuel at an incredible rate. During lift-off the Shuttle burns nearly 10 tonnes of fuel a second from its external fuel tank.

▼ *The winged Space Shuttle lifts off and rides into orbit attached to a giant external fuel tank with boosters either side. In 1986* Challenger *exploded just 72 seconds after lift-off, killing its seven crew.*

▼ Shuttle astronauts work in space wearing a jet pack called a 'manned manoeuvring unit' or MMU, which propels them through space.

▶ Lift-off! The Shuttle is blasted upwards by its three main engines, aided by the two solid fuel rocket boosters. These burn out after two minutes, at a height of 45 km, and fall back to Earth by parachute to be used again. After eight minutes the external fuel tank, now empty, also falls into the ocean. It too can be reused.

▼ When the Shuttle re-enters Earth's atmosphere, it glows red-hot from the heat of friction. Special tiles absorb the heat. It lands on a runway, ready to be used again on another mission.

SHUTTLE FIRSTS		
Columbia	1981	First test flight
Columbia	1982	First 4-person flight
Columbia	1983	First 5-person flight and first US woman
Challenger	1984	First free walk in space using a jet-pack
Challenger	1985	First 8-person flight

SPACE STATIONS

The first space station was *Salyut 1*, launched by the Russians in 1971. A series of *Salyuts* followed before the Russians built the larger *Mir* space station in 1986. *Mir* had six docking ports to which other modules or visiting spacecraft could be attached. In 1995 cosmonaut Valeriy Poliyakov spent 437 days in orbit in *Mir*, setting a space record. Russia and America are now working with Japan, Canada and Europe to build the new *International Space Station (ISS)*.

▲ *Building the* International Space Station *will take over 5 years and will require 45 Shuttle flights. The cost is put at 100 billion US dollars, making it the most expensive object ever built! The* ISS *is being put together in sections. When complete, it will be as big as a football pitch.*

MIR FACTS

- The main section of *Mir* was 13.13 m long, 4.2 m wide and weighed 21 tonnes.
- The *Kvant* module was joined to *Mir* in 1987, doubling the room inside.
- *Kvant 3* (1990) had equipment that turned *Mir* into a space factory.

▲ *The American* Skylab, *launched in 1973, had problems with a solar panel, forcing the crew to put up a 'sunshade' to keep it cool. Despite the snags, three 3-man crews visited* Skylab, *the longest mission lasting 84 days. The 75-tonne space station burned up in the atmosphere in 1979.*

▶ *This artist's impression shows the Shuttle docking with the* International Space Station. *The Shuttle will be used to transport astronauts, equipment, provisions and visitors to the space station once building is complete.*

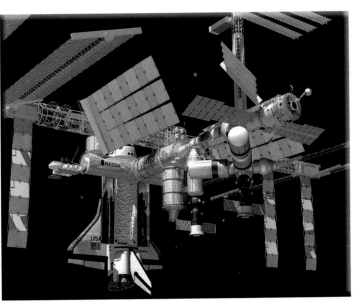

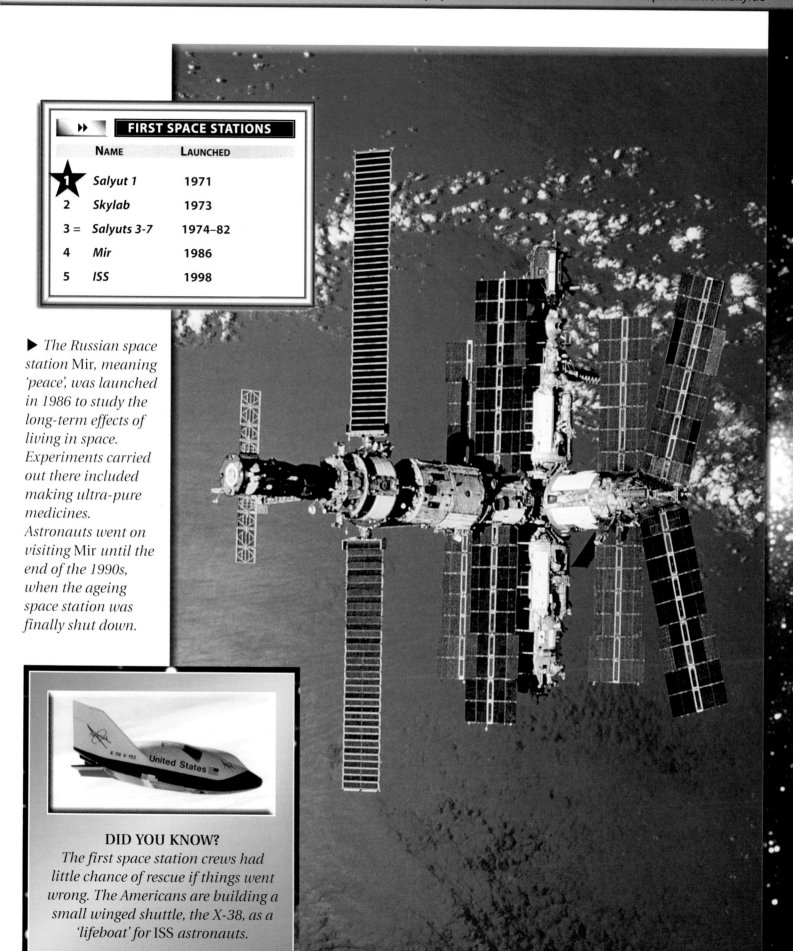

FIRST SPACE STATIONS

	NAME	LAUNCHED
1	Salyut 1	1971
2	Skylab	1973
3 =	Salyuts 3-7	1974–82
4	Mir	1986
5	ISS	1998

▶ *The Russian space station* Mir, *meaning 'peace', was launched in 1986 to study the long-term effects of living in space. Experiments carried out there included making ultra-pure medicines. Astronauts went on visiting* Mir *until the end of the 1990s, when the ageing space station was finally shut down.*

DID YOU KNOW?
The first space station crews had little chance of rescue if things went wrong. The Americans are building a small winged shuttle, the X-38, as a 'lifeboat' for ISS astronauts.

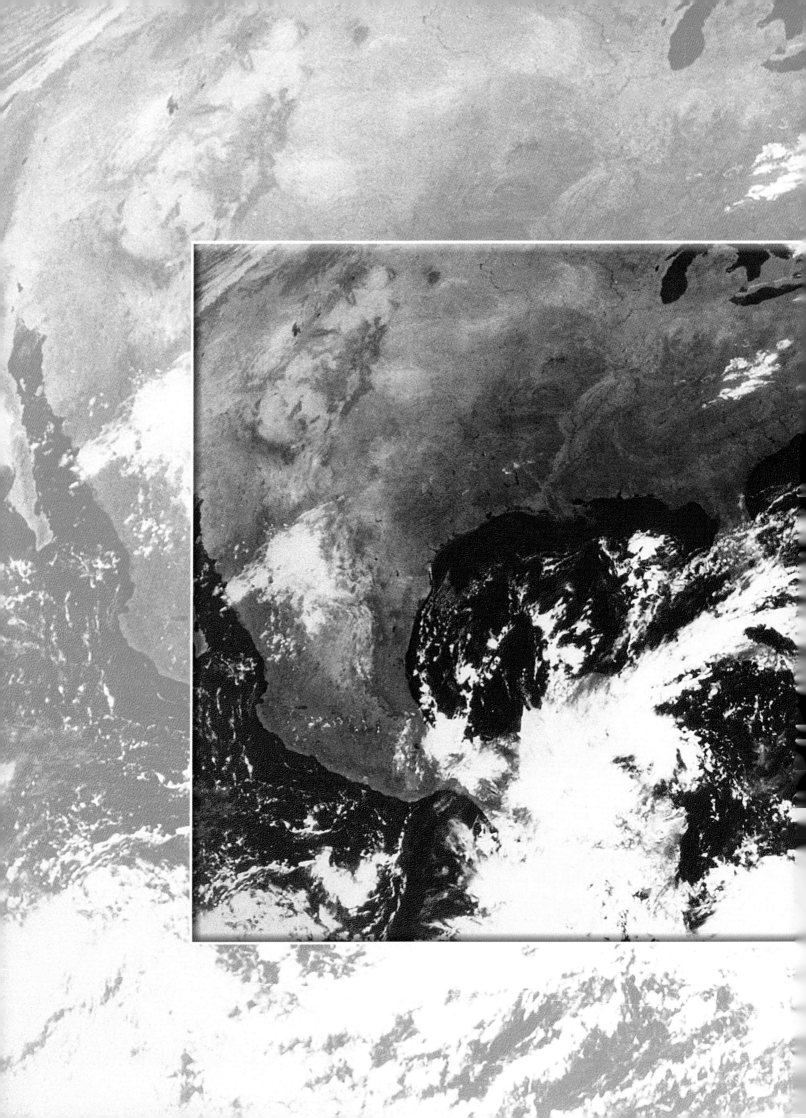

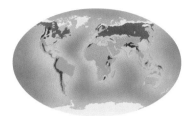

PLANET EARTH

*O*ur planet really is an amazing place. More than two thirds of it is covered by oceans, yet there are vast areas of burning desert, mountains of unimaginable height, hot, steamy rainforests and an exotic array of animal life.

It is these fantastic features of the Earth that provide us with some amazing statistics. For instance, our planet is solid ball of rock, 6,400 km thick. Yet the inner core is so hot, the rock within it is molten, reaching an incredible temperature of more than 4,000ºC. All around us are amazing things we take for granted; water recycling and falling as rain, the movement of the Earth's plates beneath our feet, grumbling volcanoes and beautiful rainbows. Within this book stunning images of these amazing natural features are accompanied by facts you'll never forget.

Explore the biggest and best facts about *Planet Earth* and rediscover your planet. There are the big, serious facts – for reference – and less serious ones, too, for fun. These pages are packed with the biggest and best, oddest and strangest, smallest and funniest facts around!

EARTH FACTS

Earth is a ball of rock mostly covered by water and wrapped in a thin, protective layer of gases – the air. It was formed at the same time as the Sun and the other planets, about 4.6 billion years ago. The outer layer of Earth is called the crust. All the continents and seas lie on the crust. Underneath the crust is the mantle, made of molten rock that moves very slowly. As it moves, huge pieces of the crust, called continental plates, move too.

▲ *Zircon crystals found in Australia are 4,276 million years old – the oldest part of Earth's crust ever discovered.*

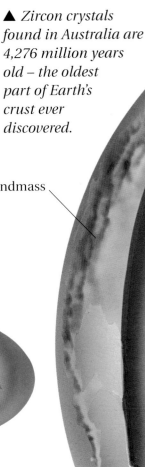

crust,
5 to 50 km thick

landmass

ocean

◄ *Some 280 million years ago all the continents were joined in one huge landmass, called Pangaea. Over time, this 'super-continent' broke up and the landmasses drifted apart to form the continents we know today.*

▼ *Earth's rocky skin, the crust, is thickest – about 50 km thick – beneath 'young' or recently built mountain ranges such as the Himalayas in Asia. The crust beneath the oceans is much thinner, between 5 to 11 km thick.*

continental plate movement

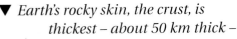

➡➡	**EARTH'S LAYERS**	
Atmosphere	Gases	80 to 1,600 km thick
Earth's crust	Rocks	5 to 50 km thick
Mantle	Rocks	About 2,800 km thick
Core	Melted rocks	About 3,550 km thick

» Most abundant chemical: oxygen » Age: 4.6 billion years » Surface area: almost 510 million sq km

quartz   galena   pyrite   gypsum   barite   calcite

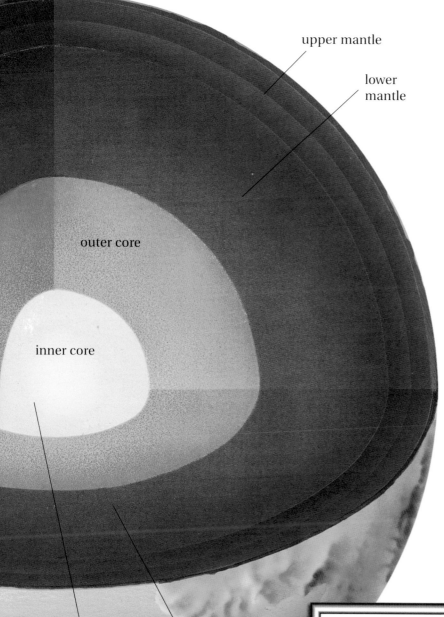

upper mantle

lower mantle

outer core

inner core

distance to the centre of Earth is 6,400 km

deepest hole yet drilled was 1,200 km deep

▲ *Earth is made of rocks. Rocks are themselves made of a mass of minerals like the ones shown here. Usually minerals are formed as crystals. Some, such as gypsum, are soft. Others, like quartz, are very hard and can scratch glass.*

▸▸ LARGEST LANDMASSES		
CONTINENT		**AREA**
1	Asia	44,009,000 sq km
2	Africa	30,246,000 sq km
3	North America	24,219,000 sq km
4	South America	17,832,000 sq km
5	Europe	10,443,000* sq km
6	Australia	7,713,000 sq km

* Europe is joined to Asia, so the two are sometimes called Eurasia

◀ *Although Earth looks round, it has a bulge just south of the Equator. It spins on its axis – an imaginary line between the Poles. The centre of Earth is about 6,400 km from the surface. The deeper down inside Earth, the hotter it gets. At Earth's core it is so hot – over 4,000°C – that the rocks there are molten rather than solid.*

▸▸ EARTH FACTS	
Equatorial circumference	40,075 km
Polar circumference	40,008 km
Surface area	509,700,000 sq km
Land area	29 percent
Water area	71 percent
Most abundant chemical	oxygen (47% of mass)

AWESOME OCEANS

Viewed from space, Earth looks like a watery world. More than 70 percent of the planet is covered by water, and about 97 percent of all Earth's water is in the oceans. These cover more than 360 million sq km. The Pacific is the biggest ocean. It is twice as big as the next largest ocean, the Atlantic. It also has the biggest waves and the deepest deeps, but not the highest tides. These are in the Bay of Fundy on the Atlantic coast of North America.

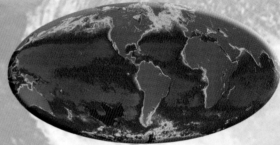

	THE BIGGEST OCEANS	
	OCEAN	**AREA**
★ 1	Pacific	181 million sq km
2	Atlantic	94 million sq km
3	Indian	74 million sq km

▲ *The world's oceans are not all the same temperature. This map shows the warm and cold waters in the top 100 m of the oceans. Deeper down, warm and cold currents swirl a few metres a day in great circular patterns, driven by the saltiness of the water.*

▲ *Sunlight never reaches below 200 m, but thousands of metres down in the darkest depths, some fish have bodies that glow. Some even have luminous tentacles used to lure prey.*

▶ *In 1961 the US navy sent a manned deep-sea diving machine, a bathyscaphe called* Trieste, *to the bottom of the Marianas Trench in the Pacific. At 10,911 m deep, this is the deepest point in any of the world's oceans.*

bathyscaphes are used to explore the ocean bed 6,000 m below the surface of the sea

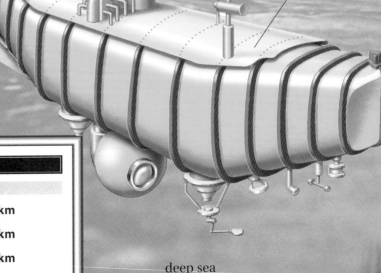

deep sea trench

	LONGEST OCEAN TRENCHES		
	TRENCH	**OCEAN**	**LENGTH**
★ 1	Peru-Atacama	Pacific	3,540 km
2	Aleutian	Pacific	3,200 km
3	Tonga-Kermadec	Pacific	2,575 km
4	Marianas	Pacific	2,250 km
5	Philippine	Pacific	1,325 km

» Biggest bay: Bay of Bengal » Longest shoreline: Canada » Clearest water: Weddell Sea » Highest cliffs: Hawaii

		DEEPEST OCEAN TRENCHES		
		TRENCH	**OCEAN**	**DEPTH**
★	1	Marianas	Pacific	10,911 m
	2	Tonga-Kermadec	Pacific	10,882 m
	3	Philippine	Pacific	10,497 m
	4	Bonin	Pacific	9,994 m
	5	New Britain	Pacific	9,940 m

▲ *Waves are blown along by winds. The highest wave ever seen was in 1933, when a US navy ship was caught in a Pacific hurricane and survived a wave estimated to be 34 m high. Waves three times higher can be caused by undersea earthquakes.*

	EXTREME WATERS
Deepest	Pacific Ocean
Shallowest	Atlantic Ocean
Coldest	Arctic Ocean
Warmest	Persian Gulf

◄ *Canada has the longest coastline of any country. Including the many islands, the coast is more than 244,000 km long – that is six times longer than the coast of Australia.*

▼ *Underneath the oceans is a dramatic landscape that is rarely seen. Mountains rise up, sometimes breaking the surface of the water as islands. There are also deep trenches. The Marianas Trench in the Pacific is the deepest, dwarfing the famous Grand Canyon in the USA.*

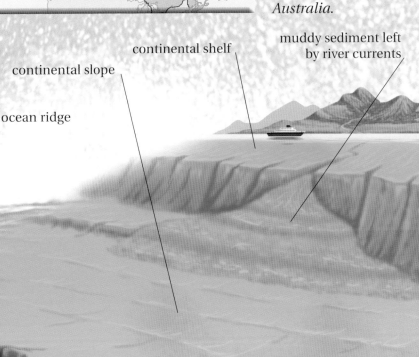

continental shelf

muddy sediment left by river currents

continental slope

ocean ridge

RECORD RIVERS

Did you know that all the water on Earth is constantly recycled? The first downpour lasted for thousands of years, more than three billion years ago. It filled the oceans and seas. The warmth of the Sun makes water in the oceans 'evaporate' or turn into water vapour in the air. The water vapour is blown over land by the wind. As the moist air rises over hills, it cools and turns into water droplets that fall as rain or snow. The rainwater finds its way into streams and rivers, which return it to the oceans.

»	LONGEST RIVERS	
	RIVER	**LOCATION**
★ 1	Nile	Africa
2	Amazon	S. America
3	Chang Jiang (Yangtze)	China
4	Huang He (Yellow)	China
5	Congo (Zaire)	Africa

◀ The Colorado River flows for 2,200 km across the United States and into Mexico. Over millions of years it has gouged out the spectacular 1.6-km-deep Grand Canyon.

▲ The Amazon River in South America, shown here, carries more water than any other river, although it is slightly shorter than the Nile River in northern Africa.

water from oceans and lakes evaporates

DID YOU KNOW?
The Suez canal was opened in 1869. This 'river through the sand' was the biggest engineering feat of its time, linking the Mediterranean and Red Seas. Ships steaming from Europe to India no longer had to go around Africa – a saving of 7,000 km.

▲ White water rafting through rapids is thrilling and dangerous. Rapids occur where rivers flow fast over soft rock, from which boulders of harder rock stick up, making the water swirl.

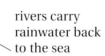
» River carrying most water: Amazon » Longest estuary: Ob » River with most tributaries: Amazon

	LENGTH
	6,670 km
	6,448 km
	6,300 km
	4,572 km
	4,667 km

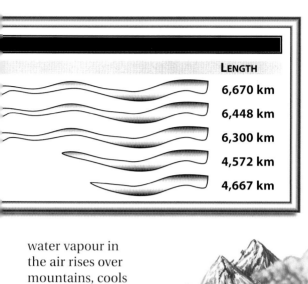

water vapour in
the air rises over
mountains, cools
and condenses,
forming water
droplets

water droplets
fall as rain
or snow

rivers carry
rainwater back
to the sea

plants give
off water

RECORD RIVERS

● The longest river in Europe is the
  Volga, at 3,531 km.
● The longest river in the United States
  is the Missouri, at 4,090 km.
● The longest river in Australia is the
  Darling, at 2,739 km.
● The muddiest river is the Huang He,
  or Yellow River, in China.

◄ *People have
travelled up and
down rivers,
transporting goods,
ever since the
ancient Egyptians
first sailed craft
like this boat,
called a felucca,
along the Nile
River more than
5,000 years ago.*

◄ *Most of the rain that
falls is carried by rivers to
the oceans. Heat from the
Sun makes the seawater
evaporate, turning it into water
vapour. Water is also returned to
the atmosphere by plants. When
water vapour cools it forms clouds,
which release the water as rain, and
the cycle begins again.*

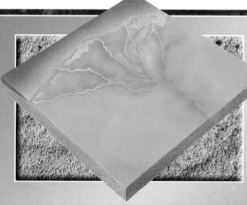

IT'S A FACT
*The first great civilizations all grew
up beside rivers, because crops could
be grown in the fertile soils. Egypt's
civilization developed along the
Nile River (its delta is shown here).
Mesopotamia's civilization started
between the Tigris and Euphrates
Rivers, and the Indus civilization
grew along the Indus River.*

WATERFALLS

Waterfalls happen when a river flows over a band of hard rock that is lying on top of softer rock. Because the softer rock wears away more quickly than the hard rock, the hard rock sticks out like a ledge with nothing underneath it. As the river flows over the ledge, the water falls with a thunderous roar and clouds of drenching spray in a thrilling spectacle.

HIGHEST FALLS

	Falls	Country	Drop
⭐ 1	Angel	Venezuela	979 m
2	Tugela	Africa	947 m
3	Utigård	Norway	800 m
4	Mongefossen	Norway	774 m
5	Yosemite	USA	739 m
6	Østre Mardøla Foss	Norway	656 m

▲ The highest falls are the Angel Falls in Venezuela, South America. One 'drop' is 807 m, and the total drop is 979 m – more than twice the height of the Empire State Building.

▲ The Victoria Falls on the Zambezi River in Zimbabwe, Africa, are 108 m high. They were named 'the smoke that thunders' by the local people.

▲ *The Iguaçu Falls between Argentina and Brazil are spectacularly wide at 3 km. They have a total drop of 80 m.*

DID YOU KNOW?

When salmon are fully grown, they return from the sea to breed in the same rivers in which they were born. After finding their way back to the river's mouth, they swim upstream, defying rapids and small waterfalls. They leap and twist to find a way through the cascading torrents of water. If a dam blocks their way, the fish swim through its tunnels to reach the higher stretch of river.

	FALLS WITH THE MOST WATER			
	Falls	**River**	**Country**	**Flow**
1	**Boyoma**	Congo	Congo	17,000 cu m per sec
2	Guaira	Paraná	Brazil/Paraguay	13,000 cu m per sec
3	Khone	Mekong	Laos	12,000 cu m per sec
4	Niagara	Niagara	Canada/USA	6,000 cu m per sec

▼ *The world-famous Niagara Falls are on the border between the USA and Canada. There are two sections, the American Falls, at 320 m wide, and the Canadian or Horseshoe Falls, at 675 m wide. The falls are gradually retreating upstream. Over the last 10,000 years they have worn away 11 km of rock. The Terrapin Tower, shown here, was built next to the Horseshoe Falls in 1829, but was blown up in 1872!*

LAKES AND INLAND SEAS

A lake is a big expanse of water surrounded by land. Some lakes are so big they are called inland seas. Most lake water is fresh rather than salty, but in some lakes so much water is lost by evaporation – it turns into water vapour as it is heated by the Sun – that the remaining water tastes very salty. The saltiest inland sea is the Dead Sea. Evaporation can cause some inland seas to shrink in hot weather. Australia's biggest lake, Lake Eyre, is dry for years and fills with water only after unusually heavy rains.

▲ *The 725-km-long St Lawrence Seaway, a great commercial waterway, links the Great Lakes of North America and the Atlantic Ocean.*

▼ *Loch Ness – loch means lake – in Scotland, is best known for its 'monster'. There have been many reported sightings and hoax pictures of the strange creature, but no firm evidence of its existence.*

▶▶	LARGEST LAKES/INLAND SEAS	
	LAKE/SEA	**AREA**
★ 1	**Caspian Sea**	**371,000 sq km**
2	**Lake Superior**	**82,350 sq km**
3	**Lake Victoria**	**69,500 sq km**
4	**Aral Sea**	**66,500 sq km**
5	**Lake Huron**	**59,600 sq km**

NORTH AMERICA

Lake Huron

Lake Superior

SOUTH AMERICA

▶ *High in the Andes Mountains of Peru, straddling the border with Bolivia, is Lake Titicaca – the highest navigable lake in the world. It is 3,810 m above sea level.*

▲ *Lake Titicaca is a vast expanse of blue water surrounded by snow-capped peaks. It is home to the native Indians, who live in floating villages made from huge reed rafts. They also make crescent-shaped boats from the reeds that grow thickly in the marshy shallows.*

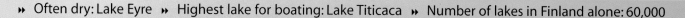
▶ *Lake Baikal in Siberia, Russia, is about 25 million years old. It is 1,637 m deep and contains about one-fifth of all the world's fresh water. The water is carried there by 336 rivers that flow into it. Lake Baikal has the world's only freshwater seals, and among its many unique animals is a fish that bears live young.*

▼ *The Dead Sea in Israel and Jordan is well named. This saltwater lake is the lowest lake on Earth – about 400 m below sea level. In summer scorching heat causes high evaporation, making the water so salty that a person cannot sink, and any fish entering the lake from the Jordan River die instantly. Only bacteria can survive.*

EUROPE

ASIA

AFRICA

Caspian Sea

Aral Sea

Lake Baikal

Lake Victoria

Lake Tanganyika

Lake Nyasa

AUSTRALASIA

LONGEST LAKES/INLAND SEAS

	Lake/Sea	Length
★ 1	Caspian Sea	1,201 km
2	Lake Tanganyika	676 km
3	Lake Baikal	636 km
4	Lake Nyasa	580 km
5	Lake Superior	563 km

▼ *The Caspian Sea is the biggest lake in the world. But it is getting smaller because more water is being taken out for irrigation than flows into it from rivers.*

►► THE GREAT LAKES OF NORTH AMERICA

	Lake	Rank
★ 1	Superior	World's biggest freshwater lake
2	Huron	5th largest freshwater lake
3	Michigan	6th largest freshwater lake
4	Erie	6th largest in North America
5	Ontario	8th largest in North America

ISLANDS AND REEFS

Islands are made in different ways. Some are the tops of undersea mountains or volcanoes. Others, such as the British Isles, were once part of a large landmass, but became surrounded by sea when the water level rose. A chain of islands is called an archipelago. The world's biggest archipelago is Indonesia, with more than 13,000 islands. Reefs are made from the bodies of millions of tiny coral animals. In warm seas they often form rings around small islands.

▲ *The biggest island in the world is Greenland, at 2,670 km long and 1,210 km wide. It is owned by Denmark, but is 50 times bigger. Greenland is 85 percent covered by ice and has very little greenery!*

ISLAND OR CONTINENT?

● Australia is bigger than Greenland, but is usually classed as a continent, not an island.

● The 13,000 islands of Indonesia stretch over a distance of 5,600 km.

▶ *New islands can appear out of the sea. Surtsey Island off Iceland rose from the waves following a volcanic eruption as recently as 1963. It grew to a height of 170 m in three years.*

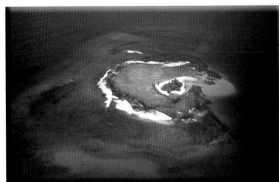

◀ *There are thousands of tiny islands in the Pacific Ocean. Many are ringed by coral reefs. Sometimes a volcanic island sinks, and all that is left is a ring of coral, called an atoll.*

▼ *When volcanoes erupt under the sea, new islands may appear. 1) Molten rock breaks through Earth's crust. 2) As more lava is deposited on the sea bed, a cone shape builds up. 3) When this breaks the water's surface, a new island appears. The volcano may go on erupting.*

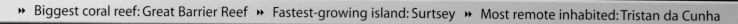
➤ Biggest coral reef: Great Barrier Reef ➤ Fastest-growing island: Surtsey ➤ Most remote inhabited: Tristan da Cunha

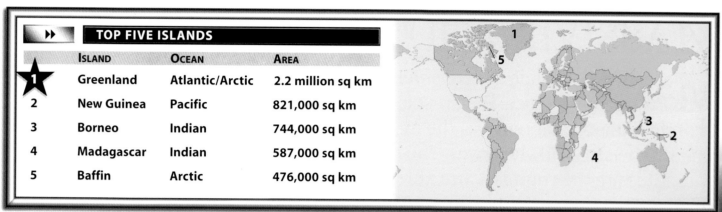

TOP FIVE ISLANDS

	ISLAND	OCEAN	AREA
★ 1	Greenland	Atlantic/Arctic	2.2 million sq km
2	New Guinea	Pacific	821,000 sq km
3	Borneo	Indian	744,000 sq km
4	Madagascar	Indian	587,000 sq km
5	Baffin	Arctic	476,000 sq km

▲ *The tiny 20-km-long Manhattan Island in the heart of New York City, USA, is now a forest of skyscrapers, where once there were only trees. A Dutch settler bought the island in 1626 from some Native Americans for a few dollars-worth of trinkets.*

▶ *The biggest coral reef on Earth is the Great Barrier Reef off eastern Australia. It is 2,000 km long, and is made from over 400 different corals. The reef has taken more than 2 million years to form.*

▲ *A coral reef is a rich habitat for wildlife. It provides food and shelter for dazzling tropical fish.*

▲ *Coral is the skeletons of tiny sea animals called polyps. Some polyps can grow to be 30 cm across.*

MASSIVE MOUNTAINS

Mountains are made by movements within Earth's rocky crust. The crust is made up of rigid plates that move as the mantle beneath the crust slowly moves. The highest mountains are the youngest and are still growing. They are pushed up by enormous pressure from deep inside Earth. The highest mountain on land is Mount Everest in the Himalayas of Asia. An even higher peak, Mauna Kea in Hawaii, rises out of the sea and is a volcanic mountain. The longest range or chain of mountains is the Andes in South America.

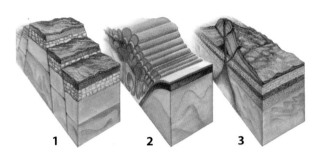

▲ 1) A fault mountain is made when weak points in Earth's crust crack and whole areas sink or are forced upwards.
2) A fold mountain is made when parts of Earth's crust shift and layers of rock are forced up into folds.
3) A volcano mountain is made as the lava that flows out cools and hardens.

THE BIG FIVE PEAKS	
MOUNTAIN	**HEIGHT**
1 Everest (shown here)	8,848 m
2 K2	8,610 m
3 Kanchenjunga	8,598 m
4 Lhotse	8,511 m
5 Makalu	8,481 m

Note: All these mountains are in the Himalayas

▶ The Eiger in Switzerland is 3,970 m high, and it challenges the very best climbers. First climbed in 1858, its towering north face was not scaled until 1938.

◀ Everest, the world's highest mountain, was climbed in 1953 by Tenzing Norgay and Edmund Hillary.

▼ The Rocky Mountain ranges run north–south across most of western North America. These sharp peaks in Montana have been shaped by sheets of ice called glaciers.

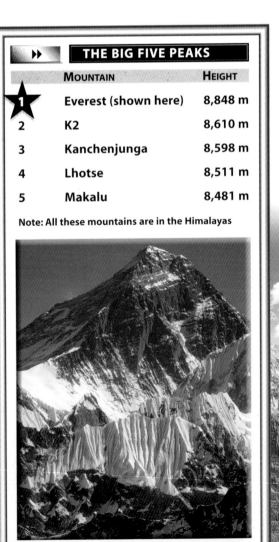

HIGHEST MOUNTAINS BY CONTINENT

	MOUNTAIN	LOCATION	HEIGHT
★ 1	Everest	Asia	8,848 m
2	Aconcagua	South America	6,960 m
3	McKinley	North America	6,194 m
4	Kilimanjaro	Africa	5,895 m
5	Elbrus	Europe	5,633 m
6	Vinson	Antarctica	5,140 m
7	Cook	Oceania	3,764 m

MOUNTAIN MARVELS

● The Himalayas have the world's 20 highest mountains. They are all over 8,000 m high.

● The Andes range has 50 peaks over 6,000 m high, making it the biggest in the Americas.

● Snowcapped Mount Kilimanjaro (shown here) in Tanzania is the highest mountain in Africa.

● The highest mountains in North America are in Alaska, USA, and the Yukon, Canada.

▶ The Andes is the longest mountain range, stretching for 7,200 km along the western side of South America. The highest peak is Aconcagua in Argentina. It is 6,960 m high.

▼ Mountain goats live on the steep cliffs and glacier edges of the Rocky Mountains. They prefer areas of high snowfall.

▼ The Grand Tetons of Wyoming, USA, are the youngest and most spectacular of the Rocky Mountain ranges.

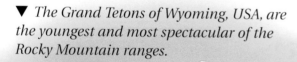

▲ Wild cattle called yaks can survive the harshest mountain conditions. They live on the ice deserts of the Tibetan Plateau at altitudes of 4,000 to 6,000 m.

▲ The chamois is a European goat-antelope. Incredibly agile, it can run along the narrowest ledges and near-vertical slopes.

CAVERNOUS CAVES

Caves are holes in the ground, usually hollowed out by water. Rainwater trickles down through the ground and dissolves the minerals in rocks such as limestone, forming hollows and tunnels. Some caves are very long passages, and some are huge open spaces called caverns. But much more common are 'pot-holes', which are deep, narrow passages, sometimes leading to caverns. Explorers crawl through pot-holes on hands and knees, or even swim through flooded sections of a cave, using flashlights to penetrate the gloom.

▲ *Prehistoric people lived in caves, and some caves contain pictures of animals made by these cave-dwellers. Stone Age people drew cave paintings of hunting scenes at Lascaux in France more than 15,000 years ago.*

◀ *Cave explorers, or cavers, wear helmets and tough clothing, as caves are often wet and cold, and rocks can be sharp. For safety they explore in groups. Each caver carries at least two torches, one fixed to the helmet so the caver's hands are free.*

▲ *The world's longest caves are the Mammoth Caves of Kentucky, USA, first explored in 1799. This cave system has 560 km of caves and passages, with underground lakes and rivers. The second-longest cave system, in Ukraine, extends for 156 km.*

◀ *In the limestone Carlsbad Caverns of New Mexico, USA, the most weird and wonderful stalactites and stalagmites can be seen. The Big Room is a huge underground chamber measuring 550 m long and 335 m wide.*

Most famous cave paintings: Lascaux, France ▸ Longest underwater cave: Mexico ▸ Longest stalagmite: 30 m

▶ *Cave animals include bats, birds and even fish. Bats roost in caves, often in huge numbers, sleeping upside down by day and leaving the cave at dusk to feed. Rarely disturbed by people, some caves have been home to bat colonies for thousands of years.*

Stalactites hang own like huge cles from the ofs of caves. They rm as water drips wn and deposits lcium carbonate. ne of the longest alactites on record easured more an 12 m long. It as in a cave in azil.

	WORLD'S DEEPEST CAVES		
	CAVE	**COUNTRY**	**DEPTH**
★1	Reseau Jean Bernard	France	1,602 m
2	Lamprechtsofen-Vogelshacht	Austria	1,537 m
3	Gouffre Mirolda/Lucien Bouclier	France	1,520 m

▼ *Stalagmites grow up from the floors of caves as water drips down from the roof and deposits calcium carbonate. A stalagmite more than 30 m tall – higher than a house! – was measured inside a cave in Slovakia.*

VIOLENT VOLCANOES AND GEYSERS

A volcano is a hole in Earth's crust. Hot, melted rocks are pushed out through the hole from time to time. When this happens, the volcano erupts. Active volcanoes erupt often. Dormant volcanoes do so only occasionally. Extinct volcanoes are safely dead and will not erupt again. There are more than 800 known active volcanoes in the world. The country with the most is Indonesia, which has about 200.

▲ Geysers are spouts of steam and hot water, found in volcanically active regions. In 1903 a New Zealand geyser spurted to 460 m high – the highest ever measured. The tallest geyser 'blowing' today is Steamboat Geyser in Yellowstone National Park, USA, shown here. It blasts out hot steam to a height of about 115 m.

▼ A volcano erupts with immense force, sending hot molten rock, ash, steam and gas into the air.

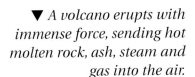

DID YOU KNOW?
Kilauea, a volcano on Hawaii, is the world's biggest-ever active volcano. Since its most recent outburst began in 1983, it has been spouting fountains of fire and a river of red-hot lava. Hawaii also has the world's biggest volcano. Called Mauna Loa, it rises about 9,000 m from the sea floor. More than 80 percent of Mauna Loa is beneath the ocean.

▶ *Magma, or melted rock, rises up a vent tube from a chamber deep inside the volcano. Lava bursts out like boiling tar and hardens as it cools on the slopes of the volcanic cone. Volcanic bombs of rock are hurled into the air.*

cloud of ash

volcanic bomb weighing up to 90 tonnes

volcanic cone

magma chamber

◀ *The biggest release of noise and energy from a volcano was in 1883, when Krakatoa Island, Indonesia, blew up. The noise was heard up to 5,000 km away, 4 hours later.*

VOLCANO FACTS

Biggest volcano	**Mauna Loa**	**Hawaii**	**Crater 180 m deep**
Highest active volcano	**Ojos del Salado**	**South America**	**6,887 m high**
Most restless volcano	**Kilauea**	**Hawaii**	**Erupting since 1983**

A HUGE DISASTER

- In 1815 the Tambora volcano in Indonesia spewed out nine times more dust, ash and rock than Krakatoa.
- Some 92,000 people were killed by the Tambora volcano, its tidal wave, or by famine afterwards.

▶ *The most destructive volcano to erupt in North America in recent times was Mount St Helens in Washington state, in 1980. Ash spread over 800 km, avalanches were triggered, and 66 people were killed.*

EARTHQUAKES

Earthquakes shake the ground so powerfully that city buildings can topple and bridges and roads can be shattered. The energy released is many times greater than from an atomic bomb. Like volcanoes, earthquakes mostly happen where the plates that make up Earth's crust meet. The movement of the plates puts such stress on the rocks that they break apart. The world's worst earthquake of recent times was in northeast China in 1976, when at least 250,000 people were killed.

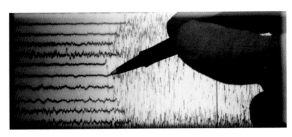

▲ *A seismograph measures the strength and direction of earthquake waves. It records the tremors and compares their strength on the Richter scale. A scale of one is a minor earthquake, while a scale of seven is severe.*

HOW OFTEN DO EARTHQUAKES HAPPEN?

● There are as many as 500,000 earthquakes every year. Luckily most of them are too small to be felt.

● Each year, on average, there are about 1,000 earthquakes that cause damage to buildings.

▼ *Earthquakes (and volcanoes) are most likely to happen along faults in Earth's crust, where two of the plates meet. The movement of the plates puts the rocks from which they are made under such pressure that they can no longer hold together. Massive amounts of energy are released in shock waves as the rocks break apart. The result is an earthquake.*

▶▶ KILLER EARTHQUAKES		
COUNTRY	DATE	KILLED
★ 1 Egypt	1201	1 million
2 China	1556	830,000
3 India	1737	300,000
4 China	1976	250,000
5 China	1920	200,000
6 Japan	1923	142,000
7 Sicily	1908	75,000
8 Iran	1990	40,000
9 Martinique	1902	38,000
10 Armenia	1988	25,000

ocean plate and continental plate meet; the thin crust under the ocean is forced beneath the thicker crust under the mountain range – an earthquake occurs

▼ *When rock is pushed and pulled in opposite directions by the movement of Earth's crust, it can shear and break apart. A crack along which rocks move is called a fault.*

arrows show movement of land

mountain range

active volcano

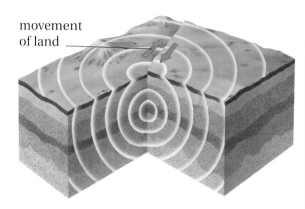

movement of land

▲ *Shock waves from an earthquake spread out in waves deep below the surface. The point on the surface directly above is called the epicentre. Aftershocks, sometimes hours later, can cause just as much damage.*

1   2

▲ *There are two kinds of surface shock waves: 1) Rayleigh, or R, waves make the ground roll. 2) Love, or Q, waves shake the ground from side to side.*

BIG EARTHQUAKES OF THE 20TH CENTURY

	PLACE	COUNTRY	DATE	RICHTER SCALE
★1	Aleutian Islands	USA	1957	9.1
2 =	Assam	India	1950	8.6
2 =	Gansu	China	1920	8.6
3 =	San Francisco	USA	1906	8.3
3 =	Kanto Plain	Japan	1923	8.3
4	Tangshan	China	1976	8.2
5	Mexico City	Mexico	1985	8.1

▶ *It takes a really big earthquake to make cracks open up in the ground. This seismologist is recording the size of the gaps that have appeared.*

◀ *The city of Los Angeles on the west coast of the USA is built on the San Andreas fault, one of the most active faults in the world. The city was badly damaged by an earthquake in 1994.*

▼ *Japan lies on a boundary of two plates. A major earthquake occurs there about every five years. Without special reinforced foundations, few buildings can survive. In 1995 an earthquake in Kobe and Osaka flattened 100,000 buildings – while one in 1923 wrecked five times that number.*

EARTHQUAKE STRENGTH ON RICHTER SCALE

	RICHTER SCALE	DEGREE OF DAMAGE
★1	11–12	Catastrophic, ground rises and falls in waves
2	8–11	Disastrous, ground cracks, serious damage and loss of life within 200–300 km radius
3	7.0–7.9	Major earthquake, serious damage and loss of life over a large area
4	6.0–6.9	Damage to buildings within 100 km radius
5	5.4–6.0	Major damage to poorly built buildings
6	3.5–5.4	Often felt, but rarely cause damage
7	3–3.5	Tremors felt, like a heavy truck passing

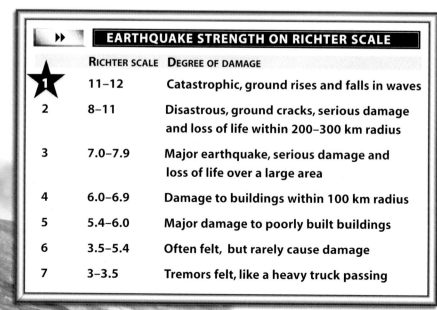

DESERTS

Almost one eighth of Earth's surface is dry desert, receiving less than 250 mm of rainfall in a year. The biggest desert is the Sahara in north Africa, at 5,000 km across and up to 2,250 km north to south. It has the world's biggest sand dunes, some more than 400 m high. Temperatures can be scorching hot by day and near-freezing at night. Not all deserts are sandy though. Most deserts are stony or icy. The continent with the most deserts is Asia.

▲ *An oasis is a green 'island' in the desert. Underground water allows plants and trees to grow. Some oases support small towns.*

◀ *Wind and sand have eroded, or worn away, these famous desert rocks in Monument Valley, Arizona, USA, giving them strange shapes.*

▶ *The driest place on Earth is the Atacama Desert in Chile, South America. Intervals between showers may be as long as 100 years, and in some areas it has not rained for more than 400 years!*

FUR COATS IN THE GOBI

● In the Gobi Desert temperatures drop below freezing for half the year. No wonder the camels in the Gobi have thick woolly coats.

▼ *Camels are the most useful desert pack animals. They can live for weeks on a few mouthfuls of thorns or dried leaves, and go for several days without water.*

▶▶	BIGGEST DESERTS		
	DESERT	LOCATION	AREA
★ 1	Sahara	North Africa	9 million sq km
2	Australian	Australia	3.8 million sq km
3	Arabian	Southwest Asia	1.3 million sq km
4	Gobi	Central Asia	1 million sq km
5	Kalahari	Southern Africa	520,000 sq km

saguaro cactus

elf owl

elf owl

woodpecker

bat

humming bird

jack rabbit

▶ *The vast Sahara takes in 11 countries of northern Africa, including Algeria and Tunisia, where there are 'seas of sand', called ergs.*

▶ *Desert plants such as cacti store water in leaves or stems, and some have very deep roots for finding water underground. They flower and set seeds quickly after rain has fallen. Many desert animals, such as the fennec fox, come out in the cool of night to find food. Some never drink, getting all the moisture they need from their food. Others, like the gila monster, run about in the fierce heat, raising their bodies above the sand to keep as cool as possible.*

cactus wren

gila monster

fennec fox

cactus flower

SNOW AND ICE

Temperatures at the South Pole fall below those at the North Pole – they can reach -50°C during an Antarctic winter. But the snowiest place in the world is not at either of the poles. It is on the west coast of the United States! During the winter of 1971–72, Paradise, in the mountains of Washington state, received 31,000 mm of snow. The deepest snowfall ever measured was in nearby California, also on the west coast of the USA, where in 1911 snow lay 11.46 m deep – enough to bury a house.

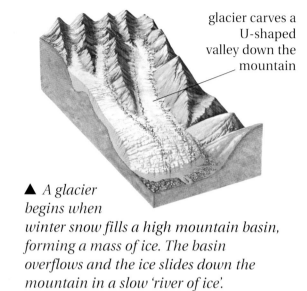

glacier carves a U-shaped valley down the mountain

▲ *A glacier begins when winter snow fills a high mountain basin, forming a mass of ice. The basin overflows and the ice slides down the mountain in a slow 'river of ice'.*

◄ *The biggest hailstone fell in Coffeyville, Kansas, USA, in 1970. It was 44.5 cm round, and weighed nearly 1 kg – bigger and much heavier than a tennis ball. Freak hailstones have been known to kill.*

▼ *The frozen waters of Antarctica support huge colonies, or rookeries, of fish-eating penguins and several kinds of seal.*

▲ *The ice covering Greenland is about 1.5 km thick, but the ice in Antarctica, shown here, is three times thicker, at up to 4.8 km thick! Scientists measure it by using echo-sounding equipment.*

southern elephant seals (bull, cow and pup)

» Biggest snow sculptures: Japan » Biggest hailstone: Kansas, USA » Oldest frozen dinner: mammoth

LONGEST GLACIERS

	Glacier	Location		Length
★ 1	Lambert-Fisher	Antarctica		515 km
2	Novaya Zemlya	Russia		418 km
3	Arctic Institute	Antarctica		362 km

Note: Eight of the ten longest glaciers in the world are in Antarctica

◀ An iceberg is a huge chunk of ice in the sea that has broken off a glacier. Big icebergs tower 120 m above the sea – but this may be only one-ninth of the total ice. The rest is under the water.

▲ The most snow to fall in 24 hours was 1.93 m in Silver Lake, Colorado, USA, in 1921. It was enough to cover a tall, upright man from head to foot.

▲ Roald Amundsen of Norway led the first expedition to the South Pole in 1911.

ANTARCTIC ICEBERGS

● Antarctic icebergs are flatter than Arctic ones.
● The biggest iceberg was spotted in the Antarctic in 1956. It was 335 km long and 97 km across. Belgium would have fitted on top of it!

▲ Permafrost is frozen soil that never thaws. The thickest permafrost was measured in Siberia in 1982, and was 1,370 m deep. Deep-frozen, extinct mammoths are dug out of the Siberian permafrost from time to time!

adult emperor penguin

Adélie penguin

young penguin

Weddell seal and pup

WEATHER

Regular weather charts have been kept for only about the last 250 years, and accurate temperature readings date from the 1800s. But people have always liked talking about weather. Chinese histories show that 903 BC was a very bad winter in China, and the Romans commented on the weather when they landed in Britain in 55 BC. The 7th century in England was unusually warm, while the winter of 1683–84 was so cold that the River Thames froze. The 1990s had several of the hottest years recorded in the 20th century.

▲ *Most rainbows last for only a few minutes, but the longest lasted for up to 6 hours. A rainbow forms when sunlight is bent and split by raindrops into the colours of the spectrum that make up light: violet, indigo, blue, green, yellow, orange and red.*

▸▸ WEATHER RECORDS			
Hottest place	Death Valley, California, USA	Above 49°C for 43 days	1917
Hottest all-year-round	Dallol, Ethiopia	34°C average	1960–66
Highest temperature	Al Aziziyah, Libya	58°C	1922
Highest-measured wind speed	New Hampshire, USA	371 km/h	1934
Coldest place	Vostok base, Antarctica	-89.2°C	1983

◀ *In the tropics, the region spanning the Equator, the weather is hot and wet all year round, and there are no seasons. Rainfall in the tropics can be incredibly heavy, falling at about 32 km/h! Many fruits, such as bananas, coconuts, mangoes and pineapples, flourish in the warm, wet tropical conditions.*

▲ *Much of North America, Europe and far eastern Asia has mild weather and spring and autumn seasons. In autumn the leaves of the 'deciduous' trees turn to brilliant colours, and in winter they drop off.*

▶ *The aurora borealis, or Northern Lights, makes the night sky glow green, gold, red or purple. The effect is caused by solar wind – radiation from the Sun – hitting Earth's atmosphere.*

▲ *All of Earth's weather, including clouds, is produced in the lowest layer of the atmosphere, called the troposphere. The troposphere extends to about 15 km above the surface of Earth. In the next layer up, the stratosphere, a thin layer of 'ozone' blocks the harmful radiation from the Sun.*

MAP KEY
Polar
Cool temperate
Mountains
Warm temperate
Tropical
Desert and semidesert

▶ *On Mount Wai-'ale-'ale in Hawaii you need an umbrella on all but 15 days of the year, while a record 38 mm of rain fell in one minute in Guadeloupe in the West Indies in 1970!*

DID YOU KNOW?
The highest clouds are nacreous clouds, which form at 24,000 m. Cumulonimbus clouds, shown here, can tower as high as 19,000 m. Cirrus clouds form at about 8,000 m, and the lowest stratus clouds form from 1,100 m to ground level.

▼ *The USA (not counting Alaska) has about 105 major snowstorms a year, and its snowiest major city is Buffalo, New York state. It is thought that no two snowflakes are the same!*

STORM FORCES

Storms are extremes of weather, ranging from hailstorms and blizzards to sandstorms and duststorms. The most destructive storms are hurricanes, known as cyclones in the Indian Ocean and typhoons in the Pacific Ocean. Wind strength is measured by the Beaufort scale. A scale of one is light air movement, while a scale of 12 is hurricane force. Hurricane winds can spiral at more than 400 km/h around a calm centre, called the 'eye'. Hurricanes cause terrible damage on land, as do tornadoes, or twisters, which are common in the United States. At sea, tornadoes create whirling waterspouts.

BEAUFORT SCALE

	WIND FORCE		WIND SPEED
1	12	Hurricane	118+ km/h
2	11	Violent storm	103–117 km/h
3	10	Storm	89–102 km/h
4	9	Strong gale	75–88 km/h
5	8	Gale	62–74 km/h
6	7	Near gale	50–61 km/h
7	6	Strong breeze	39–49 km/h
8	5	Fresh breeze	29–38 km/h
9	4	Moderate breeze	20–28 km/h
10	3	Gentle breeze	12–19 km/h
11	2	Light breeze	6–11 km/h
12	1	Light air	1–5 km/h
13	0	Calm	1 km/h

◀ *Britain's worst storm of modern times was the hurricane of October, 1987. High winds uprooted and blew down 15 million trees in southern England, blocked roads, and brought down roofs and power lines.*

◀ *The winds are influenced by the spinning of Earth. Either side of the Equator there are steady winds, called 'trade winds' by sailors. Between the trade winds lie the gentler doldrums. Westerly winds are common the farther north or south of the Equator you go, while in the polar regions easterly winds prevail.*

WEATHER RECORDS

Most thunder	Tororo, Uganda, Africa – average of 250 thundery days a year
Worst hailstorm	A hailstorm in 1888 battered to death 246 people in India
Highest waterspout	A waterspout 1,500 m high was seen off New South Wales, Australia, in 1888
Hottest flash	Lightning heats the air around it to more than 33,000°C – five times hotter than the Sun
Worst cyclone	In 1991, 138,000 people were killed when a cyclone and tidal wave hit Bangladesh
Worst hurricane	Hurricane Flora in 1963 killed 6,000 people in the Caribbean

▶ *Thunderclouds build up to great heights, dark and laden with rain. Thunder is the sound air makes when it expands, warmed by the heat of a lightning flash. Because sound travels more slowly than light, we see the lightning seconds before we hear the clap of thunder.*

» Biggest headache: outsized hailstones » Biggest waterspout: Australia » Most thundery days: Uganda

▼ *A tornado can lift and scatter cars as if they were toys, and can literally burst a building apart from the inside.*

◄ *A tornado is a windstorm that creates a huge funnel of whirling air stretching down to the ground. The tip of the funnel sucks up everything in its track. In the United States tornadoes are called 'twisters'. They roar across the Midwest at speeds of 50 km/h.*

◄ *Hurricanes form over the Atlantic Ocean and move westward through the Caribbean and across the southern United States. Most years, such giant storms strike the coasts, flattening trees and buildings, flooding towns and wrecking communications.*

◄ *When a hurricane hits, many people lose the roofs of their homes. Floods can do as much damage as the high winds.*

◄ *Satellites in space track hurricanes over the ocean, and so provide early warning for people to move to safety. You can even watch a hurricane's progress live on the Internet.*

RAINING FISH

● Storm winds create strong up-draughts of air over water that can suck up fish and frogs. The animals rain down from the sky, to the surprise of people below!

THE NATURAL

WORLD

The natural world surrounds us. Yet for most of the time we are not aware of the plant and animal kingdoms living, growing reproducing and changing right before our eyes.

From the minutest toadstool spores – up to five million are released in one go and carried by the wind – to enormous tree trunks – the sequoia measures more than 30 metres in diameter, the natural world provides us with amazing records and feats. For instance the common house spider can run at nearly 2 km per hour – that's the equivalent of a human being running 800 m in 10 seconds. Pretty fast. And parrots are so clever, they can work out simple sums.

Explore the biggest and best facts about *The Natural World* and get in touch with nature. There are the big, serious facts – for reference – and less serious ones, too, for fun. These pages are packed with the biggest and best, oddest and strangest, smallest and funniest facts around!

LIVING THINGS

Life on Earth began more than 3.5 billion years ago, when tiny cells divided and made copies of themselves. Scientists have named more than 2 million species of living things, and every year they find hundreds more new species. Living things range from microscopic bacteria to giant trees. Some live only for a day, others survive for thousands of years.

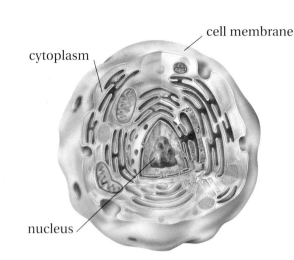

cytoplasm

cell membrane

nucleus

▼ *There are two main groups of animals: vertebrates and invertebrates. Vertebrates are animals with backbones, such as a tiger. Invertebrates, such as a sea slug, do not have backbones. About 96 percent of all animals are invertebrates.*

▲ *All living things are made of cells. Cells are like tiny chemical factories. There are millions of them in our bodies. Different-shaped cells do different jobs. This is a typical animal cell.*

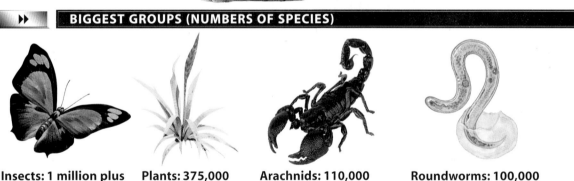

▶▶ BIGGEST GROUPS (NUMBERS OF SPECIES)

Insects: 1 million plus | **Plants: 375,000** | **Arachnids: 110,000** (SPIDERS AND RELATIVES) | **Roundworms: 100,000** (ESTIMATED) | **Molluscs: 50,000**

▶ *Insects are the biggest success story in the animal world. There are at least 1 million species.*

▶ *In this picture the size of each living thing is shown in proportion to how many species there are on Earth. There are at least 1 million insect species, so the ladybird is shown very big. But there are only 4,500 mammal species, so the elephant is tiny.*

mammal

▸ Largest weed: giant hogweed ▸ Quickest life cycle: bacteria ▸ Longest plant roots: winter rye

OLDEST LIVING THINGS

	NAME	MILLION YEARS AGO
★ 1	Primitive algae and bacteria	3.5 billion years ago
2	Crustaceans	600
3	Molluscs	500
4	Fish	480
5	Land plants and millipedes	400
6	Insects and spiders	370
7	Amphibians	350
8	Reptiles	290
9	Mammals	190
10	Flowering plants	140

▶ *The Amazon rainforest in South America is home to more species of plants and animals than any other place on Earth.*

harpy eagle

spider monkey

bromeliad flower

anaconda

blue-grey tanager

◀ *Unlike plants, animals such as this mole must find their own food. Animals eat plants or other animals. For most animals, finding food is their main activity.*

Fishes: 27,000   **Crustaceans: 26,000**   **Birds: 9,000**   **Reptiles: 5,000**   **Mammals: 4,500**

insect

bromeliad

flaming poison arrow frog

PLANTS AND FUNGI

There are about 375,000 species of plants. Some, such as mosses, ferns and lichens, never have flowers or make seeds. But most plants do make flowers – there are more than 250,000 flowering species. The earliest-known flowering plant grew 142 million years ago and a fossil of it was found in China in 1998. Plants make their own food, using sunlight, in a process called photosynthesis. Fungi are different from plants because they cannot make their own food. There are about 100,000 species of fungi.

poison ivy

nettle

water hemlock

saguaro cactus

◀ The Rafflesia *of Southeast Asia has the biggest flower, measuring 90 cm across. It also has a most disgusting smell, but flies love it!*

▲ *Plant defences discourage animals from eating them. Poison ivy gives off an oil that causes a painful itch. The hairs on nettle leaves cause a sting by injecting a fluid. The spines of cacti are too sharp to eat, and hemlock is so poisonous that animals eating its leaves or berries develop stomach ache and may even die.*

FUNGUS FEATS

- A single underground fungus mass beneath a forest in Washington state, USA, covers 6 sq km.
- A fungus mass in Michigan, USA, weighed more than 100 tonnes – as much as a blue whale.

» TALLEST, BIGGEST, LONGEST		
Tallest grass	Bamboo	25 m
Tallest cactus	Saguaro	18 m
Biggest fern	Norfolk Island tree fern	20 m
Biggest seed	Coco-de-mer palm	20 kg
Biggest carnivorous	*Nepenthes* vines	10 m
Longest leaf	Raffia palm	20 m
	Amazonian bamboo palm	20 m
Longest seaweed	Giant kelp	60 m

◀ *The most deadly fungus is the death cap* Amanita phalloides. *If eaten, less than 50 g can kill a person in just six hours.*

IT'S A FACT

Some seeds can lie dormant for hundreds of years before they start to grow. In 1966 some frozen seeds of the Arctic lupin thawed and started to grow after they had been in deep freeze, scientists reckoned, for about 10,000 years.

▲ Bamboo, a giant grass, is the fastest-growing plant. It shoots up almost 1 m a day.

▲ A Malaysian orchid has the longest petals, each one measuring almost 1 m long.

▲ Measuring 2 m across, the leaves of the giant water-lily of tropical South America are so big and strong that a large dog can stand on them and walk across water!

▼ Toadstools, such as the ones shown here, are formed by a fungus when it is ready to reproduce. A single toadstool can contain 5 million tiny spores. These are released and blown away by the wind. When they land, they begin to grow into new fungi.

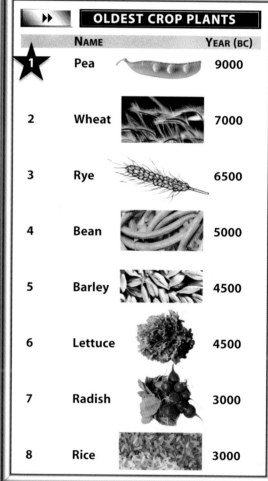

OLDEST CROP PLANTS

	Name	Year (BC)
1	Pea	9000
2	Wheat	7000
3	Rye	6500
4	Bean	5000
5	Barley	4500
6	Lettuce	4500
7	Radish	3000
8	Rice	3000

TOWERING TREES

Trees are the biggest plants, and the biggest single living thing on Earth is a tree. Trees live much longer than any animal. Some trees can survive for hundreds, and even thousands, of years. There are trees alive today that began growing long before the Roman Empire. Trees act as the Earth's 'lungs', enriching the air with oxygen. The trunks provide timber, and rubber is made from tree sap.

IT'S A FACT
The African baobab has a barrel-shaped trunk that stores water. The trunk can measure up to 54 m around the outside. Thirty people holding hands could just about make a circle around the trunk.

◄ *The banyan or Indian fig tree puts out wide-spreading branches that send down hundreds of hanging roots. These take hold of the soil and act as supports for the branches. The biggest-known banyan is in the Botanical Gardens in Calcutta, India. It has an estimated 1,775 hanging roots, and its huge canopy covers an area the size of a small forest.*

TREE SEEDS
- The fruits of the elm, ash, lime and hornbeam are fitted with aerofoils or wings that enable them to glide very long distances.
- The largest seed in the world comes from the giant fan palm or coco-de-mer, which grows only in the Seychelles. One seed can weigh 20 kg.
- Giant redwoods grow from tiny seeds less than 2 mm long.
- It would take 271,000 redwood seeds to make 1 kg!

	SUPER GIANTS – THE TALLEST TREES EVER MEASURED	
	NAME AND COUNTRY	**HEIGHT**
★ 1	Eucalyptus (Australia)	132.6 m
2	Douglas fir (USA)	126.5 m
3	Douglas fir (USA)	116 m
4	Mountain ash (Australia)	114 m
5	Coast redwood (USA)	112 m (STILL GROWING)

1   2   3   4   5

» Greatest trunk girth: baobab » Heaviest: sequoia » Tallest ever: eucalyptus » Tallest and oldest living: redwood

▶ *The most massive tree is a giant sequoia named 'General Sherman' growing in Sequoia National Park, California, USA. This forest giant is almost 84 m high and measures 31.4 m round its trunk. It weighs an estimated 2,500 tonnes – as much as 350 elephants. Redwoods grow taller than giant sequoias, but their trunks are not as thick. They can reach heights of 100 m or more.*

DID YOU KNOW?
The oldest living trees are bristlecone pines (left), in the USA, some of which are more than 4,000 years old. Giant sequoias probably have a lifespan of 5,000 to 6,000 years.

▲ *Counting tree leaves is not a job everyone would enjoy. The average oak grows and sheds at least 250,000 leaves every year.*

SLIDERS AND CRAWLERS

The creepy crawlies of the animal world – insects, spiders, crustaceans, molluscs, worms, starfish and corals – are hugely varied, but they all have one thing in common: they lack backbones. They belong to the group called invertebrates. About 96 percent of all animals are invertebrates. The mollusc species alone number more than 100,000, and there are at least 1 million known insect species, though some scientists think there may be up to 10 million!

▶ *The house spider can run at nearly 2 km/h. Relative to its size, that is like a human sprinter running 800 m in 10 seconds – much faster than an Olympic athlete.*

◀ *The Gippsland giant worm is a 4-m-long Australian earthworm. It makes a slurping, gurgling sound as it slides its way through its burrow.*

▶ *The animals with the most legs are centipedes and millipedes. Millipedes, with up to 370 pairs, have the most, but centipedes can run faster.*

millipede

centipede

DID YOU KNOW?
The mantis shrimp can punch a hole in a glass tank. Called a stomatopod, this crustacean uses its spring-action smasher-claw to crack open crab shells and to hit other mantis shrimps in fights. Losers learn to back off when they meet a bigger rival, rather than risk being killed.

▶ *Some people keep African giant snails as pets. These leaf-munchers are the biggest land snails. The record-holder weighed 900 g and measured 39 cm across (as big as a football). Some sea snails are even bigger than the average African snail!*

▼ *The sea wasp jellyfish is the most venomous jellyfish. Its sting can kill a person in less than 4 minutes.*

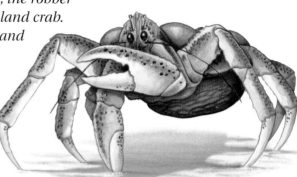

▶ *At 30 cm across, the robber crab is the biggest land crab. It can climb trees, and is so much a land animal that it drowns if kept in water.*

▸▸	LONGEST, BIGGEST, DEEPEST		
Longest worm	North sea bootlace worm		55 m
Biggest spider	Bird-eating spider		28 cm
Biggest sea snail	Horse conch		60 cm
Biggest starfish	*Midgardia xandaros*		1.38 m
Biggest jellyfish	Arctic giant jellyfish	body diameter:	2.28 m
		tentacle length:	36.5 m
Deepest-living sponge	*Hexactinellida* (class)		8,500 m

▼ *The giant squid is the largest-known invertebrate, measuring up to 6.1 m in body length, with tentacles up to 10.7 m long. Scientists believe these giants fight fierce battles with sperm whales, which hunt squid for food in the ocean depths.*

◀ *Pacific giant clams have the biggest shells of any mollusc. They can measure over 1 m across and weigh more than 300 kg. Clams grow very slowly – one tiny North Atlantic species takes 100 years to grow just 8 mm long.*

INTRIGUING INSECTS

Insects can live almost anywhere and eat almost anything. Fortunately their body design limits their size, so insect giants exist only in horror films! Many insects are amazingly strong. Some can drag objects many times heavier than themselves; others, such as termites, construct enormous homes; and fleas can jump 130 times their own height. Caterpillars may not look muscle-packed, but they have six times as many muscles as a person and they eat far more for their size.

BUTTERFLIES AND BEES

● A butterfly flaps its wings between 5 and 12 times per second.

● A queen bee lays 1 million eggs during her 5-year life.

● In spring a queen bee lays one egg every 40 seconds.

▶ There are more beetles than any other kind of insect. The bombardier beetle has one of the most unusual weapons – it sprays a jet of hot, itch-making gas at attackers.

IT'S A FACT
The fastest flyers in the insect world include dragonflies (left), which can reach speeds of up to 58 km/h. The bumblebee, by contrast, slowly buzzes along at less than half this speed – about 18 km/h.

▶ The African Goliath beetle is the world's heaviest insect. It weighs about 100 g and at 11 cm long is almost as big as an adult person's hand.

▶▶ NUMBERS OF INSECT SPECIES

Beetles: 400,000

Butterflies, moths: 165,000

Ants, bees, wasps: 140,000

Flies: 120,000

Bugs: 90,000

▸ Fastest: Australian dragonfly ▸ Best survivor: cockroach ▸ Heaviest: Goliath beetle ▸ Shortest lived: mayfly

▼ *Locusts swarm in huge numbers. A small swarm may contain 50 million locusts. The largest-ever swarm, in Nebraska, USA, in 1875, had an estimated 12.5 trillion insects.*

INSECT RECORD-HOLDERS

Heaviest	**Goliath beetle**	**100 g**
Lightest	**Bloodsucking banded louse (male)**	**0.005 mg**
Longest legs	**Stick insect**	**54.6 cm**
Biggest mass	**Locust swarm**	**25 million tonnes**
Fastest runner	**Tropical cockroach**	**5 km/h**

▶ *Some locust species can eat their own body-weight in food every day.*

▶ *Stick insects closely resemble twigs, making them hard for hungry birds to spot in the forests. The largest-known stick insect came from the rainforests of Borneo. It had a body length of 32.8 cm and its legs measured 54.6 cm – longer than a man's arm from elbow to fingertips!*

▶ *Termites make amazing mound nests. The tallest mound measured almost 9 m high. Termite queens live up to 50 years, making them the longest-lived insects.*

FISH FACTS

Fish live in salty seas and freshwater rivers and lakes. Some are fast, streamlined swimmers, some have flat bodies and live on sea and river beds, some generate electricity, and some can even fly. Most fish have skeletons made of bone, but sharks have skeletons of cartilage. The biggest fish is the rare whale shark. The longest on record measured 12.6 m in length. This 15–20 tonne gentle giant eats only tiny plankton and small fish, but some of its relatives are among the most powerful predators in the world.

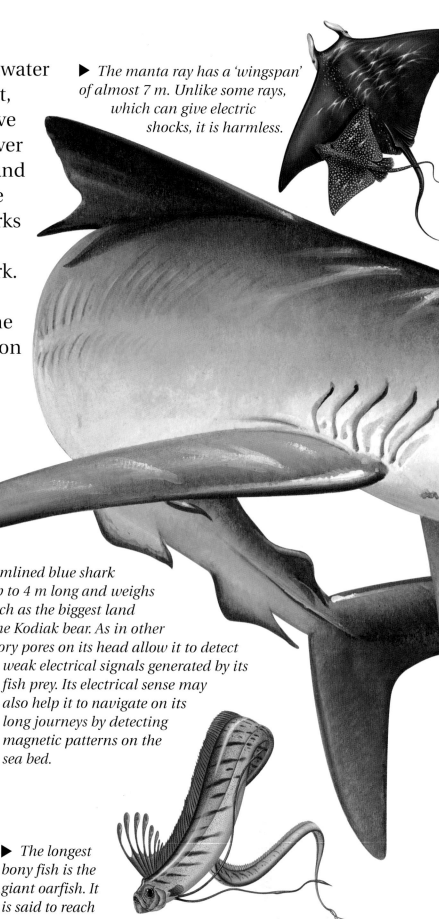

▶ *The manta ray has a 'wingspan' of almost 7 m. Unlike some rays, which can give electric shocks, it is harmless.*

▼ *The ocean sunfish, the heaviest bony fish, lays the most number of eggs at a single spawning – about 300 million. Only a tiny fraction of these develop. Most are eaten by other fish.*

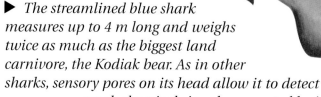

▶ *The streamlined blue shark measures up to 4 m long and weighs twice as much as the biggest land carnivore, the Kodiak bear. As in other sharks, sensory pores on its head allow it to detect weak electrical signals generated by its fish prey. Its electrical sense may also help it to navigate on its long journeys by detecting magnetic patterns on the sea bed.*

▶ *The longest bony fish is the giant oarfish. It is said to reach 15 m long.*

▼ *The 15-tonne whale shark, which lives in the warmer areas of the Atlantic, Pacific and Indian oceans, weighs almost as much as two big African bull elephants.*

◀ *The coelacanth is an ancient fish that became famous in 1938, when a specimen was caught off East Africa. Until then, scientists thought this primitive-looking fish had died out 70 million years ago. Since its discovery, coelacanths have been found on the other side of the Indian Ocean, off Indonesia.*

▶ *The sailfish is the fastest swimmer, reaching just over 100 km/h in short bursts.*

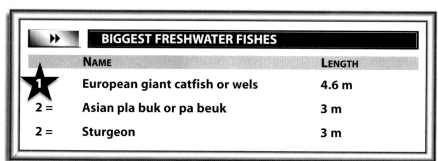

▸▸ BIGGEST FRESHWATER FISHES

	Name	Length
★ 1	European giant catfish or wels	4.6 m
2 =	Asian pla buk or pa beuk	3 m
2 =	Sturgeon	3 m

▸▸ SIX DANGEROUS SHARKS

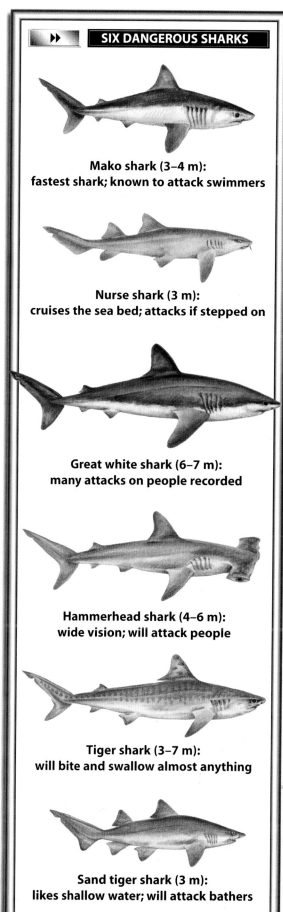

Mako shark (3–4 m):
fastest shark; known to attack swimmers

Nurse shark (3 m):
cruises the sea bed; attacks if stepped on

Great white shark (6–7 m):
many attacks on people recorded

Hammerhead shark (4–6 m):
wide vision; will attack people

Tiger shark (3–7 m):
will bite and swallow almost anything

Sand tiger shark (3 m):
likes shallow water; will attack bathers

AMPHIBIANS

There are about 3,000 species of amphibians altogether. Most of them – about 2,700 – are frogs and toads, which have no tails. Frogs hunt by shooting out their long, sticky-tipped tongues to grab insects. The largest of this group is the African Goliath frog. The second-biggest group is the newts and salamanders, which do have tails. The members of the smallest group are called caecilians. They have no legs and look like worms. All amphibians are cold-blooded animals and most can live on land or in water.

FROG FACTS AND FEATS

- Some frogs hardly ever leave the water.
- Some frogs burrow in the ground.
- Some frogs climb trees using sucker discs on their toes.
- There is even a gliding frog, which leaps between branches.

▼ *The Pacific giant salamander is the largest of the salamanders in northwestern North America. It grows to 28 cm long.*

▶▶ FATTEST, BIGGEST, SMALLEST		
Fattest toad:	Cane toad	2.6 kg
Biggest amphibian:	Chinese giant salamander	1.8 m
Biggest frog:	African Goliath frog	3.6 kg
Biggest tadpole:	Mexican axolotl	25 cm
Smallest frog:	*Eleutherodactylus limbatus*	12 mm

▶ *A frog jumps by lifting its front legs off the ground and pushing off with its strong back legs. Almost any frog can leap 20 times its own length. The record jump is 10.3 m by a pet South African sharp-nosed frog.*

▶ *The red eyed tree frog of Central America lives on the undersides of leaves in lowland rainforests. The distinctive vertical black pupils in the frog's eyes, like those of a cat, give it excellent night vision. Frogs generally have horizontal pupils for daylight vision.*

▶ *The frogs of today are descended from much larger creatures that first crept onto land around 300 million years ago. Like the first amphibians, they have to return to water to reproduce.*

▲ *The oddest amphibian is the Mexican axolotl, a salamander that never completes its metamorphosis from a tadpole to an adult. It remains a giant tadpolelike creature all its life, breathing through gills. The axolotl can never leave the water to explore dry land.*

▼ *The cane toad is the greatest amphibian pest. It was introduced to Australia from tropical South America in the 1930s to eat beetles. Unfortunately it also gobbles up native frogs and lizards, and even birds. The largest known was 53.9 cm long.*

◀ *The California newt of the United States is about 15 cm long, just smaller than Europe's biggest newt, the warty newt. Newts are salamanders that spend most of their adult lives in water.*

▶ *Amphibians have some strange names. The mudpuppy, shown here, is a salamander. Perhaps more oddly named still is the bumpy rocketfrog, which lives in Australia.*

DID YOU KNOW?
In British English frogs go "croak". In American English they go "ribbit". Korean frogs say "gae-gool, gae-gool", and Russian frogs go "kva-kva".

REPTILES

There are about 3,700 species of lizards, making this the biggest group of reptiles. The next largest group is snakes. But the biggest living reptile is neither a lizard nor a snake. It is the estuarine or saltwater crocodile, which can be up to 7 m long. The largest crocodiles weigh as much as 450 kg and can live to be 100 years old. Only a leatherback turtle outweighs a crocodile. One specimen that washed up on a beach in Wales, UK, in 1988 weighed more than 960 kg. The heaviest snake is the anaconda at 200 kg.

DID YOU KNOW?

There are only two poisonous lizards, the Mexican beaded lizard and the gila monster (right) of the southwestern United States. The gila monster's favourite food is birds' eggs. It bites humans only in self-defence. Its brittle teeth may remain in the wound.

▼ *The leatherback turtle is the heaviest reptile and also one of the fastest, reaching speeds of 35 km/h when scared.*

hawksbill

loggerhead turtle

green turtle

leatherback turtle

▼ *One of the most venomous snakes is the king cobra. It is also the longest poisonous snake. It can grow to more than 4.5 m long.*

DEADLY SNAKES

- Without treatment, victims of the taipan, black mamba, tiger snake, common krait and king cobra have a 50 to 100 percent risk of dying.
- Sea snakes in the Timor Sea have venom 100 times stronger than the taipan's.

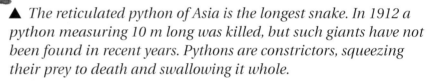

▼ *The Komodo dragon, an Indonesian monitor lizard, can grow to 3 m in length. (Animals three times this size have been reported, but not proved.) Komodos use their sawlike teeth to tear meat from their prey, which includes water buffaloes. Human victims have also been reported.*

▲ *The reticulated python of Asia is the longest snake. In 1912 a python measuring 10 m long was killed, but such giants have not been found in recent years. Pythons are constrictors, squeezing their prey to death and swallowing it whole.*

★	BIGGEST CROCODILES AND ALLIGATORS	
	NAME	**LENGTH**
1	Estuarine crocodile	7 m
2	Indian gavial	6 m
3 =	Nile crocodile	5 m
3 =	American crocodile	5 m
4	American alligator	4 m

◄ *Geckos have an unusual adaptation – hairy feet. Each foot has about 500,000 hairs, and each hair tip has thousands of microscopic 'stickers', creating a powerful adhesive. This enables the gecko to walk on any surface and even hang by one toe.*

▲ *The estuarine crocodile often swims far out in the Indian Ocean. At up to 7 m long, it is the biggest of all the crocodiles.*

BIRDS

Birds are the only animals with feathers and they all have wings, though not all of them can fly. Among the biggest expert flyers are the storks, condors, swans and albatrosses. Record-breaking flyers are the peregrine falcon, the fastest of all birds, and the Arctic tern, which makes the longest migratory flight of any bird, from the Arctic to Antarctica and back again. The ostrich is the biggest living bird, but it is flightless. It can run at speeds of up to 50 km/h.

▲ *The wandering albatross glides effortlessly across thousands of kilometres of ocean. It has the longest wing-span of any living bird, measuring up to 3.6 m.*

LONGEST-LIVED BIRDS

	Name	Age (years)
1	Siberian white crane	82
2 =	Sulphur-crested cockatoo	80
2 =	Goose	80
3 =	Ostrich	68
3 =	Eagle owl	68
4	Macaw	64

▶ *With their long necks and stilt-like legs, flamingos stand up to 1.5 m tall. They live in lakes and marshland in eastern and southern Africa, and use their curved bills to catch small water creatures. Parent birds feed their single chick on liquidized babyfood from their stomachs.*

IT'S A FACT
Birds' feathers are light, waterproof and provide insulation, slowing down heat loss. A swan (left) has about 25,000 feathers. Hummingbirds have the fewest: less than 1,000. Their feathers resemble scales.

◄ *In a dive a peregrine falcon can reach an estimated speed of 270 km/h, making it the fastest of all creatures. It knocks its prey out of the air, killing it instantly.*

▶ *Bird-brains are quite bright. Ravens and pigeons can work out simple counting sums. Parrots (right) and mynahs can mimic human speech, and some parrots can name and count objects.*

» BIGGEST EAGLES		
	NAME	**LENGTH**
★ 1	**Harpy eagle (South America)**	100 cm
2 =	**Monkey-eating eagle (Philippines)**	90 cm
2 =	**Crowned eagle (Africa)**	90 cm
2 =	**Steller's sea eagle (Pacific coasts)**	90 cm

◄ *The bald eagle is the national bird of the United States. Its huge nest can be up to 2.9 m wide and 6 m deep.*

◄ *The ostrich can be as tall as 2.7 m and weigh more than 150 kg. It lays the biggest of all birds' eggs. At up to 20 cm long, one egg would make about 12 omelettes!*

▶ *The 10.2-cm-long beak of the sword-billed hummingbird is longer than its body, making it the longest beak in relation to body length.*

▼ *The lesser flamingo of eastern Africa lives in huge flocks that can number several million birds.*

» LONGEST WING-SPANS		
	NAME	**LENGTH**
★ 1	**Wandering albatross**	3.6 m
2	**Marabou stork**	3.2 m
3 =	**Andean condor**	3 m
3 =	**Swan**	3 m

MAMMALS

The biggest animals in the world on land and in the sea are both mammals: elephants and whales. Amazingly adaptable, mammals live in a diverse range of habitats from deserts and rainforests to mountains, caves and ocean depths. They have bigger brains in relation to their body size than other animals. Many have hair or fur and some have scales or spines. But all mammals have one thing in common: they suckle their young with milk.

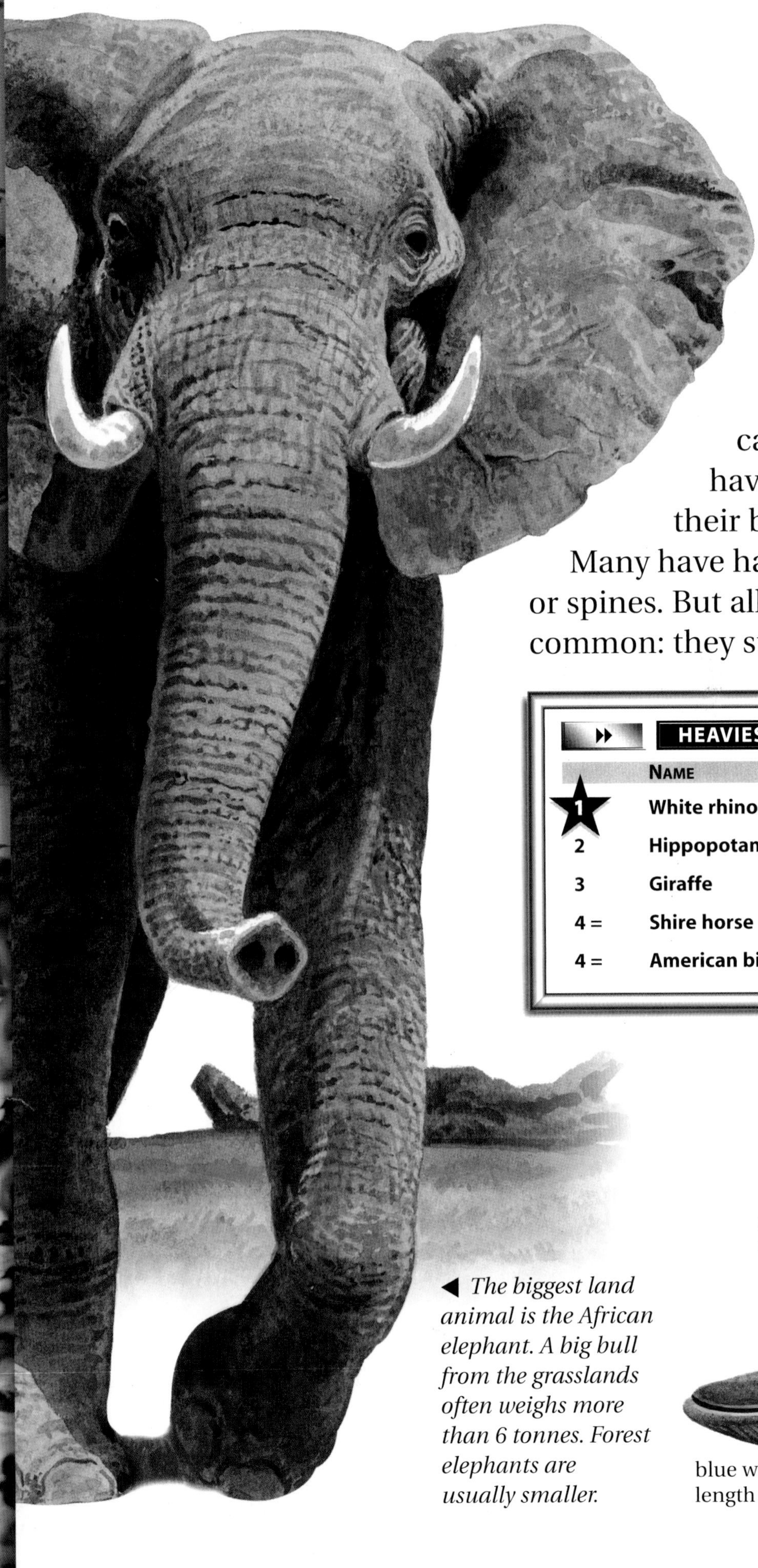

HEAVIEST HOOFED MAMMALS

	Name	Weight	Height
1	White rhinoceros	3,000 kg	1.8 m
2	Hippopotamus	1,400 kg	1.5 m
3	Giraffe	1,200 kg	5.5 m
4 =	Shire horse	1,000 kg	1.7 m
4 =	American bison	1,000 kg	1.5 m

▼ There are about 4,500 mammal species, ranging in size from the giant blue whale at 33.5 m long to tiny shrews and bats. Shown here to scale, the blue whale dwarfs the biggest land mammals and a human.

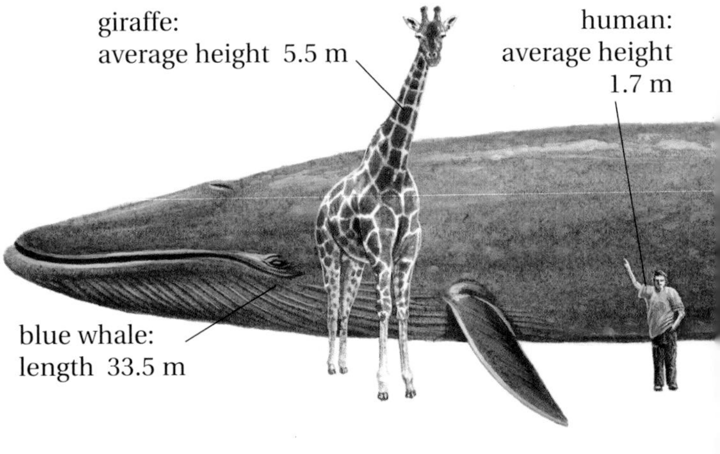

giraffe: average height 5.5 m

human: average height 1.7 m

◄ The biggest land animal is the African elephant. A big bull from the grasslands often weighs more than 6 tonnes. Forest elephants are usually smaller.

blue whale: length 33.5 m

◆ Biggest: blue whale ◆ Fastest: cheetah ◆ Longest nose: elephant

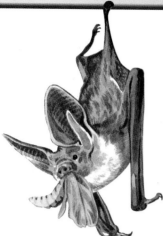

◀ *Bats are the only true flying mammals. In size they range from tiny bats no bigger than a bumblebee to flying foxes, which are as big as guinea pigs with wing-spans of 1.5 m. The small insect-eating bats, such as this long-eared bat, hunt by night using high-frequency echolocation. This means they collect sound reflections in their ear flaps.*

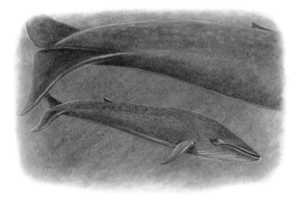

▲ *The blue whale is the biggest of all the mammals and gives birth to the biggest baby. At birth, a blue whale calf already measures 6 to 8 m long.*

▲ *The elk, or moose, is the biggest of all the deer, weighing 800 kg. Its antlers can be up to 1.5 m across. An elk eats the equivalent of about 20,000 leaves a day.*

▶ *The giraffe is the tallest mammal and has the longest neck. At full stretch a full-grown giraffe can reach juicy leaves up to 6 m above the ground.*

LARGEST WHALES

	Name		Length
★ 1	Blue whale		33.5 m
2	Fin whale		25 m
3 =	Sei whale (shown), Humpback whale		19 m
4	Sperm whale		18.5 m

brown bear:
average height 2.4 m

African elephant:
average height 3.3 m

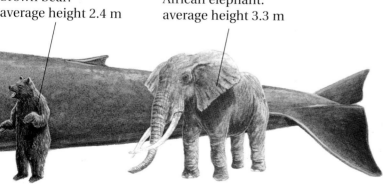

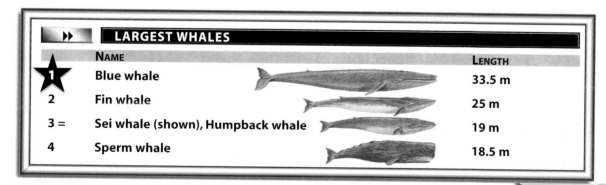

SLOW SLOTH

● The sloth is the slowest mammal. It crawls at 2 m a minute on the ground, speeding up to twice that when hanging upside-down from a tree.

PREDATOR POWER

The carnivores, or meat-eaters, include some of the most powerful predators in the animal world. The most feared hunters of the ocean are the great sharks and the killer whale, which can tackle even the biggest male seals and sea lions. The biggest land carnivores are the bears and the big cats. But smaller predators also show great determination and strength when hunting.

CATS ON THE PROWL

- Tigers hunt alone.
- Lions hunt in groups, driving prey into ambush.
- Jaguars often hunt in water.
- Leopards climb trees.
- Cheetahs chase prey at high speed.

▼ *The biggest bears in the world are the polar bear and the brown Kodiak bear (shown here) of Kodiak Island off Alaska. These huge North American bears can stand 3 m tall on their hind legs and weigh about 750 kg.*

▲ *The great white shark can attack at more than 40 km/h, biting chunks out of its prey with its enormous jaws.*

▶ *Killer whales hunt in groups called pods. They will pursue fleeing seals into the shallows and even charge through the surf to grab seals from the beach.*

▸▸ TOP PREDATORS IN THE SEA AND ON LAND

**Killer whale:
9 m; 9,000 kg**

**Great white shark:
4.5 m; 3,300 kg**

**Elephant seal:
5 m; 2,300 kg**

**Estuarine crocodile:
7 m; 450 kg**

**Steller's sea lion:
3.3 m; 1,000 kg**

» Most solitary and fattiest diet: polar bear » Most sociable: wolf » Most feared: shark » Most fearless: wolverine

▲ *Wolves (above) and African hunting dogs hunt in packs, chasing bigger animals such as deer or antelope until the prey is exhausted and can be killed.*

▲ *The male Siberian tiger is the biggest of the big cats, measuring 3.2 m from nose to tail tip. It is the most northern species of tiger, and is at home in the snow. Only about 400 are alive in the wild today.*

Note: This list does not include other sharks and marine mammals, which are bigger than the biggest land predators

Kodiak bear:
3 m; 750 kg

Polar bear:
2.6 m; 900 kg

Grizzly bear:
2.5 m; 400 kg

Siberian tiger:
3.2 m; 300 kg

Lion:
3 m; 250 kg

RECORD BREAKERS

The record-breakers of the natural world come in all shapes and sizes. Many animals are unbelievably strong. Some insects and mammals have incredible appetites. The fastest animals can easily outstrip a human sprinter, and the noisiest can outshout the loudest soccer fans. But for sheer size, the prize goes to the majestic blue whale. No creature in the history of the Earth has been bigger than this giant of the oceans. It eats only tiny, shrimplike krill, but swallows millions in one mouthful.

IT'S A FACT
Some caterpillars eat more than 100 times their own weight of food every day during the first 8 weeks of life. Shrews also have huge appetites and eat nearly all the time.

◀ *The noisiest land animals are the red and black howler monkeys of South America, the biggest of the New World monkeys. Living in troops of 10 to 30 animals, the monkeys howl to define their territory. The sound is made louder by the echo chambers beneath their chins, and can be heard 5 km away.*

▶ *The sperm whale is the biggest toothed whale, reaching 18 m in length and weighing 70 t. It dives to great depths, plunging to 3,000 m to hunt for food.*

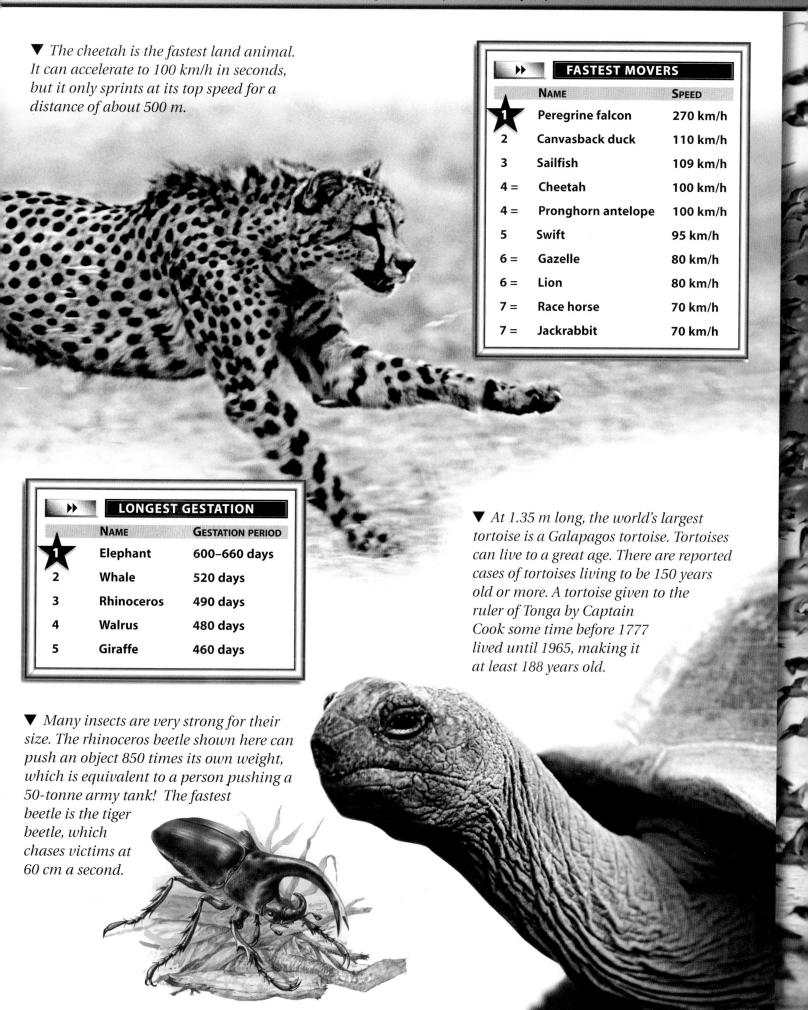

▼ The cheetah is the fastest land animal. It can accelerate to 100 km/h in seconds, but it only sprints at its top speed for a distance of about 500 m.

FASTEST MOVERS

	Name	Speed
1	Peregrine falcon	270 km/h
2	Canvasback duck	110 km/h
3	Sailfish	109 km/h
4 =	Cheetah	100 km/h
4 =	Pronghorn antelope	100 km/h
5	Swift	95 km/h
6 =	Gazelle	80 km/h
6 =	Lion	80 km/h
7 =	Race horse	70 km/h
7 =	Jackrabbit	70 km/h

LONGEST GESTATION

	Name	Gestation period
1	Elephant	600–660 days
2	Whale	520 days
3	Rhinoceros	490 days
4	Walrus	480 days
5	Giraffe	460 days

▼ At 1.35 m long, the world's largest tortoise is a Galapagos tortoise. Tortoises can live to a great age. There are reported cases of tortoises living to be 150 years old or more. A tortoise given to the ruler of Tonga by Captain Cook some time before 1777 lived until 1965, making it at least 188 years old.

▼ Many insects are very strong for their size. The rhinoceros beetle shown here can push an object 850 times its own weight, which is equivalent to a person pushing a 50-tonne army tank! The fastest beetle is the tiger beetle, which chases victims at 60 cm a second.

DINOSAURS

For about 160 million years, from 225 million years ago to 65 million years ago, dinosaurs were the most successful animals on Earth. The giant dinosaurs were the biggest reptiles of all time, and some of the prehistoric reptiles were the biggest flying animals ever. The word dinosaur means 'terrible lizard', and the names of the different dinosaurs describe something about them. *Tyrannosaurus*, for example, means 'tyrant lizard'.

▼ *Among the most fearsome dinosaurs were the 'slashing-claw' hunters such as the 4-m-long* Deinonychus, *the human-sized* Velociraptor *and the smaller* Stenonychosaurus. *These species were probably among the most intelligent too.*

Deinonychus

Velociraptor

Stenonychosaurus

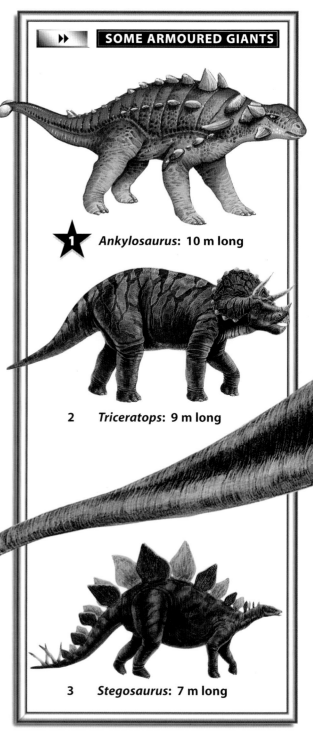

►► SOME ARMOURED GIANTS

★1 **Ankylosaurus:** 10 m long

2 **Triceratops:** 9 m long

3 **Stegosaurus:** 7 m long

►► **SOME DINOSAUR GIANTS**			Note: This list is a selection of some of the biggest dinosaurs
NAME	**LENGTH**	**WEIGHT**	
★1 *Seismosaurus*	30–50 m	50–80 tonnes	
2 *Brachiosaurus*	25 m	50 tonnes	
3 *Diplodocus*	23–27 m	12 tonnes	
4 *Mamenchisaurus*	20 m	uncertain	
5 *Apatosaurus (Brontosaurus)*	20 m	20–30 tonnes	1

▲ *Pterosaurs lived at the same time as dinosaurs and were related, but were not dinosaurs themselves. They flew on wings of skin. The largest, with a wing-span of 15 m, was* Quetzalcoatlus. *It was as big as a small aeroplane.*

▲ *The loudest dinosaurs were probably the duck-billed hadrosaurs. Like blowing trumpets, they blew air through cavities in their bony heads to make bellowing calls.*

◀ *The most terrifying carnivorous dinosaurs were* Tyrannosaurus Rex *(shown here) and the earlier* Allosaurus. *These hunters were up to 12 m long, weighed 6 tonnes, and had enormous jaws lined with sharp teeth.*

DID YOU KNOW?
Why the dinosaurs died out remains a mystery. The likeliest explanation is that a comet or meteorite hit the Earth, sending up huge dust-clouds on impact that caused a climate change. This killed off the plants on which many dinosaurs fed, and may have affected the hatching of dinosaur eggs.

2 3 4 5

» Longest tusks: straight-tusked elephant » Largest mammal: *Baluchitherium* » Longest stabbing teeth: sabretooth

EXTINCT AND VANISHING

Thousands of animals have died out naturally during the course of evolution. Most extinctions happen when animals cannot adapt to changes in the environment. Several mass extinctions happened in prehistoric times. The largest took place 240 million years ago, when perhaps 96 percent of living things vanished. The best-known mass extinction, 65 million years ago, saw the disappearance of the dinosaurs. Extinctions have greatly increased in the last 200 years, because of human activities.

» BIGGEST PREHISTORIC ANIMALS	
Baluchitherium	Giant rhinoceros
Megatherium	Ground sloth
Glyptodon	Armadillo
Diprotodon	Giant Australian wombat
Diatryma	Carnivorous bird

◀ *The dodo lived undisturbed on the island of Mauritius in the Indian Ocean until European sailors arrived in the 1500s. Sailors killed the birds for food and rats and cats ate the eggs. By 1680 the dodo was extinct.*

giant moa

Baluchitherium

▲ *The North American mammoth had huge, curling tusks. At 4 m high, it was bigger than any elephant living today.*

◀ Baluchitherium *was bigger than any land mammal alive today, and the giant moa was taller than any living bird. A human would be dwarfed by these giants.*

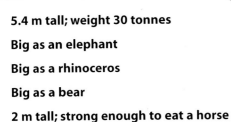

- 5.4 m tall; weight 30 tonnes
- Big as an elephant
- Big as a rhinoceros
- Big as a bear
- 2 m tall; strong enough to eat a horse

◀ *Billions of passenger pigeons lived in North America during the 19th century. But hunters began killing them in their breeding colonies, and between 1850 and 1880 the pigeon flocks vanished. The last passenger pigeon died in a zoo in 1914.*

◀ *Big cats are becoming rare as humans encroach on their hunting grounds. Among the rarest is the snow leopard of western China. It has a territory of up to 100 sq km.*

GONE FOREVER

- Steller's sea cow, a giant sea mammal, weighed 10 tonnes.
- The giant Irish deer had antlers with a span of 4 m.

◀ *Hunted for their horns, which some people value as a medicine, all the world's rhinoceroses are endangered. No more than 50 one-horned Javan rhinos are left in the wild.*

▼ *The North American buffalo, or bison, had a narrow escape. Two hundred years ago millions of buffalo wandered the Great Plains, but hunters in the 1800s killed most of them and by 1881 only 551 were left. Now protected, numbers have increased and there are more than 30,000 in the United States and Canada.*

RARE EUROPEAN BROWN BEARS

European brown bears are among the rarest animals, with only scattered populations.

	COUNTRY	POPULATION
1	France (Pyrenees)	10
2	Austria	30
3	Italy	80
4	Spain	85
5	Greece	120

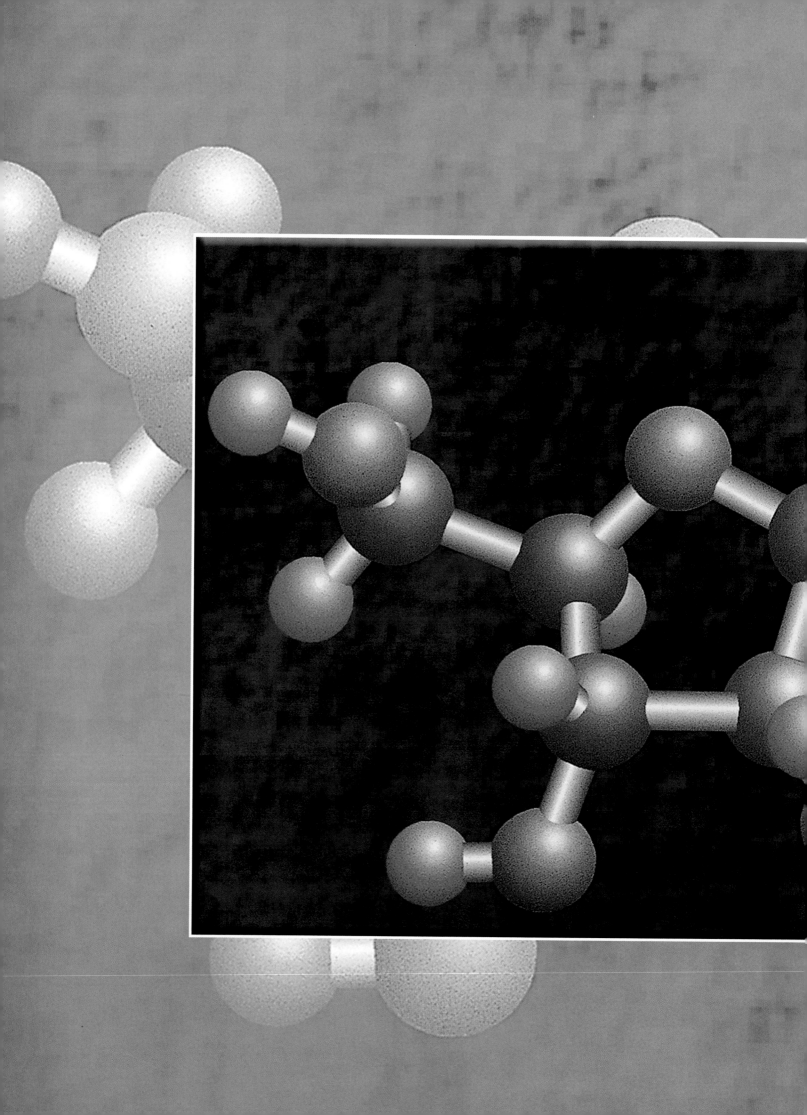

SCIENCE AND

TECHNOLOGY

Science helps us to understand our world. The different branches of science encourage us to question how things work, why things happen or what things mean. Science makes us inquisitive.

For example, how did we find out that the human body has 97,000 km of arteries, veins and capillaries making up its circulation system? Or that atoms are so tiny a minute speck of dust contains millions upon millions of them? In our modern age of complex technology, what else is there left to discover or invent?

Explore the biggest and best facts of *Science and Technology* and satisfy your natural curiosity. There are the big, serious facts – for reference – and less serious ones, too, for fun. These pages are packed with the biggest and best, oddest and strangest, smallest and funniest facts around!

BODY PARTS

Humans may not be as strong as animals of a similar size, such as chimpanzees, but they have the most advanced brains of all living things. The brain is the body's control centre. It controls all the body's systems. The main systems are the skeleton and muscles, the nervous system, circulation (blood supply), respiration (breathing), digestion, reproduction and the immune system.

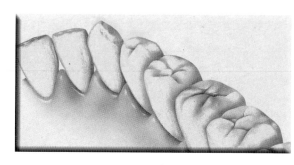

▲ *Children have 20 teeth, adults 32. The earliest false teeth date from 700 BC. They were carved by the Etruscans from bone or ivory, or came from other humans!*

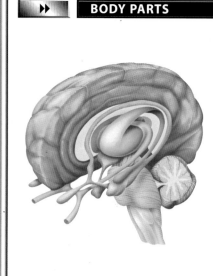

◀ *Hair grows at a rate of about 12 mm a month and falls out all the time. A Norwegian named Hans Langseth never cut a part of his beard. When he died in Iowa, USA, in 1927, it measured an incredible 5.33 m long!*

muscles make up 40 percent of a body's weight

bicep raises arm

the bulkiest muscle is the buttock muscle

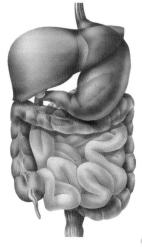

BODY PARTS

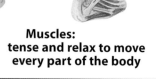

Brain:
control centre, with more than 8 billion cells

Digestive system:
breaks down food into small molecules

Muscles:
tense and relax to move every part of the body

Lungs:
soft bags full of tiny airways

▸ Bulkiest muscle: *gluteus maximus* (buttock) ▸ Longest-living cells: brain cells ▸ Most common blood group: O

▶ *Our bodies are made of 100 million million cells. Each cell contains the genetic code that makes us unique. The code is found in a chemical called DNA. Each DNA molecule is shaped like a coiled ladder.*

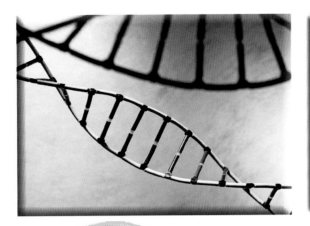

▸▸	**LARGEST ORGANS**	
	ORGAN	**AVERAGE WEIGHT**
★ 1	**Skin**	**11,000 g**
2	**Liver**	**1,600 g**
3	**Brain**	**1,400 g (male)**
4	**Lungs**	**1,100 g**
5	**Heart**	**300 g**

▼ *At birth a baby weighs, on average, 3.5 kg, though babies of 10 kg or more are on record. By two years old a baby has tripled its weight, can walk and talk, has grown teeth and is learning very fast.*

oxygen-rich blood (red) travels through arteries

oxygen-poor blood (blue) travels through veins

heart

skull

ribcage

hipbone

VITAL STATISTICS

● Adult lungs hold 3 litres of air.
● An adult's body has about 5 litres of blood.
● Walking uses over 200 muscles.
● Skin is thickest, about 3 mm, on hand palms and soles of feet.

arteries carry blood out from the heart

veins carry blood back to the heart

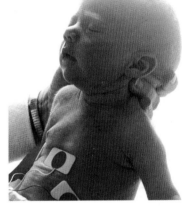

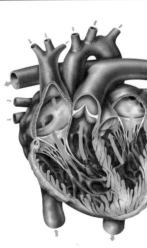

Blood supply:
arteries, veins and capillaries, up to 97,000 km in all

Heart:
power source, beating 100,000 times a day

Skeleton:
adults have, on average, 213 bones, babies over 300

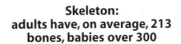

Kidneys:
have 1 million filters called nephrons

SUPER-HUMANS

A few exceptional people break through the 'average' barrier in their size or age and grow to be incredibly tall, remain very short, become enormously heavy or reach an extremely old age. But 'average' also changes. In the Western world and Japan, increasingly people are living to be 85 years or more instead of 70, and children are maturing younger and growing bigger than their grandparents as healthcare and diet improve.

▲ *Wheelchair athletes compete in all the major sports at international athletics competitions such as the Paralympics. Blindness, deafness or other medical problems are no longer barriers to success.*

▶ *The world's tallest man, an American named Robert Wadlow, grew to be 2.47 m tall. Sadly he died aged just 32 years old. The world's shortest person, an Indian named Gul Mohammad, was 0.57 m tall – about as high as Robert Wadlow's knees!*

▲ *Cloning animals such as calves can have the effect of making their cells live longer. Six cloned cows born in 1999 have cells that will last 50 percent longer than normal. A cloned human might live to be about 150.*

IT'S A FACT
The world's oldest person is usually a woman aged between 110 and 120, though the oldest ever known reached 122 years and 164 days. Only one person in five over 100 is a man. Many claims for 'oldest person' are false. In 1933 a Chinese man was reported to have died at the age of 233!

▶ *The fastest sprinters can run 100 m in just over 9 seconds, a speed of 43 km/h. When new world records are set, just fractions of a second are trimmed off the previous fast time. In 1968 the fastest time taken to run 100 m was 9.9 seconds. By 1999 it had been reduced to 9.79 seconds!*

» Strongest muscle: masseter (biting) » Oldest: 122 » Longest standing: 17 years » Largest feet: size 28 (UK)

▶▶ RECORD FEATS

Heaviest person	635 kg	Jon Minoch, USA (1941–83)
Most hiccoughing	68 years	Charles Osborne, USA
Biggest feet	28 (UK size)	Matthew McGrory, USA
Most children	1,000 +	Sultan of Morocco (1672–1727)
Longest necks	40–65 cm	Padaung women of Myanmar
Heaviest baby	10.8 kg	Anna Bates's son, Canada, 1879
Biggest biceps	77.8 cm	Denis Sester, USA
Longest sneezing fit	978 days	Donna Griffiths, UK

DID YOU KNOW?
Albert Einstein was the greatest scientist of the 20th century. After he died in 1955, his brain was donated to science to see if it gave any clues as to why he was so intelligent. Einstein's brain turned out to be wider than average, so perhaps it had greater thinking-capacity!

◀ *People have climbed Mount Everest without oxygen apparatus – a feat thought impossible when the mountain was first climbed by Edmund Hillary and Tenzing Norgay in 1953.*

MEDICAL MARVELS

Medicine made a giant leap forward during the 19th century with the introduction of anesthetics and antiseptics, which made operations much safer. Antibiotic drugs in the mid-20th century did much to fight diseases, wiping out some of them in large parts of the world. Nowadays doctors are able to replace limbs successfully, restore sight to many blind people, give deaf people hearing aids, and transplant hearts and other organs. Doctors can also tell if a human embryo is healthy or whether it contains 'abnormal' cells.

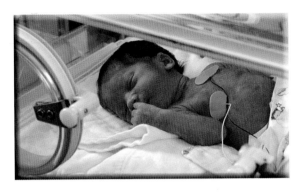

▲ *Most newborn babies weigh about 3.5 kg. Premature babies, born before the 36th to 37th weeks of pregnancy, when most births occur, can be much smaller. They are given special care in hospital until they are strong enough to go home.*

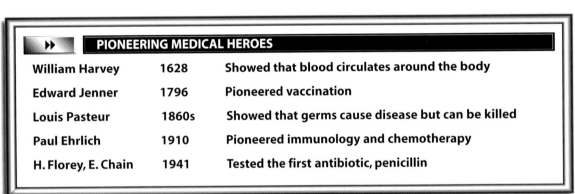

►► PIONEERING MEDICAL HEROES		
William Harvey	1628	Showed that blood circulates around the body
Edward Jenner	1796	Pioneered vaccination
Louis Pasteur	1860s	Showed that germs cause disease but can be killed
Paul Ehrlich	1910	Pioneered immunology and chemotherapy
H. Florey, E. Chain	1941	Tested the first antibiotic, penicillin

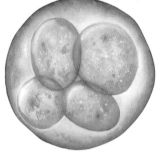

▲ *After an egg cell has been fertilized by a sperm cell, the egg cell divides and forms a cell-ball – four cells are shown here. This develops into a tiny embryo, and then a 2.5-cm foetus with organs.*

▼ *People are given a vaccine – a small dose of a disease – to prevent them getting a full attack. Louis Pasteur developed vaccines against cholera and rabies.*

◄ *In 1928 Alexander Fleming (above) found that penicillium mould, shown here in green, killed bacteria – a chance discovery that led to the first antibiotic, penicillin.*

▶ *Louise Brown, born in 1978, was the first 'test-tube' baby. She was conceived outside her mother's body, and the fertilized egg was then implanted in her mother's womb to continue growing normally.*

▶ *Joints such as hips, elbows and knees are hard-working parts of the body. But they can easily be shattered in accidents, or become damaged through age. Replacements need to be very tough. Doctors implant plastic and titanium metal joints that are fixed in place either with bone cement or by allowing the bone to grow into a mesh around the joint.*

▸▸ MEDICAL FIRSTS	
First blood transfusions	1905
First heart operation – on a dog	1914
First heart–lung machine	1951
First kidney transplant	1954
First birth control pill	1956
First IVF treatment for infertility	1965
First heart transplant	1967
First artificial heart	1969
First 'test-tube' baby born	1978
First embryo transfers (one woman to another)	1983
First heart, lung and liver transplant	1986
First time all of the human DNA gene-map read	2000

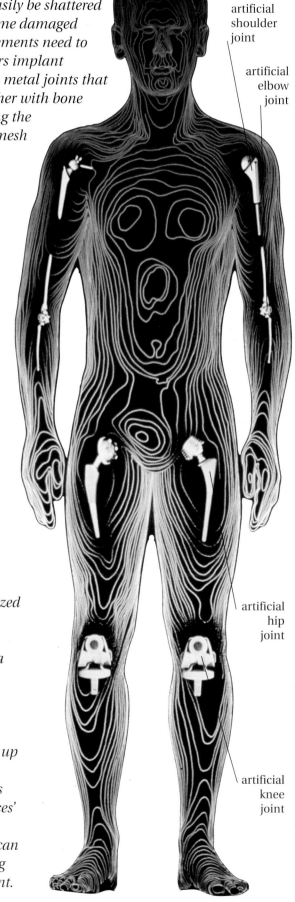

artificial shoulder joint

artificial elbow joint

artificial hip joint

artificial knee joint

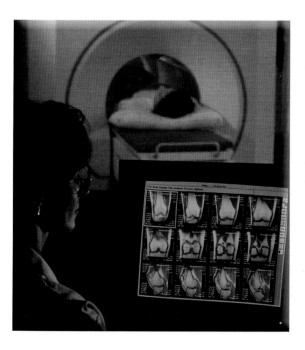

◀ *A CAT (Computerized Axial Tomography) scanner can show doctors the inside of a person's body in amazing detail. The scanner combines X-rays and computer technology. It records up to 1.5 million X-ray readings and displays them as very thin 'slices' of tissue. Doctors looking at the 'slices' can see if there is anything wrong with the patient.*

SCIENTIFIC DISCOVERIES

All kinds of advances were made in science from the 16th century on, when scientists began to realize the importance of observing, recording and experimenting. The French philosopher René Descartes (1596–1650) made the claim that the world was made up of two things: mind and matter. Matter can be liquid, solid or gas, but whatever its state, it is made of the same basic units, atoms, which are too tiny to be seen without special equipment.

▲ *In June 2000 scientists read all of the DNA code, or gene-map, contained in our body cells – genes are what make each person unique. The DNA code shows which genes affect different processes in the body. Scientists now hope to be able to develop new methods for preventing diseases.*

◀ *Sir Isaac Newton (1642–1727) was a great scientist. He invented the reflector telescope and is said to have worked out gravitation by watching an apple fall from a tree.*

▶ *Diamond is the hardest substance in nature and is used in industry for cutting. Cut diamonds sparkle so brilliantly that they make valuable gems. The British Imperial State Crown has over 3,000!*

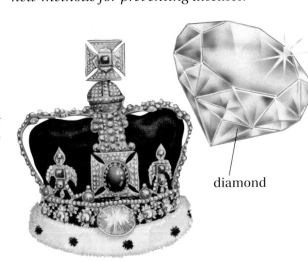

diamond

▶▶ GREAT SCIENTISTS			
Aristotle	384–322 BC	Greek	His ideas influenced most scientists until the 1700s
Galileo Galilei	1564–1642	Italian	Experimented with falling objects, discovered the pendulum, and used a telescope to study the Moon and planets
Robert Boyle	1627–91	Irish	Chemist, studied gases; founder of modern chemistry
Antoine Lavoisier	1743–94	French	Listed the known elements and introduced the metric system
Michael Faraday	1791–1867	British	Pioneer of electricity
Marie Curie	1867–1934	Polish	Discovered radium and studied radioactivity
Albert Einstein	1879–1955	German	Changed the way people think about space and time

» Lightest gas: hydrogen » Strongest element: boron » Most liquid substance: helium » Brightest light: laser

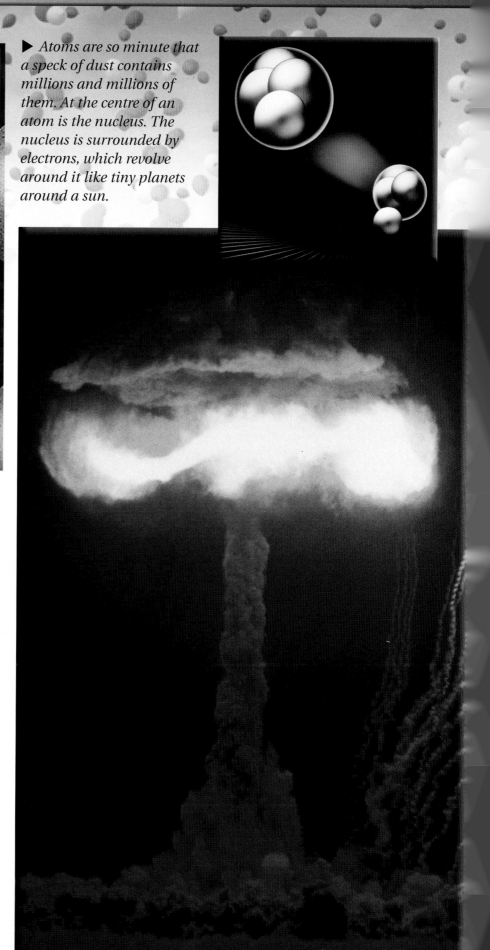

▶ *Atoms are so minute that a speck of dust contains millions and millions of them. At the centre of an atom is the nucleus. The nucleus is surrounded by electrons, which revolve around it like tiny planets around a sun.*

IT'S A FACT

Every substance is either an element or a combination of elements. There are 112 elements altogether. The commonest in Earth's crust are oxygen and silicon. Neither was known in ancient times, though people knew about gold (above), carbon, copper, lead, mercury and tin. Oxygen was discovered in 1774, silicon in 1823.

▶ *The discovery that the centre of an atom, its nucleus, could be split into even tinier particles was made in 1917 by New Zealand-born Ernest Rutherford. Splitting atoms releases the most powerful force in nature. A nuclear explosion changes matter to energy, with colossal destructive power. The first atomic bombs were dropped in Japan to end World War II in 1945.*

BRIGHT IDEAS

● About 1600, Galileo watched a lamp swinging and discovered the laws of the pendulum.

● In 1679 Leibniz worked out how to count big numbers using 0s and 1s – binary code.

● In 1901 Hubert Booth sucked dust from a carpet and discovered how to make a vacuum cleaner.

REALLY USEFUL INVENTIONS

What do you think the most useful invention has been? Perhaps the wheel? Without wheels there would be no bikes or cars, and very few machines. Electricity, plastics, fast foods and the Internet have also transformed our lives. But the list is endless, because people have been inventing since ancient times. The pace of inventions speeded up in the 1700s, with the Industrial Revolution, and has carried on getting faster and faster, changing the way we live in less than a generation.

▶ *Thomas Edison invented the electric light bulb, as did Joseph Swan. But Edison had the big idea of building a power station to light the homes and streets of New York.*

◀ *The Chinese invented the wheelbarrow in the 1st century AD. Later the wheel was moved to the front, which made tipping out the load easier. Some garden barrows have a ball instead of a wheel – balls do not get stuck in mud!*

» TOP TEN INVENTIONS AND THEIR INVENTORS, 1870–1910

Telephone:
Bell, 1876

Sound recording:
Edison, 1877

Light bulb:
Edison, 1879

Motor car:
Benz, 1885

Skyscraper:
Le Baron Jenney, 1885

▶ *Unlike old-style vacuum cleaners, invented in 1901, the Dyson vacuum cleaner of 1992 has no bag – it sucks up air like a whirlwind into a plastic container. Before 1901 people used brushes.*

▼ *The first true electronic digital computing began in 1943. During the 1970s and 1980s computer designers developed integrated circuits so small that an ant could carry one between its jaws.*

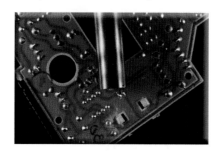

▶ *Mobile phones first appeared in 1979, 103 years after the first telephone of 1876. Now they are used on the street, while travelling, or in remote places all over the world.*

» Postage stamp: 1840 » Typewriter: 1868 » Pneumatic tyre: 1888 » Hearing aid: 1935 » Laser: 1960

» USEFUL AND ODD FIRSTS	
First chewing gum	1848
First potato crisp	1853
First tin opener	about 1860
First margarine	1869
First drinking straw	1888
First breakfast cereal	1892
First vacuum cleaner	1901
First frozen fish	1924
First electric toaster	1926
First contact lens	1948
First post-it note	1973
First clockwork radio	1991

▼ *Power is supplied to cities by power cables carrying electric current. The USA produces and consumes more electricity than any other country, followed by Russia, Japan and China.*

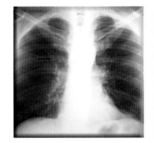

X-ray: Röntgen, 1895

Radio: Marconi, 1895

Tape recording: Poulsen, 1899

Aeroplane: Wright brothers, 1903

Family car: Ford, 1908

▼ *Miniaturization – making things smaller – has revolutionized business. Laptop computers, unknown before the 1980s, are now so slim they can be carried anywhere, allowing people to do business on trains, in aeroplanes, or anywhere they choose. The thinnest is just 1.7 cm thick when folded.*

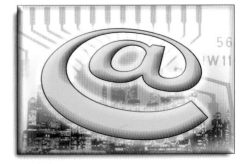

▶ *The Internet began in 1969 as a US defence network of linked computers. By the 1990s an international network was operating as a cyberspace route for e-mails, web sites (the world wide web) and e-commerce – buying and selling on line.*

COMMUNICATIONS AND COMPUTERS

A revolution in communications completely changed the modern world in little more than 50 years. In 1950 the computer was unknown outside a few hi-tech laboratories. Now it is hard to imagine a world without computers, videos, CDs, telephones, television or the Internet. These inventions have changed forever the way people live, work and play.

◀ The telephone, invented in 1876, was a huge breakthrough in communications. For the first time people miles apart could speak directly to one another.

▶ In 1895 Guglielmo Marconi realized it was possible to transmit messages without the need for wires. By the 1920s 'wireless', or radio, made it possible for one person to communicate with millions at the same time.

▶▶ EARLY BREAKTHROUGHS IN COMMUNICATION	
Writing	about 3500 BC
Paper	AD 105
Numbers 0 to 9 (modern forms)	about 500
Mechanical clock	1000s
Printing press	1400s

▼ In July 1997 the US Sojourner robot, shown here, was the first vehicle to roam another planet – Mars. It was recorded by the Mars Pathfinder lander, which was controlled by a computer able to carry out 22 million instructions per second. Some 100 million Internet users logged on to NASA's mission website.

▸▸ First TV broadcast: 1937 ▸▸ Marathon phone call: 550 hours (1966) ▸▸ Longest undersea cable: 27,000 km

▶ *The computer games industry is a multi-million pound business selling fantasy worlds peopled by digitally animated characters. Most of the games test quick reactions or strategy, and are played on personal computers at home.*

▶▶ TOWARDS THE COMPUTER AGE

Charles Babbage's analytical engine	1830s
Punched card machine for vote-counting	1888
ENIAC, the first all-purpose computer	1946
First transistorized computer	1958
The Internet begins as a military network	1969
Pocket calculator	1971
First personal computer (Altair 8800)	1975
Compact disc	1981
First Apple Macintosh computer	1984
The World Wide Web	1992

◀ *Today's portable CD players have an 'electronic shock protection' device that 'fills in the gaps' if the CD is jolted, so joggers can listen to music on CD while running.*

◀ *A smartpen provides electronic security for people buying goods via the Internet. It contains pressure pads and a computer processor that can verify a signature against a copy held in a database.*

▶ *The personal handyphone is a wristwatch-sized Japanese system designed to give low-cost, cordless communication and 60 minutes worth of talk time.*

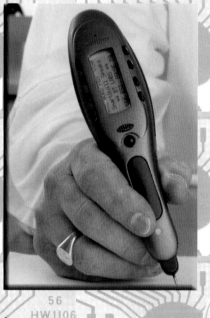

▶▶ GREAT LEAPS FORWARD

Electric telegraph	1837
Typewriter	1868
Telephone	1876
Voice radio	1906
Photocopier	1938
Transistor	1947
Microchip	1958
Laser	1960
Telecommunications satellite	1960
Computer mouse	1964

▶ *With a Lego Mindstorm kit you can build an electronic robot capable of following a trail, moving around obstacles and even hiding in dark corners!*

WEAPONS

Wars have got bigger as weapons have become more deadly. Each new weapon sparks off a race to invent a counter-weapon. The first big armies marched into battle in Egypt and Assyria 3,000 years ago. Two kinds of bows were used in ancient warfare – the crossbow and the longbow. Wars changed dramatically, first with the invention of gunpowder and guns in the Middle Ages, and secondly with the use of aircraft, rockets and nuclear weapons during the 20th century.

▼ *Radar, first used in World War II (1939–45), can locate aircraft at any height, but it cannot detect the B-2 Stealth bomber. Built at huge expense for the US Air Force, the Stealth bomber casts such a faint radar 'shadow' that it can sneak through most air defences.*

▼ *The first cannon fired large darts or round stones. They were used to batter down castle walls, but often they blew up their own gunners. Cast-iron cannonballs were first fired in the 1400s.*

▼ *The tank was invented during World War I (1914–18). Designed to smash through barbed wire and climb over trench defences, it became a formidable weapon in World War II. Tanks were also used in the Gulf War (1991).*

▲ *The aqualung was a 1940s wartime invention of the French navy. It gave divers an automatic supply of air at the same pressure as the surrounding water. It was later adapted for peaceful use by scuba divers such as this naturalist.*

▸▸ DEADLY INVENTIONS	
Gunpowder rockets	pre-1000
Cannon	1300s
Rifle and machine gun	1860s
Submarine	1898
Bomber plane	1914
Guided missile (*V2*)	1944
Atomic bomb	1945
Nuclear submarine	1955
Smart bombs	1990s

WARS, DEATHS, ARMIES AND BATTLES

Longest war	1346–1453	Hundred Years' War between England and France
Most casualties	1939–45	World War II, 55 million people killed
Greatest invasion	June 6, 1944	D-Day landings; Allied forces sent 1 million troops into northern France to oppose German occupation
Longest siege	1941–44	Leningrad (now St Petersburg), Russia, lasting 880 days
Biggest army	present-day	China's state army, numbering more than 3 million soldiers
Bloodiest battle	1916	World War I Battle of the Somme, 1 million soldiers killed

▼ *Rocket missiles can be launched from underground – where they are kept for secrecy – or from submarines. They can carry nuclear warheads or other weapons halfway around the world.*

▶ *The world's fastest warplane is the Russian MiG-25 'Foxbat', which has been tracked by radar flying at well over 3,000 km/h. This twin-engine fighter has been flying since the 1970s, and is now used mainly for 'reconnaissance' – examining an area to locate the enemy or gather information.*

▼ *Six* Typhoon *class submarines were built in Russia between 1977 and 1989. The* Typhoons *carry a crew of 170, and can dive to a depth of 400 m. They are armed with 20 ballistic nuclear missiles. Typhoons are the world's biggest submarines, at over 25,000 tonnes.*

◀ *The fastest plane ever was the North American X-15, used to explore the fringes of space. Dropped from under a B-52 bomber, it reached 7,274 km/h in 1967.*

BUILDINGS AND STRUCTURES

The age of tall buildings began in 1885 with the first skyscraper. Although only 10 floors high, the steel-framed Home Insurance Building in Chicago, USA, was truly the world's first skyscraper. There were many huge buildings or structures before this, notably the pyramids of ancient Egypt, Roman temples and medieval castles and cathedrals, but none rose as high as modern skyscrapers, which are being built ever taller and taller.

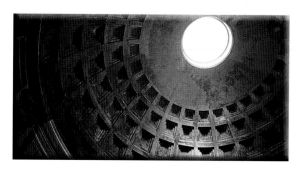

▲ *The Pantheon in Rome, rebuilt about AD 119–125, has the largest brick and concrete dome of ancient times. Measuring 43 m across, it is exactly as wide as it is high and has no visible supports. A 9-m-wide hole in the centre lets in sun and rain.*

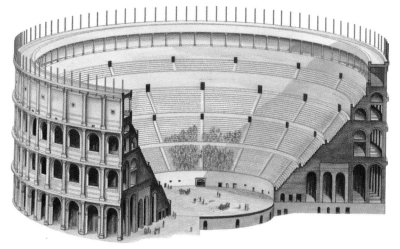

▲ *The Colosseum is a vast amphitheatre in Rome, Italy. Ancient Romans flocked there – it held up to 50,000 spectators – to watch gladiators fighting each other or wild animals. There was even a mock sea battle in the arena, which was flooded for the occasion.*

▲ *The high-rise city of Hong Kong in southern China covers an area of just 1,075 sq km, but houses an incredible 6.3 million people in its forest of skyscrapers.*

Sears Tower,
443 m, 110 floors

▼ *The United States has more skyscrapers than any other country, though China is fast catching up. New York and Chicago, shown here, have long been rivals in the tallest-buildings race. New York has 140 major skyscrapers and Chicago has 70, including the 443-m-high Sears Tower.*

▸ Tallest building being built: Shanghai World Financial Centre, Shanghai ▸ Biggest church: St Peter's, Rome

THE WORLD'S TALLEST BUILDINGS AND STRUCTURES

BUILDING OR STRUCTURE	DATE	HEIGHT
1 The CN Tower, Toronto, Canada	1976	555 m
2 Shanghai World Financial Centre, China	*2003	460 m
3 Petronas Towers, Kuala Lumpur, Malaysia	1996	452 m
4 Sears Tower, Chicago, USA	1974	443 m
5 Jin Mao Building, Shanghai, China	1999	420 m
6 World Trade Center, New York, USA	1973	417 m
7 Empire State Building, New York, USA	1931	381 m
8 Eiffel Tower, Paris, France	1889	300 m

Note: * = due for completion

◀ *The Houston Astrodome in Texas, USA, was the first stadium to have a roof over its playing field. Built in 1965, the stadium's dome soars 63 m above the players – as high as an 18-floor building. When the grass died under the semi-transparent roof, plastic grass, called Astroturf, was invented, and laid for the opening day.*

▶ *The record for the world's tallest building without a mast is broken every few years. The twin Petronas Towers in Kuala Lumpur, Malaysia, became the tallest in 1996. The 96-floor towers are 452 m high.*

TOUCHING THE SKY!

● The tallest TV mast is in Fargo, North Dakota, USA. It is 629 m high. There was an even taller mast in Poland (646 m), but it fell down in 1991!

● Although no longer the tallest skyscrapers, the Sears Tower, Chicago, and the World Trade Center, New York, still have the most floors – 110 each.

● The Baiyoke II Tower Hotel in Bangkok (319 m) is higher than Europe's tallest office building, the Messeturm in Frankfurt (256 m).

● From Lake Point Tower in Chicago residents have an amazing view – the ground is 197 m below the 70th-floor apartments.

ROADS AND VEHICLES

The first roads were paths and trails made for feet rather than wheels. The longest ancient road was the Silk Road, a series of trails almost 10,000 km long used by merchants travelling between China and Europe. The best road-builders of the ancient world were the Romans, who built 80,000 km of paved roads across their empire. Today the longest road network is the Pan-American Highway, with a total length of 47,000 km. Most roads are now too crowded, resulting in the smelliest traffic jams in history.

▲ *Karl Benz built the world's first petrol-engine car in 1885. It had three wheels and was steered at the front by a lever. Chains from the engine drove the rear wheels. The car's top speed was about 16 km/h.*

▲ *The* McLaren F1 *is the most powerful car in production in the world. With a 6.1-litre BMW V12 engine, it can accelerate incredibly fast, attaining a speed of 95.6 km/h in just 3.2 seconds! The car's top speed is over 370 km/h. The driver and steering wheel are in the centre front, with two passenger seats in the back.*

▼ *Assembly lines were pioneered in the USA by Ransom Olds in 1901 and later by Henry Ford. They allowed cars to be built more quickly and cheaply. In 1994 a record 49.97 million cars were produced worldwide.*

	FIRST ON THE ROAD			
	VEHICLE	**DESIGNER**	**COUNTRY**	**DATE**
★ 1	Steam tractor	Cugnot	France	1769
2	Steam coach	Trevithick	Britain	1801
3	Steam dredger	Evans	USA	1805
4	Gas carriage	Brown	Britain	1820s
5	Gas carriage	Lenoir	France	1862
6	Petrol car	Benz	Germany	1885

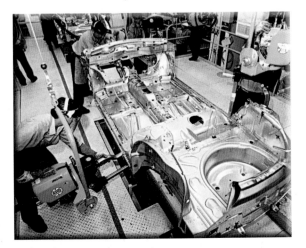

▲ *The German* Volkswagen, *or 'people's car' – the Beetle – is the most-produced car ever. It was first driven in 1938. Since then more than 21 million have been made. One record-breaking Beetle did 2.6 million km! A new-look design came out in 1998.*

»» FASTER AND FASTER

	VEHICLE	DRIVER	DATE	SPEED
★ 1	*Thrust SSC*	Green	1997	1,227 km/h
2	*Thrust 2*	Noble	1983	1,019 km/h
3	*Blue Flame*	Gabelich	1970	1,016 km/h
4	*Spirit of America*	Breedlove	1964	846 km/h
5	*Railton*	Cobb	1947	634 km/h
6	*Thunderbolt*	Eyston	1937	502 km/h
7	*Bluebird*	Campbell	1932	408 km/h
8	*Sunbeam*	Seagrave	1927	328 km/h
9	Steam car	Stanley	1907	241 km/h
10	*La Jamais Contente*	Jenatzy	1899	106 km/h

▲ *The biggest vehicles ever built are two Marion crawlers, used to move US Moon rockets like this* Saturn 5, *and later Space Shuttles, into position for launch. The crawlers weigh 8,000 tonnes and crawl along on eight caterpillar tracks.*

▶ *The United States has more than 6 million km of roads. More than 80,000 km are motorways. Americans own the most cars, too – more than 140 million in all, or one car for every 1.5 people.*

▲ Thrust SSC, *powered by two Rolls-Royce Spey 205 jet engines, became the first vehicle to break the sound barrier on land. In 1997 Andy Green drove the British jet car at 1,227.99 km/h across the flat sands of Black Rock Desert, Nevada, USA.*

118 SCIENCE AND TECHNOLOGY

» Biggest station: Grand Central, New York » Fastest train: *TGV Atlantique* » Steepest track: Mount Pilatus, Switzerland

TRAINS AND RAILWAYS

High-speed trains are five times faster than the first steam trains of the 1830s. The fastest speed reached by a steam train was 202.73 km/h by the British LNER locomotive *Mallard* in 1938. The world's fastest train is the French *TGV Atlantique*, which in 1990 achieved a record top speed of 515.3 km/h. There is enough rail track around the world to stretch from Earth to the Moon three times. The longest stretch without curves crosses the Nullarbor Plain in Western Australia – it is straight for 470 km!

▶ *France's TGV (Train á Grand Vitesse, or high-speed train) Atlantique is the world's fastest train. It runs between Lille and Roissy. In 1990 it set a record speed on a national rail system of 515.3 km/h, although in passenger service TGVs normally cruise at 300 km/h.*

▼ *The Eurostar glides between Paris and Calais in France at speeds of 300 km/h. It then travels through the Channel Tunnel and reaches the UK, where it has to slow down for the rest of the journey to London.*

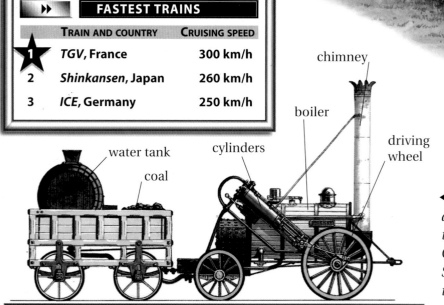

FASTEST TRAINS

	TRAIN AND COUNTRY	CRUISING SPEED
★ 1	*TGV*, France	300 km/h
2	*Shinkansen*, Japan	260 km/h
3	*ICE*, Germany	250 km/h

chimney

boiler

driving wheel

cylinders

water tank

coal

◀ Rocket *was designed and built by two British engineers, George and Robert Stephenson. In 1829 they entered it in a speed trial to find the best locomotive to run on the Liverpool and Manchester Railway.* Rocket *won the contest, reaching a speed of 58 km/h with a full load. It became the first-ever intercity steam locomotive.*

COUNTRIES WITH THE MOST TRACK

	COUNTRY	TRACK LENGTH
★ 1	USA	222,000 km
2	Russia	151,000 km
3	Germany	87,000 km
4	Canada	65,000 km
5	India	62,000 km

▼ Maglev *trains could be the trains of the future. They are suspended by powerful magnets above a guide track. Early versions were built in Germany and Japan, and in 1996 a* Maglev *train started operating at Disney World in Florida, USA, running at speeds of more than 400 km/h. It is thought* Maglevs *of the future may exceed 800 km/h!*

BIG BOY
The biggest and strongest steam locomotives ever were nicknamed 'Big Boy'. Twenty-five were built for the Union Pacific Railroad in the United States from 1941 to 1944. They were designed to haul 3,000-tonne freight trains over the Rocky Mountains.

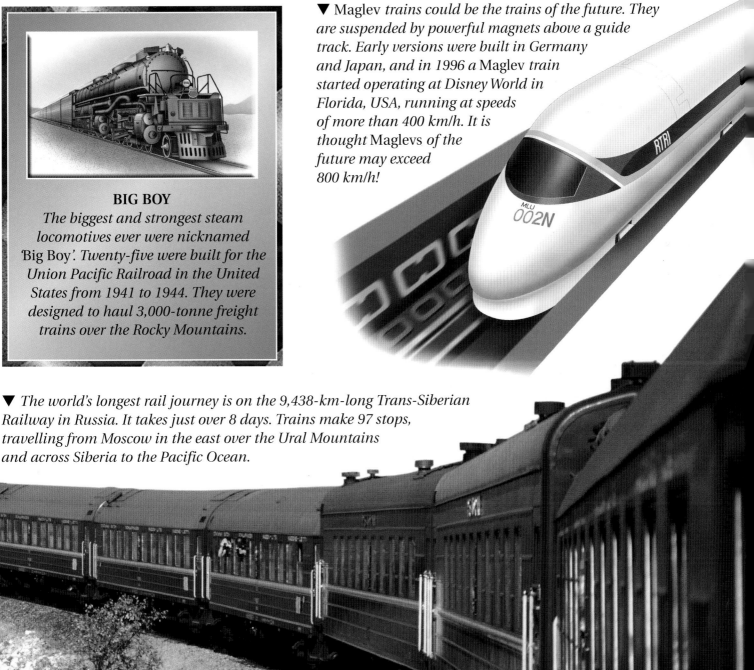

▼ *The world's longest rail journey is on the 9,438-km-long Trans-Siberian Railway in Russia. It takes just over 8 days. Trains make 97 stops, travelling from Moscow in the east over the Ural Mountains and across Siberia to the Pacific Ocean.*

BRIDGES

In ancient times the Romans built long, wooden bridges across rivers and enormous, stone-arched aqueducts to carry water from its source across country to towns. Some of their stone aqueducts are still standing after hundreds of years. The British built the first iron bridge in 1778 over the River Severn, and the first great suspension bridge in 1826 over the Menai Straits, Wales. Today all the longest bridges in the world are suspension bridges, hung from wire cables slung from high towers.

▲ *The dramatic Pont du Gard aqueduct in southern France was built by Roman engineers about 2,000 years ago. It has three tiers of arches. The topmost tier carries water. It is supported by 35 arches and is 47 m above the River Gard.*

◄ *Cantilever bridges have two beams, or cantilevers, joined in the middle and resting on piers. Quebec has the world's longest, with a main span of 549 m. Also famous is the Forth Rail Bridge, Scotland, built in 1890.*

▶ *Suspension bridges span the greatest distances – the longest is the Akashi–Kaiko Bridge in Japan. The roadway hangs from cables and can sway quite safely in a strong wind.*

◄ *The longest steel-arch bridge is the New River Gorge Bridge, West Virginia, USA, shown here. Another steel-arch bridge, Sydney Harbour Bridge in Australia, is the world's widest long-span bridge.*

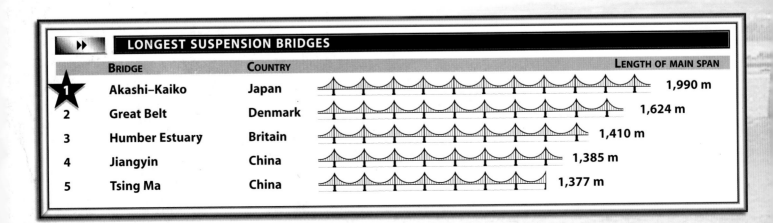

	BRIDGE	COUNTRY		LENGTH OF MAIN SPAN
★ 1	Akashi–Kaiko	Japan		1,990 m
2	Great Belt	Denmark		1,624 m
3	Humber Estuary	Britain		1,410 m
4	Jiangyin	China		1,385 m
5	Tsing Ma	China		1,377 m

LONGEST SUSPENSION BRIDGES

» Widest long-span: 48.8 m wide, Sydney Harbour, Australia   » Biggest mistaken identity: London Bridge, bought by USA

◄ *In 1883 the chief engineer of the Brooklyn Bridge, New York, tested the cables by swinging along them in a bosun's chair!*

► *The beautiful Rialto Bridge in Venice was built in the late 1500s. It crosses the Grand Canal.*

▼ *California's Golden Gate Bridge, built in 1937, was the world's longest suspension bridge until 1964. It spans 1,280 m and its towers soar an amazing 227 m above the waters of San Francisco Bay. Its total length is 2,737 m.*

LONGEST STEEL-ARCH BRIDGES

	BRIDGE	COUNTRY		LONGEST SPAN
1	New River Gorge	USA		518 m
2	Kill Van Kull (Bayonne)	USA		504 m
3	Sydney Harbour	Australia		503 m
4	Fremont	USA		383 m
5	Port Mann	Canada		366 m

DID YOU KNOW?
In 2006 a gigantic bridge is due to be completed across the Strait of Messina, linking Sicily to mainland Italy. Its centre span will be 3,320 m.

LONGEST CABLE-STAYED BRIDGES

	BRIDGE	COUNTRY		LENGTH OF MAIN SPAN
1	Tatara Ohashi	Japan		890 m
2	Pont de Normandie	France		856 m
3	Qunghzhou Minjiang	China		605 m
4	Yangpu	China		602 m
5	Meiko–Chuo	Japan		590 m

DAMS AND TUNNELS

Dams have been built since ancient times to hold back water so that it can be released gradually. Today's enormous dams are made from concrete or stone blocks. Behind the dam, the water is stored in vast artificial lakes for irrigation or to provide hydroelectric power. Tunnel engineering began much later, during the 19th century, with dynamite and tunnelling machines. The world's longest tunnel carries water to New York and is 169 km long. Others carry roads and railways through mountains.

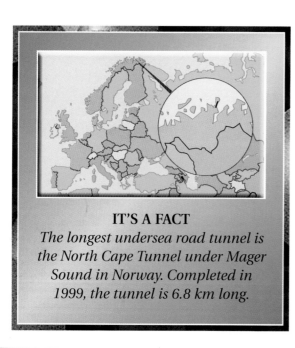

IT'S A FACT
The longest undersea road tunnel is the North Cape Tunnel under Mager Sound in Norway. Completed in 1999, the tunnel is 6.8 km long.

▲ *The Kariba Dam, built on the Zambezi River in Africa in 1959, created a lake covering 5,000 sq km. Over 30,000 people and many wild animals had to be moved as the waters rose. Hydroelectric power from the lake supplies electricity to Zimbabwe and Zambia.*

↠	**HIGHEST DAMS**		
	DAM	**COUNTRY**	**HEIGHT**
★ 1	Rogun	Tajikistan	335 m
2	Nurek	Tajikistan	300 m
3	Grand Dixence	Switzerland	285 m

▼ *The Grand Coulee Dam across the Columbia River is the biggest concrete dam in the United States. It is 1,592 m long, 168 m high and over 150 m thick at the base.*

Largest hydroelectric scheme: Turukhansk, Siberia ⟫ Most controversial dam project: Three Gorges, China

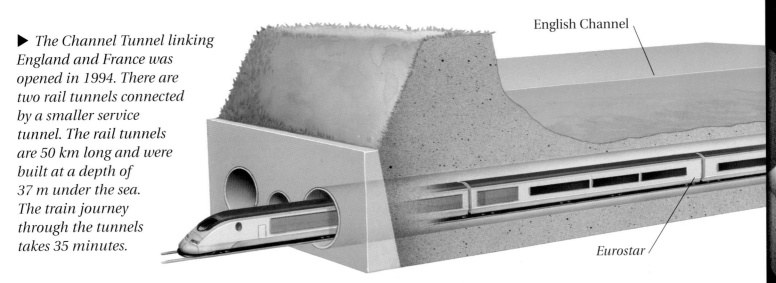

English Channel

Eurostar

▶ *The Channel Tunnel linking England and France was opened in 1994. There are two rail tunnels connected by a smaller service tunnel. The rail tunnels are 50 km long and were built at a depth of 37 m under the sea. The train journey through the tunnels takes 35 minutes.*

⟫ LONGEST UNDERGROUND ROAD TUNNELS

	TUNNEL	COUNTRY	LENGTH
★ 1	Laerdal*	Norway	24.5 km
2	St Gotthard	Switzerland	16.3 km
3	Arlberg	Austria	13.98 km
4 =	Frejus	France–Italy	12.9 km
4 =	Pinglin Highway**	Taiwan	12.9 km
5	Mont Blanc	France–Italy	11.6 km

Note: * = Completion date 2001, ** = Completion date 2003

⟫ LONGEST UNDERWATER TUNNELS (ALL RAIL)

	TUNNEL	COUNTRY	LENGTH
★ 1	Seikan	Japan	54 km
2	Channel Tunnel	UK–France	50 km
3	Dai-Shimizu	Japan	22 km
4	Shin-Kanmon	Japan	19 km
5	Great Belt	Denmark	8 km

▼ *The Thames Barrier has 10 gates that can be lowered to dam the river at times of flood alert and protect central London. Each gate can withstand a load of 9,000 tonnes.*

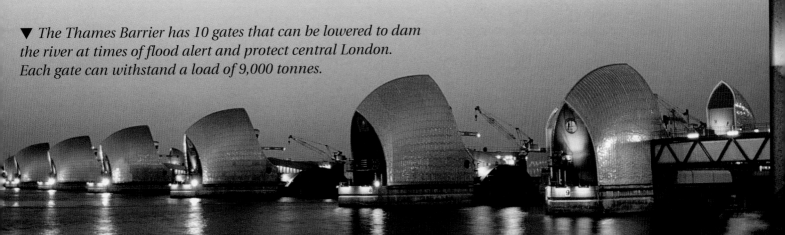

124 SCIENCE AND TECHNOLOGY

» Biggest ships: oil tankers » Biggest liner: *Queen Elizabeth* » Fastest kind of ship: hydrofoil » Busiest port: Rotterdam

SHIPS

Ships were built much the same size for 2,000 years. Galleons of the 1600s were not much bigger than Roman ships or Chinese junks. The age of the giant ship began in the 1800s with steamships. Today the biggest ships afloat are oil tankers, which dwarf even the mightiest aircraft carriers. Cruise ships of the 21st century are even bigger than the huge, elegant ocean liners of the 1910 to 1940s era.

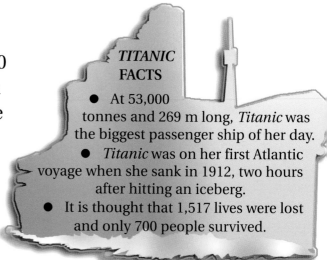

TITANIC FACTS

- At 53,000 tonnes and 269 m long, *Titanic* was the biggest passenger ship of her day.
- *Titanic* was on her first Atlantic voyage when she sank in 1912, two hours after hitting an iceberg.
- It is thought that 1,517 lives were lost and only 700 people survived.

▲ *Clippers were the fastest sailing ships between 1840 and 1870. A clipper could do 20 knots (37 km/h), 'clipping' days off the sailing time of other cargo-carrying ships.*

▶▶ BIGGEST AFLOAT

Largest ship ever	*Jahre Viking*	**564,763 tonnes**
Largest liner	*Queen Elizabeth*	**83,000 tonnes**
Longest liner	*Norway* (formerly *France*)	**315.5 m**
Largest warship	*Nimitz* class carriers	**96,000 tonnes**
Largest sailing ship	*France II*	**5,800 tonnes**

DID YOU KNOW?
Roman merchant ships were about 60 m long. They often had a carved swan's head, representing the Egyptian goddess Isis, protector of sailors.

▶ *The QE2, built in 1967, is smaller than the original great Queen Elizabeth of 1938. This elegant cruise ship is 293 m long and usually travels at about 50 km/h. It is fitted with stabilizers to ensure the passengers have a comfortable voyage.*

▶ *The aircraft carrier USS Midway (1943) served in World War II and retired from the US Navy in 1992. Slightly smaller than modern Nimitz class nuclear-powered carriers, Midway is now a museum at San Diego.*

» First trans-Atlantic steamer: *Sirius* » Biggest mystery: *Marie Celeste*, 1872 » First hovercraft: 1959

▶ *The* Great Eastern *was a giant in its day. Built in 1858, it weighed over 19,000 tonnes and was 211 m long – bigger than any ship built over the next 40 years. It was the only ship to have screw propellers, paddles and sails.*

	BIGGER AND BIGGER	
	SHIP	**LENGTH**
1	*Jahre Viking*	485 m
2	*Nimitz* aircraft carrier	333 m
3	*Queen Elizabeth*	314 m
4	*QE2*	293 m
5	*New Jersey* battleship	270 m
6	*Great Eastern*	211 m
7	*Typhoon* submarine	170 m
8	SRN-4 hovercraft	56 m
9	Viking longship	21 m

▲ *The* Grand Princess, *built in 1998, is the second-largest passenger ship in service, second only to the* Voyager of the Seas, *launched in 2000. The luxurious* Grand Princess *is a 109,000-tonne floating hotel with rooms for 2,600 passengers.*

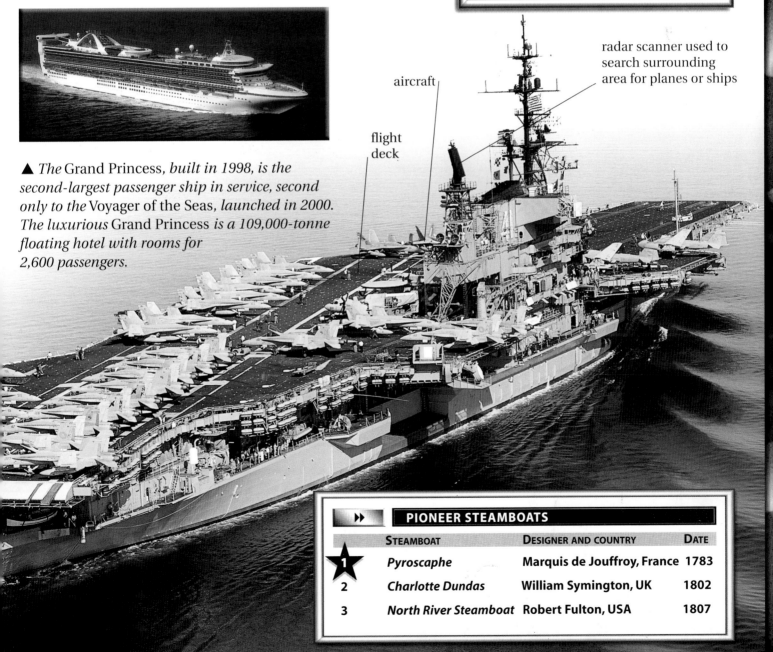

aircraft

flight deck

radar scanner used to search surrounding area for planes or ships

	PIONEER STEAMBOATS		
	STEAMBOAT	**DESIGNER AND COUNTRY**	**DATE**
1	*Pyroscaphe*	Marquis de Jouffroy, France	1783
2	*Charlotte Dundas*	William Symington, UK	1802
3	*North River Steamboat*	Robert Fulton, USA	1807

126 **SCIENCE AND TECHNOLOGY**

‣ Biggest airship: *Graf Zeppelin II* ‣ Busiest airport: O'Hare, Chicago, USA ‣ Oldest airline: KLM ‣ Heaviest bomber: *B-52*

AIRCRAFT AND FLIGHT

Some of the earliest flying machines were extremely big. The 1930s *Graf Zeppelin* airship, for example, was longer than any passenger jet of today. The size of passenger aircraft has increased as foreign holidays and business air travel have become more popular. The 400-seater *Boeing 747* is the biggest passenger aircraft. Generally speed is less important to airlines than size, which is why the very fast, but slim, *Concorde* was built in small numbers and used only on a few routes.

▲ The Hughes H-4 'Spruce Goose' *was the biggest aircraft ever to fly. Made of wood and fabric, it weighed 180 tonnes. The huge flying boat made one brief flight of 914 m in 1947 and has been on the ground ever since.*

FIRSTS IN THE AIR

1783: Montgolfier brothers fly a hot air balloon

1874: Felix du Temple's monoplane makes a hop

1903: Orville and Wilbur Wright fly their biplane

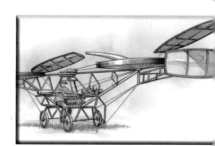

1907: Paul Cornu flies the first helicopter

▶ *In 1969 the new* Boeing 747 *jumbo jet was by far the world's biggest airliner. The 747-400, launched in 1988, has a wing-span of 65 m and can carry 400 passengers more than 12,000 km non-stop.*

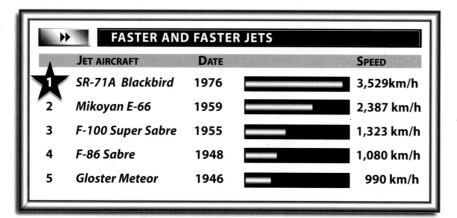

FASTER AND FASTER JETS

JET AIRCRAFT	DATE		SPEED
⭐ 1 SR-71A Blackbird	1976		3,529km/h
2 Mikoyan E-66	1959		2,387 km/h
3 F-100 Super Sabre	1955		1,323 km/h
4 F-86 Sabre	1948		1,080 km/h
5 Gloster Meteor	1946		990 km/h

➤ Fastest plane: *X-15* ➤ First supersonic: *Bell X-1* ➤ Biggest passenger load: 1,088 ➤ First jet airliner: *Comet*

➤➤ FAMOUS BALLOON FLIGHTS

First manned balloon flight	1783	**Montgolfiers' hot air balloon**
First cross-Channel flight	1785	**Blanchard and Jeffrey**
First across the Atlantic	1978	***Double Eagle II***
First across the Pacific	1981	***Double Eagle V***
First hot air crossing of Atlantic	1987	***Virgin Atlantic Flyer***
First non-stop around the world	1999	***Breitling Orbiter 3***

Hindenburg

◀ *The world's biggest airships were the* Hindenburg, *destroyed by fire in 1937, and the* Graf Zeppelin II, *last used in 1940. They were 245 m long and carried 75 passengers plus 25 crew, gliding almost silently above the oceans.*

1909: Louis Blériot flies the English Channel

1919: Alcock and Brown are first to fly the Atlantic

◀ *The* Airbus A3XX *will be the world's biggest airliner when it takes to the skies in 2003. The jumbo will carry 555 passengers on two decks.*

DID YOU KNOW?
Only 16 Concordes were ever built. The world's only commercial supersonic airliner flew at 2,300 km/h, crossing the Atlantic in under 3 hours. No Concorde had ever crashed until 2000.

SPORT AND

ENTERTAINMENT

For thousands of years, people have taken part in sports. The very first Olympic Games took place in Greece 776 BC, and still take place today. The 21st century still enjoys the thrill of sport, but people also find entertainment in thousands of other pastimes.

From roller coaster riding to rock climbing, to snowboarding and playing giant chess, people love to do different things. For instance, collecting things like teddy bears can be pretty popular – and expensive – someone once paid £110,000 for one – rather a lot of money for a cuddly toy!

Explore the biggest and best facts of *Sport and Entertainment* and enjoy your very own roller coaster ride. There are serious facts – for reference – and less serious ones, too, for fun. These pages are packed with the biggest and best, oddest and strangest, smallest and funniest facts around!

PLAYING GAMES

For more than 5,000 years people have played games. Some of the earliest were board games and games of chance, using dice or pieces like dominoes. The ancient Egyptians enjoyed wrestling and chariot racing, and Greek athletes took part in the Olympic Games more than 3,000 years ago. The rules of many modern games, such as tennis and rugby football, were drawn up in the 1800s. Today some stars are paid more than the leaders of their countries!

▲ *Polo – the name comes from the Persian word 'pulu' – was first played 5,000 years ago in India, and then Persia. Hitting a ball from a horse's back gave cavalry soldiers expert training at controlling their horses.*

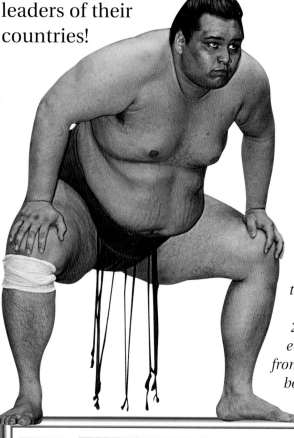

	OLDEST GAMES AND SPORTS	
	GAME OR SPORT	FIRST PLAYED
1	Wrestling	3000 BC
2 =	Horse racing	2500 BC
2 =	Dice	2500 BC

◄ *Sumo wrestling is popular in Japan. Size is important – the heaviest wrestlers weigh more than 200 kg. The heaviest-ever sumo champion, from Hawaii, weighed a body-crushing 267 kg!*

	MOST FAMOUS ALL-TIME GREATS	
Basketball	Michael Jordan	USA
Cricket	Sir Donald Bradman	Australia
Soccer	Pelé	Brazil
Golf	Jack Nicklaus	USA
Boxing	Muhammad Ali*	USA

Note: *Muhammad Ali was voted most famous sports star of the 20th century

▲ *Eldrick 'Tiger' Woods of the USA won the world's four major golf titles (the British and US Opens, the US Masters and the US PGA) by the age of just 24. He was only the fifth person to achieve this 'Grand Slam', and he was also the youngest.*

↠ Most varied: board games ↠ First card players: Chinese or Indians ↠ Rowdiest: medieval football players

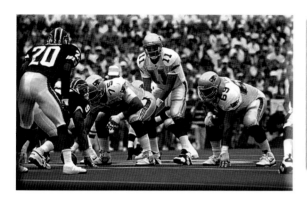

	RICHEST SPORTS STARS (ESTIMATED YEARLY EARNINGS)		
	NAME	**SPORT**	**EARNINGS**
1	Michael Jordan	Basketball	£40 million +
2 =	Michael Schumacher	Racing driver	£30 million
2 =	'Tiger' Woods	Golfer	£30 million

▲ *American football has been played by professional teams in the National Football League since 1922. Championship of the league is decided in the annual Super Bowl game, a major sports spectacle since 1967, watched by millions of viewers worldwide.*

GAME, SET AND MATCH

● Using a modern tennis racket with a fibreglass-graphite frame and tightly strung synthetic strings, a top male player can serve the ball at over 220 km/h.

▲ *Chess, shown here being played with giant pieces, was played at least 1,500 years ago. It probably began in India. The first world champion was William Steinitz of Austria, who held the title from 1866 to 1894.*

TOUGHEST CHALLENGE

● The Ironman Triathlon was first held in Hawaii in 1978. Contestants have to swim 4 km, ride a bike for 180 km and then run a marathon.

● After 8 hours only the very fittest triathletes are still running!

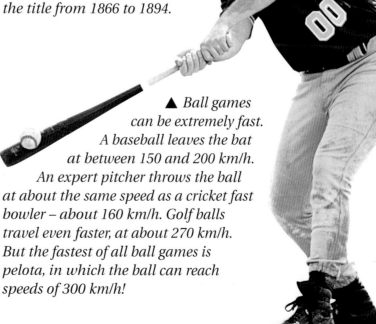

▲ *Ball games can be extremely fast. A baseball leaves the bat at between 150 and 200 km/h. An expert pitcher throws the ball at about the same speed as a cricket fast bowler – about 160 km/h. Golf balls travel even faster, at about 270 km/h. But the fastest of all ball games is pelota, in which the ball can reach speeds of 300 km/h!*

IT'S A FACT

Some games have not changed in hundreds of years. In Children's Games, *painted in 1560 by Pieter Bruegel, children are shown playing with hoops and riding piggyback.*

SOCCER GREATS

Soccer is the world's biggest spectator sport. The only continent where it does not reign supreme is North America. Both China and Europe claim to have invented football, which developed into soccer, now watched by millions of people around the world. Europe's top clubs, such as Manchester United (England), Real Madrid (Spain) and Internazionale-Milan (Italy), are so rich that they can afford to pay over £30 million for just one star player. The biggest international soccer tournament is the World Cup, held every four years.

◄ *Many children dream of playing soccer for their country, and for the fame and money that stardom can bring. In richer countries children are taught from a young age. In poorer countries they play wherever there is a patch of ground and a ball.*

	NATIONAL TEAM	WINS	YEARS
WORLD CUP: MOST WINS			
1	Brazil	4	1958, 1962, 1970, 1994
2 =	Italy	3	1934, 1938, 1982
2 =	West Germany	3	1954, 1974, 1990

◄ *Brazil's soccer star Pelé, real name Edson Arantes do Nascimento, is rated the greatest player of all time. Born in 1940, Pelé played in three World Cup-winning sides, in 1958, 1962 and 1970. Pelé scored his 1,000th goal during his 909th first-class match, and his total when he retired in 1977 was a remarkable 1,281 goals in 1,363 games!*

THE TOPS

● The first World Cup, held in Uruguay in 1930, was won by Uruguay.

● Brazil has the biggest football stadium in the world. The Maracana Municipal Stadium in Rio de Janeiro can hold 205,000 fans.

● Brazil are the only team to have won the World Cup four times.

▼ *Old Trafford in Manchester is the home of Manchester United, the world's richest club. In 1999 United won the English Premier League, the FA Cup and the European Champions Cup.*

▸▸ £30+ MILLION PLAYERS		
NAME	**TRANSFER**	**FEE**
1 ★ Luis Figo	Barcelona to Real Madrid	£37.4 million
2 Hernan Crespo	Parma to Lazio	£36 million
3 Christian Vieri	Lazio to Inter-Milan	£31 million

Note: all these deals were done in 2000

3-tier seating

pitch

entrance

seating for 67,000 spectators

luxury boxes

▼ *The World Cup trophy is presented to the winning team every four years. Countries qualify for the final stages through an elimination series. Brazil are the only nation to have played in every World Cup finals stage.*

◀ *The 1994 World Cup tournament was the first to be staged in the United States. The winners were Brazil, shown here in yellow and blue playing against Italy in blue and white. Brazil took the trophy for the fourth time.*

OLYMPIC GAMES

The Olympic Games is the biggest international sports competition on Earth. Thousands of athletes, representing nearly every country in the world, come together every four years to take part in individual and team sports. A few take home gold, silver or bronze medals. New sports are added at every Games, and billions of people watch the Olympics on television. Separate Winter Games for winter sports such as skiing and ice skating are also held every four years at snowy locations.

▲ *The first recorded Olympic Games were held at Olympia in Greece in 776 BC. They were held every four years after that until AD 393. Athletes entered the 20,000-capacity stadium through this stone arch.*

◀ *Relays of runners carry a flaming torch from Greece to the country where the Olympic Games are to be held. In the opening ceremony the torch is used to light the Olympic flame, a beacon that burns until the Games are over.*

▶▶ SUPER-OLYMPIANS

Carl Lewis	USA	9 golds in track and field	1984–96
Jesse Owens	USA	4 golds in track and field	1936
Mark Spitz	USA	7 golds in swimming	1972
Vera Caslavska	CZK	7 golds in gymnastics	1964–68
Steve Redgrave	GBR	5 golds in rowing	1984–2000
Raymond Ewry	USA	10 golds in track and field*	1900–08

Note: * = the most by any competitor

DID YOU KNOW?
In ancient Greece athletes often competed naked. (Women were not allowed to watch or take part!) Greek artists strove to capture the athletes' grace and power in works of sculpture. This famous statue is a Roman copy of a Greek statue called The Discus-thrower, *made about 450 BC. The ancient Greeks used a bronze plate for their discus.*

◀ *Long jumper Bob Beamon (USA) set an amazing world record in 1968 at the Mexico City Olympics by leaping 8.9 m. This added 78 cm to the Olympic record. His world record lasted until 1991.*

TOP FIVE GOLD WINNERS

	COUNTRY		GOLDS
★ 1	USA	🇺🇸	931
2	Russia*		572
3	Germany**		470
4	France		207
5	GBR	🇬🇧	195

Note: Summer Games since 1896, Winter Games since 1924. * = USSR until 1992;
** = East and West Germany from 1968 to 1988

▶ *After 1,500 years the Olympic Games were revived. The 1896 Games were held in the Greek capital, Athens, in the stadium shown here. The Games have been held every four years since 1896, except during wartime (1916, 1940 and 1944).*

▶ An Olympic gold medal is the most sought-after award in sport. The winner's national anthem is played as the medal is presented, and silver and bronze medals are given to the athletes who come second and third.

▼ In the 110-m and 400-m hurdles races, athletes such as Colin Jackson must exercise perfect balance, concentration and fitness. They also need flexible hip joints and strong thigh muscles to protect their knees on impact.

TOP AT SYDNEY 2000

	COUNTRY		GOLDS	MEDALS
★ 1	USA	🇺🇸	39	97
2	Russia		32	88
3	China		28	59
4	Australia		16	58
5	Germany		14	57
6	France		13	38
7	Italy		13	34
8	Netherlands		12	25
9	Cuba		11	29
10	GBR	🇬🇧	11	28
11	Romania		11	26
12	South Korea		8	28
13	Hungary		8	17
14	Poland		6	14
15	Japan		5	18
16	Bulgaria		5	13
17	Greece		4	13
18	Sweden		4	12
19	Norway		4	10
20	Ethiopia		4	8
21	Ukraine		3	23
22	Belarus		3	17
23	Canada		3	14
24	Spain		3	11
25	Kazakhstan		3	7

Atlanta 1996

HOBBIES AND PASTIMES

A hobby is something people do for fun and not because they have to. In prehistoric times people were too busy finding food and shelter to have hobbies. It was only when survival became easier and people had time to spare that hobbies and pastimes developed. Early pastimes included drawing, sewing, riding and dancing. Today people fill their leisure time with fishing, cycling, collecting (anything from Beanies to Pokémon cards), making models, playing computer games and Internet surfing.

◄ *Birdwatchers, or 'twitchers', go to extraordinary lengths to spot a bird they have not seen before. Some twitchers have spotted more than 8,000 of the 9,000 or so species.*

▼ *Fishing is one of the most popular pastimes worldwide. A monster catch like this record-breaking 700-kg marlin would need an extra-large case.*

▶▶ RECORD COLLECTIONS		
	COLLECTION	**NUMBER**
★ 1	Buttons	1 million
2	Bottle caps	82,000
3	Matchbox labels	74,000
4	Fridge magnets	15,000
5	Ties	10,000

▼ *Windsurfing, or sailboarding, is a water sport that first became popular as a hobby in 1969. The sailboard is a surfboard with a sail. A sailboarder needs a good wind to send the board racing across the water.*

◄ *The first jigsaw was cut out by mapmaker John Spilsbury in 1791. He wanted to make geography fun for children. The biggest-ever jigsaw had 44,000 pieces. Put together in France in 1992, it covered more than half a soccer pitch.*

IT'S A FACT
A penny stamp can be worth a million to a collector – if it is rare. A letter dated 1847 with two Mauritius stamps (original value 1 and 2 pence) sold in 1993 for over £2 million!

► *Model planes were flown in the 1800s, before full-sized ones. This giant model of a Russian* Antonov 225 *cargo plane, built in 1995, had a wing-span of over 5.6 m, but weighed only about 20 kg.*

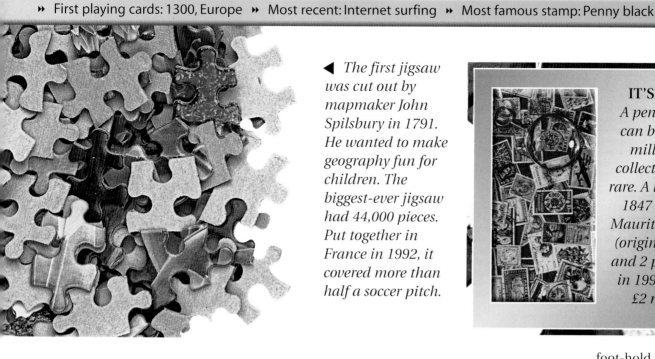

foot-hold in rock

safety harness

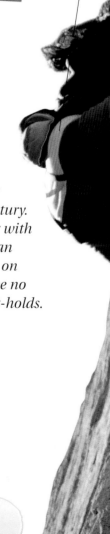

▼ *Robot modelling is a popular hobby, especially in Japan. The latest robots, like this Lego Mindstorms character, use electronics and computers to react to the world around them.*

► *People have climbed mountains since ancient times, but modern climbing began in the 19th century. A skilled rock climber with modern equipment can scale sheer rock walls on which there seem to be no obvious hand- or foot-holds.*

COLLECTING BEARS

● Collecting can be an expensive hobby. In 1994 a Steiff bear was bought by a collector for £110,000, making it the most expensive teddy ever!

● Teddy bears were named after US President Theodore 'Teddy' Roosevelt.

SPEEDY SPORTS

Record speeds in sports are always being broken. Runners run ever faster, golf balls are hit farther and tennis players serve faster – thanks to a combination of training and technology. Before 1800, the speediest sports were horse racing, real tennis, fencing and archery. But following the inventions of the car and the aeroplane, a new craze was born – breaking speed records, whether in the air, on water or on land. The fastest team game at present is ice hockey, in which players zoom around the rink at up to 50 km/h, whacking the puck at 160 km/h.

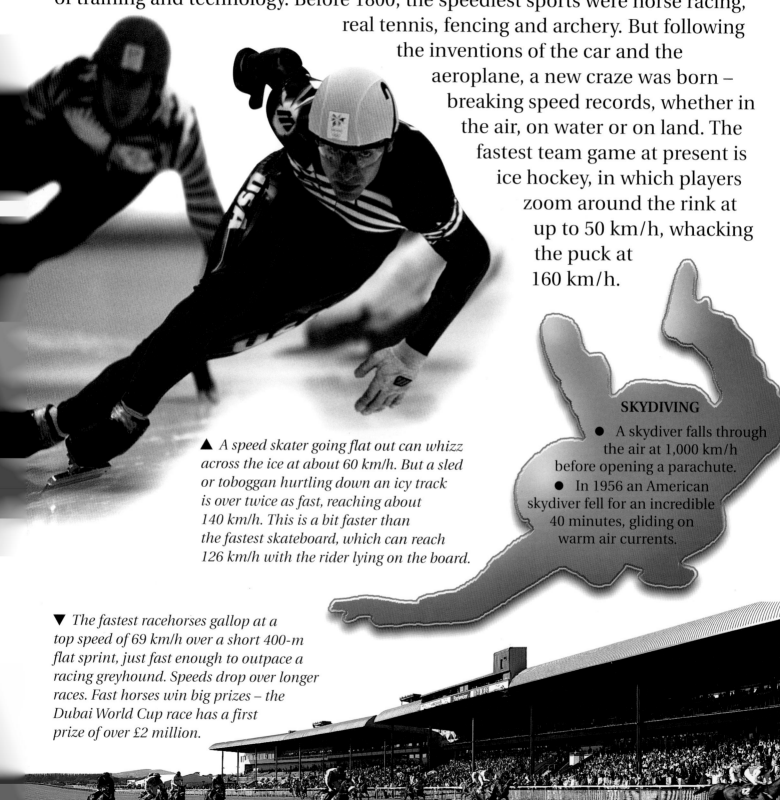

SKYDIVING
● A skydiver falls through the air at 1,000 km/h before opening a parachute.
● In 1956 an American skydiver fell for an incredible 40 minutes, gliding on warm air currents.

▲ *A speed skater going flat out can whizz across the ice at about 60 km/h. But a sled or toboggan hurtling down an icy track is over twice as fast, reaching about 140 km/h. This is a bit faster than the fastest skateboard, which can reach 126 km/h with the rider lying on the board.*

▼ *The fastest racehorses gallop at a top speed of 69 km/h over a short 400-m flat sprint, just fast enough to outpace a racing greyhound. Speeds drop over longer races. Fast horses win big prizes – the Dubai World Cup race has a first prize of over £2 million.*

▲ Ice hockey is a fast and furious game, with the heavily padded players crashing into one another on the ice while in pursuit of the puck – a rubber disc. Ice hockey was first played in Canada in the 1850s.

▶ Snowboarding is even faster than skateboarding. This 'extreme', or fast and sometimes dangerous, sport became a craze in the 1990s with people who wanted the thrill of skiing, but on a board. Other extreme sports, also called X-Games, include motocross and snow mountain bike riding.

SPEEDY SPORTS COMPARED

	PERSON OR OBJECT	SPEED
★1	Sky diver	1,000 km/h
2 =	Pelota ball	300 km/h
2 =	Racing motorbike	300 km/h
3	Golf ball	270 km/h
4	Tennis ball	220 km/h
5	Skier	210 km/h
6	Cricket ball (bowled)	160 km/h
7	Toboggan	140 km/h
8	Greyhound	67 km/h
9	Speed skater	60 km/h
10	Sprinter	37 km/h

▼ With a rocketlike serve of more than 200 km/h, US tennis star Pete Sampras won a record seventh Wimbledon singles title in 2000, his fourth win in a row. This broke the all-time record of 12 'grand-slam' title wins held by Australia's Roy Emerson (1961–67).

◀ Sailing is one of the oldest sports. The fastest sailing boats today are trimarans, which have three hulls, and catamarans, which have two. The record speed reached by a sailing vessel was 86 km/h on a 500-m run. But sailing on ice is even quicker. An ice yacht has been timed at speeds of more than 225 km/h!

A GOOD READ

The oldest printed book dates from the AD 800s, but it was not until 1454, when Johannes Gutenberg set up Europe's first printing press, that books became available cheaply and in large numbers. The first book Gutenberg printed was the Bible, still the world's number-one bestseller. In 1935 the publisher Penguin started the paperback revolution. Today's most popular titles may be printed in millions, like the most-read children's books of the 1990s and 2000, the Harry Potter series by J. K. Rowling.

▲ *The Rosetta stone was found in Egypt in 1799. On it was the same inscription in three kinds of writing – ancient Egyptian picture-writing called hieroglyphic, demotic (a simpler form of Egyptian writing) and Greek. It gave scholars the key to understanding Egyptian hieroglyphs.*

◄ *The most famous detective in literature is Sherlock Holmes. Frequently mistaken by readers for a real person, Holmes and his friend Dr. Watson first appeared in Arthur Conan Doyle's story* A Study In Scarlet *in 1887.*

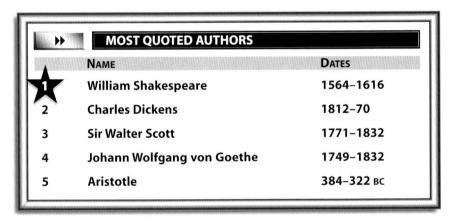

	MOST QUOTED AUTHORS	
	NAME	**DATES**
★ 1	**William Shakespeare**	1564–1616
2	**Charles Dickens**	1812–70
3	**Sir Walter Scott**	1771–1832
4	**Johann Wolfgang von Goethe**	1749–1832
5	**Aristotle**	384–322 BC

▼ *For about 3,000 years the ancient Egyptians wrote in picture-writing called hieroglyphic. Some symbols stood for single sounds, some for objects and some for actions, like walking. Hieroglyphs were used mainly for religious inscriptions on temples and stone monuments.*

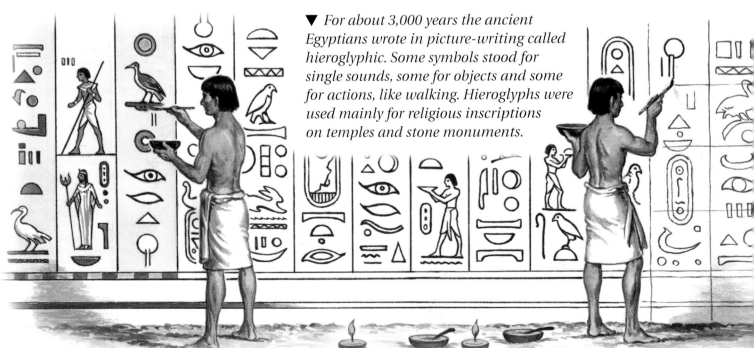

▸ Longest-running comic: *Dandy* ▸ Longest novel: 27 volumes (French) ▸ Most popular cartoon: *Peanuts*

◀ *Braille is a raised-dot alphabet used by blind people. It is read by running the fingertips over the dots, or bumps. Braille was invented by a blind French teenager named Louis Braille in the 1820s.*

▲ *Charles Dickens (1812–70) was one of the most popular novelists of all time. His books such as* A Christmas Carol *and* Oliver Twist *are full of memorable characters, humour and sadness. Dickens gave public readings from his many books.*

	BESTSELLING BOOKS
	BESTSELLERS
⭐ **1**	**The Bible**
2	**The plays of William Shakespeare**
3	**The Little Red Book of Mao Zedong**

THE LONGEST WORD

● This is a ridiculously long chemical enzyme name that starts with *methionyl-* and ends in *-serine*. In between there are 1,894 other letters, making a total of 1,909!

▲ *The first book printed using movable metal blocks of type was Johannes Gutenberg's Bible of 1456. The first printer in Britain was William Caxton, in 1476.*

▶ *Bede, an English monk who lived from about 673 to 735, is often called 'the Father of English History'. His written history of the English (731) is the best account of events in the years after the Romans left Britain.*

DID YOU KNOW?
The Bible, parts of which were written more than 3,000 years ago, contains over 3.5 million words and is the world's biggest-selling book. The shortest verse in the Bible is John 11, verse 35: "Jesus wept".

▲ *The biggest-selling writer ever is Agatha Christie (1890–1976). Her 78 crime stories, featuring detectives Hercule Poirot and Miss Marple, have been translated into more than 44 languages. Many have been made into plays such as* The Mousetrap.

	COMIC BOOK HEROES	
Dick Tracy		**1931**
Batman		**1937**
Desperate Dan, *Dandy*		**1937**
Superman		**1938**
Charlie Brown, *Peanuts*		**1950**
Dan Dare		**1950**

SOUNDS IMPRESSIVE

Music was first written down about 1800 BC. The three biggest groups of musical instruments are wind instruments, which are blown into, stringed instruments, which are plucked or played with a bow, and percussion instruments such as drums and cymbals, which are hit. They are used to play all kinds of music ranging from classical, opera and military to folk, jazz, pop and rock. Some of the most famous composers of 'classical' music wrote long pieces, called symphonies, for orchestras.

THREE GREAT COMPOSERS

Note: experts will never agree on 'the greatest-ever composer', but many music-lovers place the following as the top three:

Johann Sebastian Bach
(1865–1750)

Wolfgang Amadeus Mozart
(1756–91)

Ludwig van Beethoven
(1770–1827)

▶ *Drums are among the oldest of all musical instruments. The biggest drum kit ever built, in 1994, had over 300 pieces. Most drummers manage with less!*

▼ *No party is complete without music. The world's best-known tune is the party song* Happy Birthday, *sung just before the candles on a cake are blown out.*

SPOOKY TUNES

● In 1964 Rosemary Brown 'composed' music she said was played for her by Frans Liszt, a Hungarian pianist who died in 1886. His ghost, she said, moved her hands over the piano. She also produced music in the style of Beethoven, Chopin and Schubert.

▶ *The violin was developed from earlier stringed instruments. The finest violins were made in Italy by Antonio Stradivari in the 1600s.*

▶ *The saxophone was the invention of Adolphe Sax of Belgium. He made the first one about 1840.*

▼ *The violoncello, usually called a cello, is really a big violin. It dates from the 1600s, about the same time as the violin.*

◀ *The guitar's origins go back to ancient Egypt, but the shape of the Spanish acoustic guitar, shown here, dates from the 1800s. Most guitars have 6 strings, but some have 12. Guitars used by ex-rock stars sell for huge sums of money.*

◀ *Instruments do not get much longer than the alpenhorn. This 4-m-long wooden horn was used by herdsmen in the Swiss Alps to communicate across mountain valleys.*

▼ *In a standard concert orchestra as many as 100 musicians play more than 20 different kinds of instrument. But in 1998, in Birmingham, UK, 3,503 musicians played a piece by composer Malcolm Arnold!*

▸▸ LONGEST AND QUIETEST MUSICAL EXPERIENCES

Longest opera	*Die Meistersinger...*	R. Wagner	5 hrs, 15 mins
Longest symphony	*Symphony No.2*	H. Brian	1 hr, 39 mins
Quietest piece	*4'33"*	J. Cage	4 mins silence
Longest applause	**For singer Placido Domingo**		1 hr, 20 mins

ROCKING RECORDS

The first rock superstar was Elvis Presley, 'The King' of rock 'n' roll. Such is his popularity that although he died in 1977, there are still more than 600 fan clubs and countless lip-curling lookalikes! In the 1960s the Beatles took the world by storm and became the biggest-selling group of all time. More recent superstars include Mariah Carey, the first singer to hit the Top 5 with her first ten singles. Carey, Madonna and Whitney Houston are the biggest-selling female singers, each with over 45 platinum (million-selling) albums.

▲ *Mississippi-born singer Elvis Presley (1935–77) became the first pop superstar. Nicknamed 'Elvis the Pelvis' for his hip-twitching on stage, he made rock 'n' roll popular all over the world.*

▼ *In the 1960s 'Beatle-mania' swept the world. The Beatles, from left to right: Paul McCartney, Ringo Starr, George Harrison and John Lennon, sold more recordings than any other performers, topped the US charts 20 times, and made number 1 in the UK 17 times – a record they share with Elvis Presley.*

HUGE HITS OF THE 20TH CENTURY

White Christmas	1942	Bing Crosby	Biggest Christmas hit
Oklahoma	1949	Rogers and Hammerstein	First million-selling LP album
Rock Around the Clock	1955	Bill Haley and the Comets	Started rock 'n' roll craze
Please Please Me	1963	The Beatles	Their breakthrough single
Thriller	1983	Michael Jackson	Top-selling album
I Will Always Love You	1992	Whitney Houston	Top US single for 14 weeks
Three Lions on a Shirt	1996	Baddiel and Skinner	Most popular football song

▼ *The Spice Girls became the most successful girl-group ever with a succession of Top Ten hits from 1996 on. Their first album,* Spice, *was the biggest and fastest-selling debut album by a British group. More than 20 million people worldwide bought the album.*

» Biggest-selling group: The Beatles » Biggest single hit: *Candle in the Wind* » First million-selling singer: Enrico Caruso

▶▶	POP SUPERSTARS' FIRST HITS	
Elvis Presley	*Heartbreak Hotel*	1956
Cliff Richard	*Move It*	1958
The Beatles	*Love Me Do*	1962
Elton John	*Your Song*	1970
Michael Jackson	*Got To Be There*	1971

▲ *The Backstreet Boys were named best newcomers of 1995. By 1999 they were listed as the biggest-earning American band, scooping £37 million in a year. Fame in the pop world can bring millionaire status.*

CANDLE IN THE WIND

● Elton John rewrote his song *Candle in the Wind* for the funeral of Princess Diana in 1997. It became the biggest-selling single ever, with worldwide sales of more than 33 million.

▶▶	MOST NUMBER 1 SINGLES (UK)	
	NAME	**No. 1s**
1=	The Beatles	17
1=	Elvis Presley	17
2	Cliff Richard	13
3	Madonna	10

▶ *Madonna, born Madonna Louise Ciccone, burst onto the pop scene in 1984 with her album* Like A Virgin. *She became the biggest-selling female singer in showbiz history. Her string of over 40 hits throughout the 1980s and 1990s made more than 100 million sales. The image she projects is often outrageous, and was as important as the sound of her music in rocketing her to superstardom.*

▲ *Michael Jackson started his career at the age of five, singing in The Jackson Five with his older brothers. His* Thriller *album (1982) broke all records, and is reckoned to be the best-selling pop album of all time.*

CURTAIN-UP!

The first theatre-goers were the ancient Greeks. They sat in audiences of up to 18,000 on hillsides to watch tragedies and comedies. The Romans built bigger stone theatres that could seat 40,000 and were used to stage raucous comedies. But the most successful playwright ever was William Shakespeare (1564–1616). His plays have been translated into numerous languages and are staged all over the world. Other performing arts besides drama are musicals, ballet and mime, in which actors use exaggerated movements instead of words to convey actions and emotions.

▲ *William Shakespeare wrote 37 plays. The longest is* Hamlet, *which also has the longest solo part. An actor playing Hamlet has 11,610 words to learn! More films have been made of Shakespeare's plays than any other playwright's.*

▼ *Greek audiences sat in a terraced half-circle to watch plays – the word theatre means 'seeing place'. The actors performed in a space called the orchestra. Behind was a hut, called the skene, used as a dressing room. In time 'scenery' was added, and the actors stood on a raised stage.*

raised stage

actors

audience seating

entrance

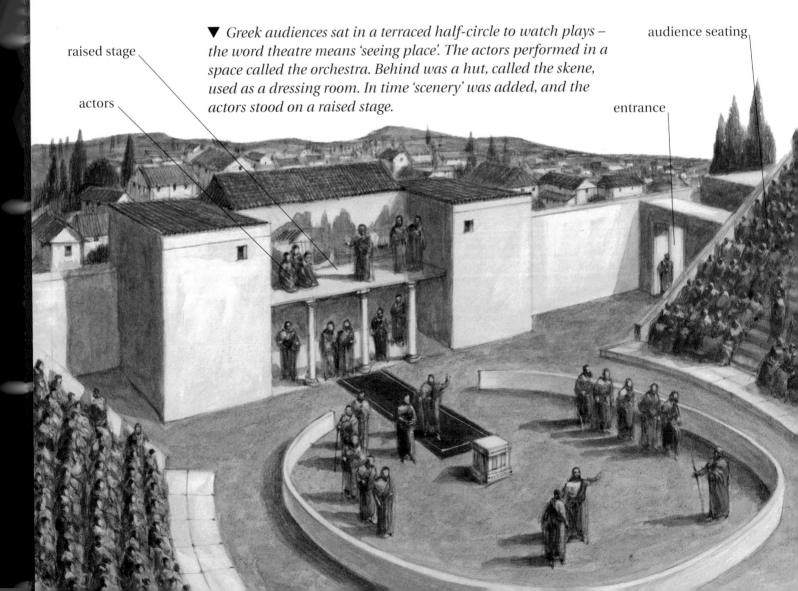

▼ *Broadway in New York is America's theatreland – the equivalent of London's West End – and is the place where British and American actors most want to perform. If a play transfers to Broadway from a West End theatre, and is praised by the critics, it is considered a hit.*

▲ *In ancient Greece, plays developed from religious ceremonies. Actors wore masks to show emotion – a happy face like this one for comedy, a gloomy one for tragedy.*

▶ *The Globe Theatre, built in 1599 beside the River Thames in London, is where William Shakespeare presented his plays. In 1613 the theatre burned down, but a replica Globe Theatre was opened in 1997 to stage Shakespeare's plays in the same way as they were originally performed.*

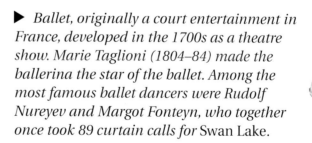

▶ *Ballet, originally a court entertainment in France, developed in the 1700s as a theatre show. Marie Taglioni (1804–84) made the ballerina the star of the ballet. Among the most famous ballet dancers were Rudolf Nureyev and Margot Fonteyn, who together once took 89 curtain calls for* Swan Lake.

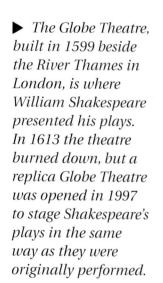

▲ *In 1999 Andrew Lloyd Webber's* Cats *overtook* A Chorus Line *as the longest-running musical in New York. During the course of more than 6,000 performances it was seen by over 6 million people.*

▶▶	OLDEST DRAMATIC ARTS		
	ART FORM	**DATE**	**COUNTRIES**
★1	Tragedy and comic drama	500 BC	Greece
2	Mime	100 BC	Rome, Italy
3	Opera	1580s	Italy and France
4	Ballet	1650s	France
5	Cinema	1890s	France and USA

FILM MAGIC

The film industry began in the early 1900s after experiments with 'kinetoscope' peepshows showed how much people loved watching moving pictures. The first big movie was D. W. Griffith's epic *Birth of a Nation*, made in 1915. The early films were silent – 'talkies' didn't appear until the late 1920s. Hollywood, California, became the home of American cinema, but today film-making is international.

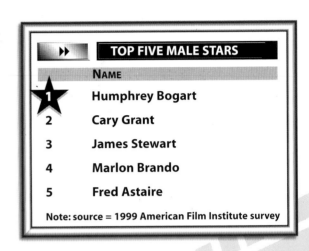

▶	TOP FIVE MALE STARS
	NAME
★ 1	**Humphrey Bogart**
2	**Cary Grant**
3	**James Stewart**
4	**Marlon Brando**
5	**Fred Astaire**

Note: source = 1999 American Film Institute survey

▶	TOP FIVE FEMALE STARS
	NAME
★ 1	**Katherine Hepburn**
2	**Bette Davis**
3	**Audrey Hepburn**
4	**Ingrid Bergman**
5	**Greta Garbo**

◀ *Voted the most popular film actor, Humphrey Bogart played tough-guy roles in 1940s films such as* Casablanca *and* The Maltese Falcon. *Bogart and Hepburn co-starred in* The African Queen, *for which Bogart won an Oscar in 1951.*

▲ *American actress Katherine Hepburn is the only star to have won four best-actress Oscars – an Oscar is the most sought-after award in the film industry. She won the first in 1933 and the last in 1981.*

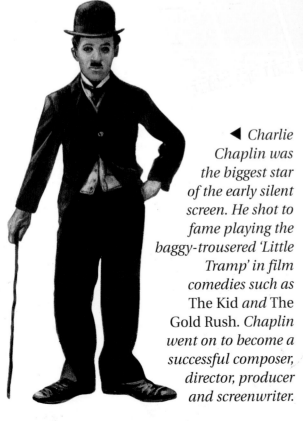

◀ *Charlie Chaplin was the biggest star of the early silent screen. He shot to fame playing the baggy-trousered 'Little Tramp' in film comedies such as* The Kid *and* The Gold Rush. *Chaplin went on to become a successful composer, director, producer and screenwriter.*

▲ *Titanic (1997) is the only film since* Ben-Hur *(1959) to have won 11 oscars. More than 100 stunt artists helped to recreate the sinking scene, shown here in an artist's impression. The stunt team spent a record 6,000 hours on the set of* Titanic *– the equivalent of almost 17 years for one person!*

HOLLYWOOD

▲ Hollywood, California, was the home of American movies for most of the 20th century. Many of the greatest films ever were made in Hollywood studios.

◄ Star Wars rocketed into movie history when the first of producer George Lucas's space adventures appeared in 1977. The menacing Darth Vader, shown here, and other Star Wars characters have appeared in books, toys, games and on all kinds of merchandise.

▲ The first movie monster to become a star was King Kong (1933). Although the giant ape had film-goers on the edge of their seats, Kong was actually a model only 45 cm tall. For close-ups the studio used a giant furry head worked by three men inside!

▶▶	BLOCKBUSTERS BY DECADE	
1940s	**Gone With The Wind**	1939
1950s	**Ben-Hur**	1959
1960s	**The Sound Of Music**	1965
1970s	**Jaws**	1975
1980s	**ET: The Extra-Terrestrial**	1982
1990s	**Titanic**	1997

▶ Jurassic Park's *nine species of dinosaurs thundered and roared through the world's cinemas in 1993. Made of latex and foam rubber, the dinosaur robots were incredibly realistic. They included the largest film robot ever made –* a 5.5-m tall Tyrannosaurus rex.

Velociraptor

Tyrannosaurus rex

▶▶	TOP FIVE FILMS	
	TITLE	**YEAR**
★ 1	**Titanic**	1997
2	**Jurassic Park**	1993
3	**Independence Day**	1996
4	**Star Wars** series	1977–97
5	**The Lion King**	1994
Note: ranked by world box office takings		

CRAZES AND FADS

Crazes, or enthusiasms for doing something in a new way, come and go all the time. A fad is another word for a craze, though fads tend to last less time. Typical crazes are for weird hairstyles, startling dress, new foods, toys or games. Teddy bears started as a craze in the 1900s, and Action Men have been popular for about 40 years. More short-lived fads were Teenage Mutant Ninja Turtles and Power Rangers. Some crazes reappear years later, like yo-yos and scooters.

▲ *Yo-yos were a craze in the 1920s, the 1960s and again in the 1990s. 'Yo-yo' is said to be a Filipino word. In the Philippines people used yo-yos as weapons!*

CROSSWORDS

● The first crossword puzzle was published in the *New York World* newspaper of 1913. It had 32 clues. The crossword craze caught on, and general knowledge or cryptic crosswords now appear in most local and national newspapers.

● The largest crossword ever had more than 12,000 clues!

▲ *'Doing the Charleston' was the great dance craze of the 1920s. In the 1940s nations twirled to the Jitterbug, and later the Jive. Rock came in with a bang in the 1950s. The Twist was a dance of the 1960s and disco hit the 1970s. Salsa was a craze of 2000.*

▶ *Punk was a fad of 1970s youth culture and it started a craze for body art that is still popular. Ripped clothes, safety-pin piercings, chains, studs and spiky coloured hair were worn as an expression of freedom and a rebellion against conformity.*

◀ A kind of pinball machine was invented in the 1400s, long before electricity. The craze for pinball was particularly popular in Spain. Today 'amusement arcades' all over the world are filled with pinball games. Among the keenest gamblers are the Chinese.

▼ High-heeled shoes came into fashion in the 1600s and have never gone out. But in the 1970s they were given a new look with the platform heel. Platforms were often worn with flared trousers, which made a comeback in the 1990s.

◀ Tattooing is done mainly for fun, love, boldness or as body-art. Designs are pricked into the skin with needles dipped in coloured inks. The most tattooed person has covered 99.9 percent of his body in a leopard skin design.

▶ The first Barbie doll, whose full name is Barbara Millicent Roberts, went on sale in 1959, and the craze continues. There have been 2,000 different Barbie dolls to collect, dress and accessorize.

◀ Every few years a new craze comes along that everyone can do. The hula hoop is so simple that even toddlers can do it. All they have to do is wiggle! 'Hula' is the name of a dance from Hawaii that also requires wiggling (though not with hoops), and the name stuck!

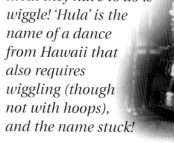

ART AND SCULPTURE

Art ranges from tiny miniature paintings to whole buildings wrapped in plastic. The earliest-known art was made by Stone Age people, who painted pictures on cave walls and made figures from stone and clay. The ancient Egyptians and Chinese put some of their finest art treasures into tombs for the dead to take to the afterlife, and the ancient Greeks decorated their temples with statues of heroes and gods. The Italians gave painting a new, lifelike look from the late 1300s. Later, French Impressionists such as Claude Monet painted atmospheric scenes and abstract painters such as Picasso developed a non-realistic style called Cubism.

▲ *The Lascaux cave paintings in France are about 17,000 years old. Discovered in 1940, the cave walls are covered with paintings of animals like this wild horse.*

▲ *John Constable (1776–1837) painted the landscape of eastern England, vividly capturing its clouds, trees, fields and the work of country people.*

▶▶ MOST EXPENSIVE WORKS OF ART		
By a man	Van Gogh's *Portrait Of Dr. Gachet*	£49.1 million
By a woman	Mary Cassatt's *In The Box*	£2.45 million
Sculpture	Canova's *The Three Graces*	£7.5 million
Photograph	Le Gray's *Grande Vague – Séte* (1855)	£507,500
Poster	Charles Rennie Mackintosh's poster advertising an art show, Glasgow	£68,200

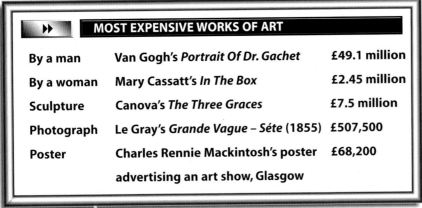

▼ *A few artists blast away at mountains to create mega-sculptures. This giant 172-m-high figure of the Sioux leader Crazy Horse is being carved on Thunderhead Mountain in South Dakota, USA.*

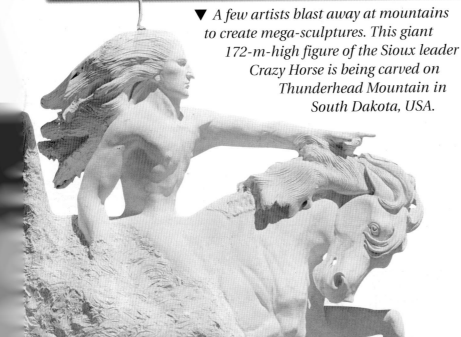

▲ *Italian artist Michelangelo (1475–1564) spent the years 1508–12 painting the ceiling of the Sistine Chapel in Rome. It includes the famous scene of God creating Adam, shown here in the centre of the picture.*

» Most successful forger: Hans Van Meegeren » Most famous painting: *Mona Lisa* » Most controversial: row of bricks

▼ *The Mona Lisa, by Leonardo da Vinci (1452–1519), is the world's most famous painting. In 1911 it was stolen from the Louvre Museum, Paris. Six fakes were sold to buyers before it was recovered in 1913.*

» GIANT STATUES AND FIGURES

Crazy Horse, stone figure*	Thunderhead Mountain, South Dakota, USA	172 m
Buddha, figure	Tokyo, Japan	120 m
The Motherland, statue	St Petersburg, Russia	82 m
The Long Man, chalk figure	Sussex, England	68 m
The Statue of Liberty	New York, USA	46 m

Note: * = begun in 1948, not yet complete

ART ON A GRAND SCALE

- The biggest painting is said to be one of Elvis Presley in Georgia, USA.
- The biggest art collection is in the Hermitage Museum, St Petersburg, Russia. It has more than 16,000 paintings.

▶ *The Dutch artist Rembrandt (1606–69), shown here in a self-portrait, left more than 2,000 paintings, etchings and drawings. He painted himself about 100 times, from youth to old age.*

▶ *The Venus de Milo, found on the island of Melos in Greece, was carved about 150 BC and is in the Louvre Museum, Paris. The famous statue shows the goddess of love, named Aphrodite by the Greeks and Venus by the Romans.*

» FAMOUS PAINTERS

Giotto (c.1266–1337)	Italian	Showed people in a more lifelike way
Leonardo da Vinci (1452–1519)	Italian	Painted the *Mona Lisa*
El Greco (1541–1614)	Spanish	Painted religious scenes
Rembrandt von Rijn (1606–69)	Dutch	Master of portraits
J. M. W. Turner (1775–1851)	English	Master of landscapes, seas and skies
Claude Monet (1840–1926)	French	Impressionist painter
Vincent Van Gogh (1853–90)	Dutch	Painted landscapes and portraits
Pablo Picasso (1881–1973)	Spanish	Many styles, including abstract Cubist

THEME PARKS AND FAIRS

The first fairs were markets where people met to buy and sell goods and enjoy street entertainments. Fairs were important in the Middle Ages. Later they developed into international World Fairs and Exhibitions. One of the most impressive was London's Great Exhibition of 1851, with more than 13,000 exhibits from around the world. The first big amusement park was Coney Island in the United States, which opened in the early 1900s. Theme parks such as Disneyland now attract tens of millions of thrill-seekers every year.

▲ In 1851 a Great Exhibition was held in the magnificent, specially built Crystal Palace in London. It aimed to show people every known machine from around the world, and was a Victorian industrial theme park!

◀ Disney World in Florida is the biggest theme park in the world. The park's attractions recreate stories and cartoon characters, such as Dumbo the flying elephant, familiar from Disney films.

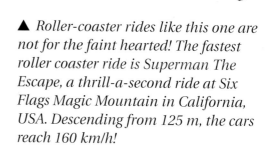

▲ *The London Eye, opened in 2000, is the world's largest observation wheel. From its slowly rotating gondolas, riders have a bird's eye view across London from 135 m above the ground.*

▶ *Acrobats are part of the fun of the circus. The most famous circus is Ringling Brothers and Barnum and Bailey's (combined in 1919). This circus had the biggest-ever Big Top, or tent, and its stars included the Wallendas, the only act to balance seven people in a human pyramid on a high wire.*

▲ *Roller-coaster rides like this one are not for the faint hearted! The fastest roller coaster ride is Superman The Escape, a thrill-a-second ride at Six Flags Magic Mountain in California, USA. Descending from 125 m, the cars reach 160 km/h!*

➤➤ GREATEST SHOWS ON EARTH	
Most visitors	Disneyland, Tokyo, Japan with more than 17 million visitors a year
Most roller coasters	United States has 427; United Kingdom has 114
Biggest theme park	Disney World, Orlando, Florida, USA
Biggest g-force	The Mindbender at Galaxyland, Alberta, Canada reaches 6.3 g
First vertical-drop ride	Oblivion at Alton Towers, UK (1998); has a 55-m drop at over 100 km/h into a black hole!

TV AND DVD

The television (TV) age began in 1936, when only a few hundred people owned television sets and black-and-white pictures flickered across the screens. Today TV is the world's biggest form of information and entertainment. Satellite and cable networks provide hundreds of channels around the world, with thousands of hours of viewing. And if you miss your favourite film or programme the first time around, you can always watch it later on DVD.

▲ *Satellite TV began in the 1960s with the first communications satellites in space. The first commercial TV satellite was* Early Bird *in 1965. Today a network of satellites circling Earth provides 24-hour live television around the world.*

▲ *CNN is one of the world's biggest news broadcasters. Based in the USA, its news reporters can cover big stories such as a war, an election or a natural disaster anywhere in the world using mobile TV cameras and satellite links that keep them in contact with the studio. Using 23 satellites, CNN can reach 212 countries.*

▼ *TV talk-show host Oprah Winfrey is a bigger celebrity than many of the politicians and showbiz stars she interviews. She is also the richest TV entertainer in the world. Her talk-show was voted the best on TV for 11 seasons in a row and has won 30 Emmys, the most sought-after award for a US TV show.*

BIGGEST TV AUDIENCES IN THE UK

	PROGRAMME	YEAR	VIEWERS
1	Royal wedding, Prince Charles and Lady Diana Spencer	1981	39 million
2	World Cup, Brazil v England	1970	32.5 million
3	World Cup Final, England v West Germany	1966	32 million
4	Funeral of Diana, Princess of Wales	1997	31 million
5	*EastEnders* Christmas edition	1987	30 million

▼ *Prince Charles and Lady Diana Spencer's wedding was watched by millions in 1981. In 1997 Princess Diana's funeral was seen by about 2.5 billion people – more than a third of Earth's population.*

◄ *George Clooney is the most popular male TV star. During the 1996–97 season of the US hospital drama* ER, *Clooney was watched in Britain and the United States by more than 24 million people per episode, and was said to have been paid £92,000 for each one!*

▼ *Historic events such as the* Apollo *Moon landing of 1969 are seen by viewers 'live' as they take place. Millions of people watched as the astronauts took their first steps and posed for the camera.*

COUCH POTATOES!

● The country with the most TV sets is China with an estimated 394 million.
● The USA has about 227 million TV sets and the UK about 38 million.

▼ *Videotape, invented in the 1950s, has been superseded by DVD digital discs that give better quality sound and images. They are played on DVD players like this one. Films and children's TV shows are most popular.*

THE WAY

WE LIVE

People around the world often lead very opposite lives. From the food they eat to the clothes they wear, people around the world do the same things differently. This is what makes our world so vibrant and interesting.

For instance, on average the people of Britain consume an amazing 16 kg of chocolate per person per year, while the Japanese have a love of eating raw fish. And while everyone knows that education is important, there is a school in India, which has more than 22,000 pupils.

Explore the biggest and best facts about *The Way We Live* and discover other cultures and traditions. There are the big, serious facts – for reference – and less serious ones, too, for fun. These pages are packed with some of the biggest and best, oddest and strangest, smallest and funniest facts around!

WORLD LEADERS

The most powerful kind of ruler is a dictator, whose word is law. Dictators rule with the support of their country's army. In democratic countries the people can vote for the political party of their choice to run the country. Democracy was first put into practice by the ancient Greeks. The most powerful democracy is the USA. Some countries have an ancient ruling family. Japan, for example, has had 125 emperors so far, dating back 2,000 years, and Britain's royal family is descended from Saxon kings who ruled over 1,000 years ago.

▲ *Traditional leaders and groups still exist in some societies. These Maoris are modern New Zealanders, but they retain links with their past, when Maoris lived in groups called* iwis, *led by chiefs.*

▼ *Britain's prime minister (PM), Tony Blair, was the youngest British PM since William Pitt the Younger held office in 1783, aged 25. Blair moved into 10 Downing Street, the PM's official home, in 1997, at the age of 43.*

▲ *Every nation has its own government, but most countries also belong to the United Nations (UN), whose flag is shown here. Since World War II ended in 1945, the UN has debated international issues and acted as a peace-keeper.*

▲ *The first black president of South Africa (1994–99) was Nelson Mandela. Mandela was imprisoned from 1962 to 1990 because he opposed the racist apartheid system that separated black and white people and gave them unequal rights.*

KINGS

● The world's longest-reigning king is King Bhumibol Adulyadej (Rama IX) of Thailand, who became king in 1946.
● The richest king is King Fahd of Saudi Arabia, whose wealth is almost twice that of the Sultan of Brunei.
● In 1976 King Taufa'ahau Tupou IV of Tonga was the heaviest king, weighing 209.5 kg. He has since lost more than 70 kg!

»	PRESIDENTS OF THE USA	
First president	George Washington	President 1789–97
Oldest elected	Ronald Reagan, age 73	President 1981–89
Youngest elected	John F. Kennedy, age 43	President 1961–63
Biggest family	John Tyler, 15 children	President 1841–45
Longest-serving	Franklin D. Roosevelt	President 1933–45

WOMEN PRIME MINISTERS

Sirimavo Bandaranaike of Sri Lanka became the world's first woman PM in 1965.

Margaret Thatcher was the first woman PM of the UK (1979 to 1990).

Indira Gandhi (India's PM 1966–77, 1980–84) was assassinated in 1984.

▲ *The White House in Washington, D.C., is the home of the president of the United States. Until 1901 its official name was The Executive Mansion, but President Theodore Roosevelt made its popular name, 'The White House', official.*

PARTIES AND VOTERS

● The world's biggest national assembly is China's National People's Congress. However, China is not yet a democracy. All 3,000 assembly members belong to the Communist Party.

● India is the world's largest true democracy, with more than 500 million voters.

● About AD 840 the Saxon kings of England had a council of advisers called the 'witan'. The use of the word 'parliament' dates from 1241.

● The first country in which women had the same voting rights as men in elections was New Zealand, in 1893.

▼ *The Palace of Westminster in London is home to the UK's two Houses of Parliament, the Commons and Lords. Elected members of the Commons discuss and vote on new laws or changes to old laws. The famous clock tower is known as Big Ben, after its great bell.*

COUNTRIES AND PEOPLE

The world is divided into seven continents: North America, South America, Europe, Africa, Asia, Oceania (including Australia) and Antarctica. Apart from Antarctica, each continent is made up of countries. The biggest is Russia, but China and India have more people – both have more than 1 billion.

▲ *The most common family name in the world is probably Zhiang – 1 in 10 Chinese (above left) are called Zhiang. In the Islamic world (centre) it is Muhammad, and in the English-speaking world (above right) it is Smith. The shortest name is O, common among Koreans.*

North America is the richest continent.

▲ On July 4 every year Americans celebrate Independence Day with flags, parties and parades.

South America is the fourth-largest continent, but it is thinly populated. Many of its people speak Spanish or Portuguese, a legacy of European settlement which started in the 1500s.

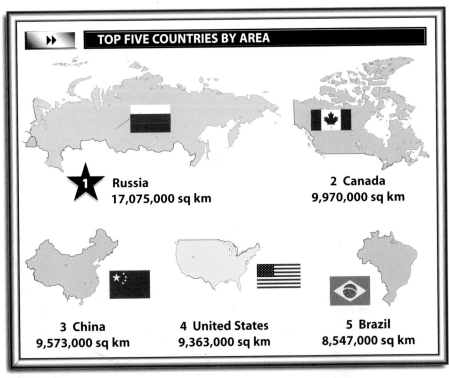

TOP FIVE COUNTRIES BY AREA

1 Russia
17,075,000 sq km

2 Canada
9,970,000 sq km

3 China
9,573,000 sq km

4 United States
9,363,000 sq km

5 Brazil
8,547,000 sq km

Europe is smaller than any other continent except Oceania, but has about one-eighth of the world's population.

Russia is the world's biggest country. Part of Russia (west of the Ural Mountains) is within Europe, the rest belongs to Asia.

◀ *Europe's oldest national flag belongs to Denmark. It has been flown since 1219 when, according to legend, the Danish king saw a white cross in a red sky before winning a battle, and so adopted the colours for his flag.*

Russia

EUROPE

•Vatican City
Rome

China

ASIA

India

AFRICA

Africa is the second-largest continent by area, but has the most countries with 53.

Asia is the biggest continent. It covers 30 percent of the world's total land area. It also has about 60 percent of the world's people. Twenty percent of the world's people are Chinese and Indians.

Indonesia

Australia

OCEANIA

▲ *Vatican City in Rome, dominated by St Peter's Basilica, is home of the pope. It is the smallest state in the world. About 870 people live within its 44 hectares.*

▶ *The first settlers in Australia over 50,000 years ago were the ancestors of the Aboriginal people, or Aborigines. About 1 in 100 Australians are Aborigines.*

⇥	TOP FIVE COUNTRIES BY POPULATION		
	COUNTRY		**POPULATION**
★ 1	China	👤👤👤👤👤👤👤👤👤👤👤👤👤	1,300,000,000
2	India	👤👤👤👤👤👤👤👤👤👤	1,000,849,000
3	USA	👤👤👤	273,000,000
4	Indonesia	👤👤	206,143,000
5	Brazil	👤👤	164,000,000

CITIES

There have been cities for over 5,000 years. The first cities with a million people were Rome in Italy and Chang'an in China. But in the last 200 years, since the Industrial Revolution began, cities have grown much bigger. About half the people in the world now live in towns and cities, whereas 200 years ago only 3 in 100 people lived in towns. Many cities are growing fast as people crowd into them from the country. The biggest cities have more people than many countries. Mexico City and Tokyo each have 20 million (including their suburbs), so these mega-cities would rank in the top 50 of the world's biggest countries by population!

TOP TEN CITIES

	CITY	POPULATION
1=	Mexico City, Mexico	10 million
1=	Cairo, Egypt	10 million
1=	Seoul, South Korea	10 million
1=	Bombay, India	10 million
2	São Paulo, Brazil	9.3 million
3	Moscow, Russia	8.4 million
4=	Tokyo, Japan	8 million
4=	Manila, Philippines	8 million
5	Shanghai, China	7.8 million
6	New York City, USA	7.3 million

Note: figures are based on cities proper, without suburbs

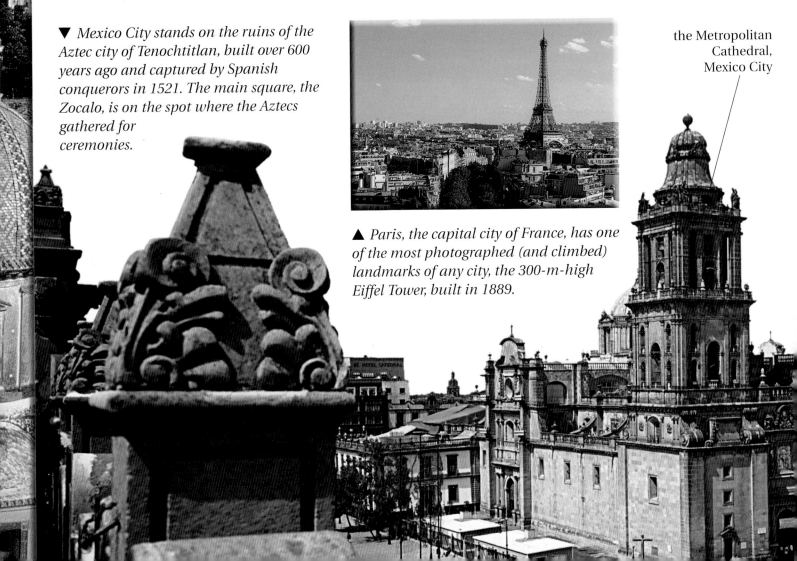

▼ Mexico City stands on the ruins of the Aztec city of Tenochtitlan, built over 600 years ago and captured by Spanish conquerors in 1521. The main square, the Zocalo, is on the spot where the Aztecs gathered for ceremonies.

▲ Paris, the capital city of France, has one of the most photographed (and climbed) landmarks of any city, the 300-m-high Eiffel Tower, built in 1889.

the Metropolitan Cathedral, Mexico City

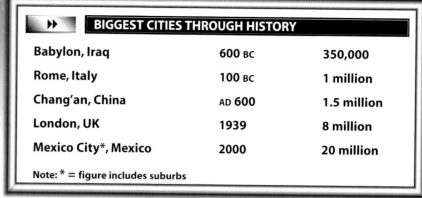

BIGGEST CITIES THROUGH HISTORY

City	Date	Population
Babylon, Iraq	600 BC	350,000
Rome, Italy	100 BC	1 million
Chang'an, China	AD 600	1.5 million
London, UK	1939	8 million
Mexico City*, Mexico	2000	20 million

Note: * = figure includes suburbs

▲ Sydney is the biggest city in Australia, though not its capital. It is also one of the world's great harbours. A landmark of the city is the Opera House with its distinctive roofs, which resemble ships' sails.

▼ The population of Los Angeles, USA, was only 1,610 in 1850. By 1890 the city had 50,000 people. Over the next 10 years the population doubled to 100,000 and by 1960 it was 2.5 million. Today Los Angeles is home to more than 3.5 million people and it covers an area of 1,207 sq km.

▲ One of the world's most crowded but exciting cities is Hong Kong in China, where tall buildings reach skywards to create more offices and living space.

◄ Cairo, Egypt's capital, is the biggest city in Africa with a population of about 10 million people. Cities first flourished along the banks of the River Nile 5,000 years ago.

» Most followers: Christianity » City holiest to most religions: Jerusalem » Oldest sacred books: Hindu *Vedas*

RELIGIONS

People around the world believe in thousands of religions. But the eight faiths with the most followers are Buddhism, Christianity, Confucianism, Hinduism, Islam, Judaism, Shinto and Taoism. Other popular religions include Sikhism and Jainism. Most religions teach a belief in a supreme god, or in many gods, and set out rules for living. They try to answer life's big questions, such as 'what happens to us when we die?' and 'what is the difference between right and wrong?'

◀ *Hinduism, one of the world's oldest belief systems, is the chief religion of India. Some Hindu gods have more than one form. The Hindu goddess Kali, shown here, is the destructive side of the mother-goddess Shakti.*

▼ *A towering statue of Jesus Christ overlooks the Brazilian city of Rio de Janeiro. Europeans brought Christianity to South America in the 1500s. Christianity is now the most widespread of all world religions, with nearly 2 billion followers in over 200 countries.*

	BIGGEST RELIGIONS		
	RELIGION	**BELIEVERS**	**PERCENT WORLD POPULATION**
★ 1	Christianity	1,974 million	33.0 percent
2	Islam	1,155 million	19.0 percent
3	Hinduism	800 million	13.0 percent
4	Buddhism	356 million	6.0 percent
5	Traditional	225 million	3.8 percent
6	Sikhism	23 million	0.4 percent
7	Judaism	14 million	0.2 percent

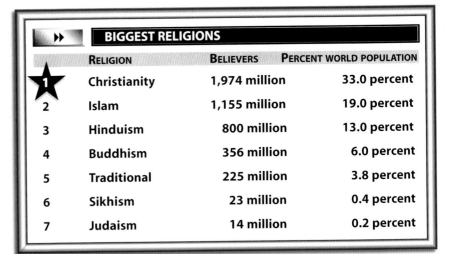

▲ *Followers of the religion of Islam are called Muslims. The holiest shrine in the Islamic world is the Kaaba (shown here) in the city of Mecca, Saudi Arabia. Every Muslim adult must make at least one pilgrimage to Mecca, the birthplace of the Prophet Muhammad in about* AD *570.*

→ Muslim holy book: Koran → Longest book in the Bible: Psalms → Continent producing most religions: Asia

▼ *Jerusalem is a city sacred to the followers of three faiths: Jews, Christians and Muslims. Jews come to pray at the Western or Wailing Wall (shown here), the last remains of the ancient Temple.*

WORLD RELIGIONS

Hinduism	**Ancient Indian religion with no known founder**
Buddhism	**Based on the teachings of Siddhartha Gautama, about 563–483 BC**
Christianity	**Based on the life and teachings of Jesus Christ, about 4 BC to AD 30**
Islam	**Founded by the Prophet Muhammad, about 570–632**
Judaism	**Ancient religion of the Jews, based on the laws of Moses and Abraham**
Sikhism	**Religion founded by Guru (teacher) Nanak, 1469–1539**

▶ *Buddhist monks live simply, following the teachings of Siddhartha Gautama (about 563–483 BC), who was later named the Buddha, or 'the enlightened one'.*

TOP RELIGIONS BY CONTINENT

Most Christians	**South America**	**474 million**
Most Hindus	**Asia**	**793 million**
Most Muslims	**Asia**	**807 million**
Most Buddhists	**Asia**	**351 million**

▶ *Salisbury Cathedral in England is one of Europe's great churches. Built between 1220 and 1258, its 123-m-tall spire is the highest in the country.*

kesh (under turban)

kangha

kara

kirpan

kachh

▲ *Sikhism was founded by an Indian, Guru Nanak (1469–1539) – a guru is a spiritual teacher. A Sikh's '5 ks' are* kesh *(uncut hair),* kangha *(comb),* kirpan *(dagger),* kara *(bangle) and* kachh *(trousers). Sikh men share a common name, Singh.*

FAVOURITE FOODS

Different parts of the world specialize in making different delicious foods – curries in India, stir-fries in China, sushi in Japan, pizza in Italy, casseroles in France, steamed puddings in Britain and hamburgers in the USA. Today most foods can be bought anywhere in the world, but five hundred years ago potatoes and tomatoes were unknown outside the Americas. In richer developed countries, many people eat far more than is good for them. Britons, for example, eat 500,000 tonnes of chocolate a year!

▲ *The hamburger is named after the German city of Hamburg, where a dish of fried minced beef steak was popular in the 1890s. Emigrants took the recipe with them to the United States, where meat in a bun soon became a national favourite.*

▼ *In India spices of all kinds are used to flavour food. Before refrigeration and canned foods were invented, spices were used to preserve food and to disguise the smell of meat dishes long past their best!*

⇥	TOP CHOCAHOLICS	
	COUNTRY	PER YEAR
1	Britain	16 kg
2	America	10 kg
3	France	9 kg
4	Japan	3 kg
Note: average amount per person per year		

SANDWICHES

● The sandwich was named after the Earl of Sandwich (1713–92). This British nobleman so loved playing cards that he ordered a snack of meat between slices of bread to be brought to the card table so that he could play and eat at the same time.

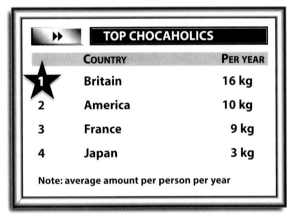

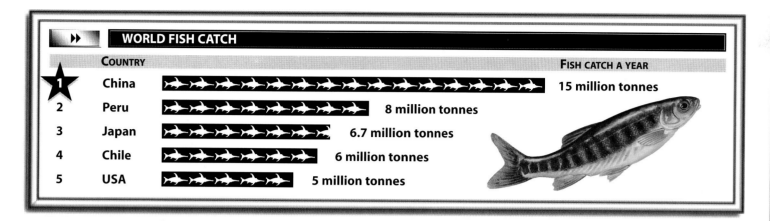

▸▸ WORLD FISH CATCH

	COUNTRY		FISH CATCH A YEAR
1	China		15 million tonnes
2	Peru		8 million tonnes
3	Japan		6.7 million tonnes
4	Chile		6 million tonnes
5	USA		5 million tonnes

UNSAVOURY DISHES

● Willing to try anything once, Dr Frank Buckland, a 19th-century British naturalist, served his dinner guests boiled elephant trunk, rhinoceros pie, slug soup and even earwigs!

▲ *Fruits are one of the best foods because they are rich in vitamin C (ascorbic acid), which helps improve our ability to heal our wounds.*

▶ *Breakfast cereals are 'starchy' foods – the main source of carbohydrates, which give us energy. The first breakfast cereal was Shredded Wheat, invented in 1892. Cornflakes, shown here, were cooked up in 1894 by Dr John Kellogg, a name now famous all over the world.*

▼ *Pizza is an Italian invention – the word pizza is Italian for pie. The cooks of Naples were especially good at baking pizzas. In America the pizza became one of the most popular 'fast foods', and it is now an international favourite.*

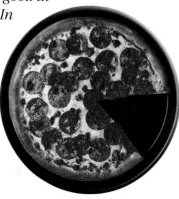

▲ *Bread is one of the oldest-known foods. Prehistoric bakers made 'flat' bread from grain flour and water. Adding yeast, first used about 5,000 years ago, made bread 'rise'. Today's traditional breads include naan (India), rye (Germany), baguette (France), bagel (Jewish) and many more.*

▸▸ FOOD FIRSTS

First potato crisp	1853
First coke	1886
First cereal – Shredded Wheat	1892
First tea bag	1904
First wrapped, sliced bread	1928
First McDonalds	1955

FARMING

Most of the food we eat comes from farms that grow crops – grains, vegetables and fruit – or raise animals. The most important foods include cereals such as maize, wheat and rice, and pulses such as beans and peas. The most numerous livestock (animals) are chickens. Europe is the world's biggest producer of dairy foods (butter, milk and cheese), while the Chinese grow the most rice and wheat. In many poor countries, more than half the people work on the land, growing at least some of their own food. This is called subsistence farming.

▲ *Farmers raise more chickens than any other animal, for meat and eggs. Many chickens spend their lives in crowded cages in battery sheds, for intensive egg-laying, but most people prefer to see them free to run about and scratch for food outdoors.*

» **WHERE VEGETABLES CAME FROM**

Potatoes:
South America

Carrots:
Afghanistan

Broccoli:
Eastern Mediterranean

Onions:
Eastern Mediterranean

Peas:
Southeast Asia

▶ *In North and South America, and in Australia, prairie grasslands provide grazing for beef cattle. The cattle are kept on huge ranches, where cowboys on horseback help with the roundup. There are about 100 million cattle in the United States alone.*

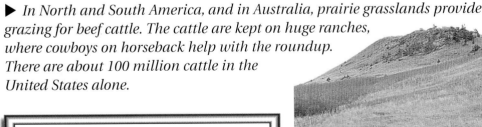

» BIGGEST WHEAT GROWERS		
	COUNTRY	AMOUNT PER YEAR
★1	China	100,000 million kg
2	USA	65,000 million kg
3	India	56,700 million kg
4	Russia	37,800 million kg
5	France	29,700 million kg

» Country with most cattle: India » Biggest cow: Chianina » Biggest farms: Australian sheep stations

▶▶ MOST ANIMALS BY COUNTRY

| Most chickens:
USA,
1.3 billion | Most pigs:
China,
485 million | Most cattle:
India,
200 million | Most sheep:
Australia,
120 million | Most goats:
China,
60 million |

▼ *Dairy foods such as cheese, butter and yogurt can be made from the milk of cattle, sheep, goats, horses, reindeer, camels and yaks. As long ago as 2000 BC people in India made butter from water buffaloes' milk.*

cheese milk butter

▶ *Rice is the basic food eaten by more than half the people in the world. The leading rice-growing countries are China, India and Indonesia, where flooded rice fields, called paddies, terrace the hillsides.*

▶▶ FARMWORKERS AS PERCENT OF POPULATION

	REGION	PERCENT OF POPULATION	MAIN TYPE OF FARMING
★1	Africa	60 percent	Subsistence, plantations
2	Asia	58 percent	Subsistence, plantations
3	Central/South America	25 percent	Ranching, subsistence
4	Europe	8 percent	Industrial, mechanized
5	USA and Canada	2 percent	Industrial, mechanized

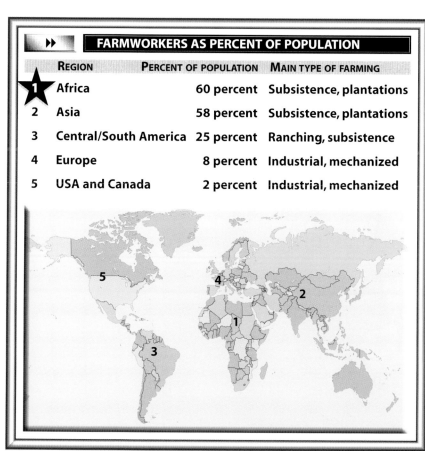

▼ *The world's largest domestic cattle are Italian Chianina, descended from the oxen used by the ancient Romans to pull carts. A Chianina bull stands 1.8 m (as tall as a man) at the shoulder and weighs 1,800 kg.*

FASHION FIRSTS

New fashions are often shocking – for the sake of glamour or comfort. Some styles have been around for thousands of years. Men in ancient Egypt and Greece wore kilts, for example. Other fashions take longer to catch on. Although the Persians and Celts wore trousers more than 2,000 years ago, trousers for men were not usual until the 1830s. Some fashions seem odd today. In the Middle Ages there were shoes with curly toes so long that they had to be held up with strings! All clothes were made by hand until the 1850s, when 'ready-to-wear' factory clothes were made possible by the invention of the sewing machine.

HEAD GEAR
- The balaclava got its name from a battle in the Crimean War (1854), where soldiers wore them to keep warm.
- The bowler hat was invented in the 1840s for horse-riding. In America it was called a derby after Englishman Lord Derby.

◀ The first top hat, worn by James Heatherington in London in 1797, caused a sensation. Women fainted, children jeered, and Mr Heatherington was arrested. Rich men wore top hats until the 1940s, after which only circus ringmasters and actors wore 'toppers'.

▶ The mini-skirt is a symbol of the 'swinging 60s'. Introduced by British designer Mary Quant in 1964, it revolutionized the fashion industry, which until then had been led by the Paris fashion shows. By 1968 mini-skirts were so short that dry cleaners charged by length!

◀ Wigs for fashion originated in France in the 1630s, when the king, Louis XIII, went bald. Wigs like the ones shown here were worn in England after 1660 – the taller a man's wig, the higher his rank. Many wigs were made from the hair of plague victims, and most were infested with headlice!

➤ Longest scarf: 32 m ➤ Tallest headdress: wimple ➤ Biggest wigs: periwigs ➤ Worst for soup-eating: ruff

▶ *Traditionally, makeup was made from any of about 5,000 natural ingredients. This Indian girl is wearing eyeliner similar to that worn in ancient Egypt. It is made from kohl or powdered antimony (a mineral). The dot between her eyes is called a* bindi *(or a* tilak *on men). It symbolizes good fortune and marriage.*

▶ *The zip was an 1893 invention for fastening boots. An easier-sliding version of 1912 caught on as a clothes fastener, replacing hooks, buttons and pins, but it was not called a zipper until 1923.*

▲ *Daring women first wore trousers in the late 1800s, to go cycling. But they were not worn much until 1940s' women factory workers started wearing them for safety and comfort. They then became a fashion item, as seen here.*

◀ *The first jeans were made in 1874 for workmen. Today jeans are worn by both sexes in every country, as working clothes or as a fashion item by superstars. 'Designer jeans' carrying a top designer label can cost over £500 a pair!*

▶ *The skimpy two-piece bikini of the 1950s got its name from a Pacific island being used as a test-site for atomic bombs. The idea was that the explosion had blown all a woman's clothes away!*

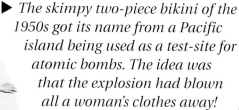

◀ *Before the 1820s sea bathing was done mostly for health, not pleasure, in heavy, itchy woollen costumes that reached the knees. Swimming for fun came in in the 1920s, when women still dressed modestly.*

TALKING AND WRITING

Many animals communicate by making sounds – some quite complex, like dolphins – but only people have developed language, expressed in speaking and writing. There are almost 4,000 languages in the world (about 845 of them in India alone). More people speak Chinese than any other language, but the language spoken in the most countries is English. Unlike English, Chinese does not have an alphabet – it uses signs to stand for words. Possibly the oldest-known alphabet, dating from 1450 BC, comes from the ancient city of Ugarit in Palestine.

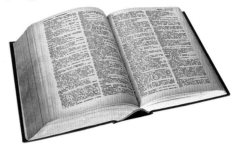

▲ Most people use about 5,000 words in speech and about 10,000 words when writing. Shakespeare used over 33,000 words in his plays, but altogether there are more than 1 million words in English!

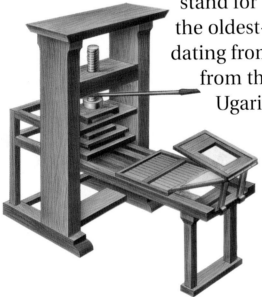

▲ Printing is a fast way to make copies of writing. The earliest printing machinery (shown here) dates from the 1450s. Today's presses print millions of books, newspapers and magazines a week.

▶ Long before stories were written down in books, people told them aloud, retelling the best tales they had heard themselves as children. In this way beliefs, ideas and stories from long ago were passed from one generation to the next, and are still told today.

◀ Language experts believe that 'apple' is one of the oldest words in the English language. It has been in use since before 3000 BC. 'Apple' and a few other words, including 'bad' and 'gold', are relics of the ancient Indo-European language from which many modern languages developed.

»	TOP FIVE LANGUAGES	
	LANGUAGE	**SPEAKERS**
★1	Chinese	Over 1 billion
2	English	510 million
3	Hindustani	500 million
4	Spanish	392 million
5	Russian	277 million

◄ *The Chinese language has about 50,000 characters or signs. Some characters look like objects, others are more complicated and stand for ideas. A Chinese reader needs to know about 5,000 characters in order to read a newspaper.*

▶ *Making speeches, an art known as oratory, is an effective way of using words to influence people. The passionate speeches of Martin Luther King Jr. inspired Civil Rights supporters in the USA in the 1960s.*

▶ *These Egyptian hieroglyphs are a form of picture-writing. The Egyptians used hieroglyphics for over 3,000 years, mainly for religious or historical inscriptions carved or written on stone. The Maya and Aztecs of Central America also wrote using picture-symbols.*

LETTERS, WORDS AND MEANINGS

Longest alphabet	Cambodian, with 74 letters
Most common vowel	'a', as in f<u>a</u>ther, in every known language
Most concise language	Japanese – longest word 12 letters
Most meanings	The word 'set' has about 200 meanings
Most common placename in English	Newton, or 'new town'

◄ *Pictures are internationally understood and can often convey information faster than words, like this road sign. In Africa drivers sometimes need to watch out for rather large obstacles!*

▲ *The oldest letter in the English alphabet (the letter written for longest in the way it is written now) is the letter O. The newest letters are J and V, which only came into use about Shakespeare's time, in the 1500s. Before then the letters I and J were the same, and so were U and V.*

MAKING MONEY

Money has been in use for about 2,500 years, ever since the people of Lydia (now Turkey) started exchanging metal coins, instead of shells and beads, for goods. By the AD 800s the Chinese had invented paper money, which was easier to carry than moneybags. The term 'millionaire' was first used to describe the world's richest people in the 1800s, when a million dollars was still a great deal of money. Today's richest industrial nations belong to the G8 group: USA, Japan, Germany, France, Britain, Canada, Italy and Russia.

▲ *The country with the most gold is the United States. Much of its gold reserves – stored as gold bars – are kept in a top security building at Fort Knox, Kentucky.*

◄ *Harrods in London is one of the world's most famous stores, selling exclusive goods. Department stores date from the 1800s. In the 1900s chainstores spread across cities. Famous among them is Marks and Spencer.*

◄ *Britain's independent central bank is the Bank of England, founded in 1694. Modern banking began in Italy in the 1400s, when moneylenders did business from benches known as 'bancos'.*

◄ *The world's big car-makers are huge multinational companies. In the USA alone people buy 17 million new cars every year.*

►► FAMOUS FOR THEIR MULTIMILLIONS

The Rothschilds	Banking family, business begun in Germany by Mayer Rothschild (1743–1812)
The Rockefellers	Fortune founded on oil business, started in the USA by John D. Rockefeller (1839–1937)
Andrew Carnegie	Scottish-born US steelworks owner (1835–1919), said to be richest man in the world in 1901
Henry Ford	American (1863–1947), founder of the Ford Motor Company
Bill Gates	Born 1955, founder of Microsoft Corporation, said to be the world's richest businessman

◀ *During the 19th century millionaires made their money from oil, steel and building railways. Today many of the world's richest people make their fortunes from hi-tech businesses, computers, computer games and e-commerce (trading on the Internet).*

▶ *The Sultan of Brunei (right) has a fortune from oil revenues estimated at over £11 billion. One of the world's wealthiest women is Britain's Queen Elizabeth II, shown here (far right) wearing the state crown.*

IT'S A FACT
The top five richest Americans aged under 40 are not pop stars or athletes, but computer whizzkids. Probably the most famous is Bill Gates of the Microsoft Corporation, estimated to be worth £38 billion in 2000.

▼ *Stock exchanges are markets where shares in businesses are bought and sold. Europe's first exchange started trading in 1531, and the New York exchange in 1792. The Tokyo exchange, shown here, was founded in 1878, but was re-established in 1949. Until then most Japanese businesses were family-owned.*

IMPORTANT CURRENCIES

Dollar: United States

Pound sterling: United Kingdom

Deutsche mark: Germany

Yen: Japan

Yuan: China

POWER AND ENERGY

Most of the energy we use comes from burning 'fossil fuels', such as coal, oil and natural gas. Fossil fuels were made millions of years ago from plants and animals, and their supply is limited. We burn these fuels in power stations to make electricity, and we also burn them to drive cars, trains, ships and planes. One day they will be used up. Most of the easily-extracted oil will be gone in 50 years, and coal in 200 years. Fortunately, other energy sources – wind, Sun and ocean waves – will never run out. In the future we will rely on these sources.

◄ *About one third of the world's oil comes from offshore wells that drill into oil reserves beneath the seabed. Standing on huge concrete legs beneath the sea, the biggest offshore rigs can be 350 m tall and weigh thousands of tonnes. A rig can produce 250,000 barrels of oil in one day.*

◄ *Miners work in deep, underground shafts drilling for coal. Coal is more plentiful than either oil or natural gas, but produces more pollution than other fossil fuels. Russia is the world's biggest producer of coal.*

COUNTRIES TOP IN OIL		
COUNTRY	OIL RESERVES	YEARS BEFORE USED UP
1 ★ Saudi Arabia	261,000 million barrels	88
2 Russia	155,000 million barrels	71
3 Indonesia	112,000	511
4 Kuwait	96,000	128
5 India	93,000	69

▶ *In an oil refinery, crude oil is broken down into various grades, including fuel for cars. Since 1900 energy use has doubled every 20 years. People in Europe and North America between them use about 65 percent of the world's energy. Asia and Australasia use about 29 percent, and Africa and South America about 6 percent.*

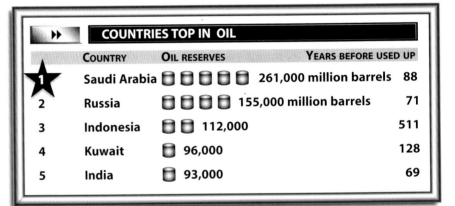

◄ Water is a limitless source of reusable energy. Released from behind dams, it drives turbines that generate electricity, producing about 10 percent of the world's power.

»	COAL RESERVES	
	COUNTRY	RESERVES
1	Russia	241 million tonnes
2	USA	240 million tonnes
3	China	114 million tonnes
4	Australia	91 million tonnes
5	India	69 million tonnes

◄ The Sun provides all our life-giving energy. Solar energy systems turn sunlight into electrical energy, using absorbent collectors and solar cells. Switzerland uses more solar energy per person than any other country in the world.

ENERGY PIONEERS

● At least 3,000 years ago the Chinese piped natural gas through bamboo poles and burned it as a fuel.

● Gaslight arrived in 1792, when a British engineer named William Murdoch lit his home by coal gas.

● The world's first electricity power station was built in New York City in 1882.

◄ Wind is an inexhaustible form of energy. It has been harnessed for at least 4,000 years. Today giant wind turbines – modern windmills – on windfarms generate electricity without causing pollution. Denmark, Germany, Britain, Spain, China, India and the USA all use wind power, the world's fastest-growing energy resource.

▼ One day the world's petroleum will run out. It is too useful – for making plastics, for example – for us to waste what remains by burning petrol in car engines. Electric cars like this one, powered by chemical batteries or solar cells, offer an excellent, clean alternative.

TOP OF THE CLASS

It was only in the 20th century that 'education for all' became usual. Throughout history, many people never went to school. One of Europe's most famous rulers, the Emperor Charlemagne (742–814) encouraged learning, but never learned to write himself. This was not unusual in the Middle Ages. Even today about a fifth of the world's people (around 1 billion) cannot read or write. The country with the most schools is China (which also has the biggest population), followed by India. Poorer countries often spend a larger part of their income on education than rich ones like the USA.

▲ One of the greatest Greek philosopher-scientists was Aristotle (384–322 BC), seen here contemplating a bust of Homer in a famous 17th-century painting by Rembrandt. Aristotle taught in Athens and was teacher to Alexander the Great.

▶ The oldest university in Europe is Bologna in Italy. Italy became a magnet for students from all over Europe from the 1300s, a time when European scholars were making new discoveries and rediscovering old knowledge.

	OLDEST UNIVERSITIES		
	TOWN	**COUNTRY**	**DATE**
★1	Karueein	Morocco	859
2	Bologna	Italy	1088
3	Oxford	England	1167
4	Paris	France	1170
5	Cambridge	England	1284

▲ Developing countries place great value on education, and poor children often walk long distances to get to school. Schools in poor countries may lack equipment, but students generally work very hard.

▶ In ancient Rome the boys of rich citizens were taught by their father or by a tutor, who was often a Greek slave. They learned arithmetic and to read and write Latin and Greek. Discipline was strict and the boys were often beaten. Girls did not go to school.

THE GREATEST MUSEUMS AND LIBRARIES

- The Smithsonian Institution and the Library of Congress, Washington, D.C., USA.
- The Metropolitan Museum of Art, New York City, USA.
- The British Museum and the British Library, London, UK.
- The Louvre Museum and the Bibliothèque Nationale, Paris, France.
- The Hermitage Museum, St Petersburg, Russia.

▲ *The most famous museum in the USA is the Smithsonian Institution in Washington, D.C. It was set up in 1846 with money left to the US government by a British scientist, James Smithson, who died in 1829.*

▼ *Many children today use computers for classwork and homework. They have access to the Internet as well, allowing them to do research using a worldwide range of information sources.*

▲ *The Bodleian Library in Oxford, England, is one of the biggest in the world, containing 6.5 million books and documents. The Radcliffe Camera (shown here), which is part of the Bodleian, was the first circular library in Britain. Part of the library's function is to preserve rare books.*

▶ *The youngest-ever university graduate was an American aged 10! Graduates wear a square hat called a mortar board.*

DID YOU KNOW?
Nobel prizes are awarded to people who make significant breakthroughs in one of six categories: physics, chemistry, physiology or medicine, literature, peace-campaigning and economics. The prize is named after Alfred Nobel (1833–96) of Sweden, who invented explosive dynamite. Two people have won twice: Marie Curie (physics and chemistry) and Linus Pauling (chemistry and peace).

▸▸ TOP FOR PRIMARY SCHOOLS

	COUNTRY	NUMBER OF SCHOOLS
★ 1	China	850,000
2	India	590,000
3	Indonesia	150,000

HOMES BIG AND SMALL

Two thousand years ago rich Romans lived in spacious villas, while poor Romans lived in six-storey tower blocks. In many countries the pattern is the same today. But for most people, until the mid-19th century when blocks of flats were built in cities, home was a small house or cottage. Two of the world's most famous homes are No. 10 Downing Street in London, home of Britain's prime minister, and the White House in Washington, D.C., home of the US President.

▶ *Frank Lloyd Wright was one of the most influential architects of the 20th century, famous for his 'prairie houses' of Illinois. His Unity Temple (1908), shown here, was one of the first US public buildings with concrete on the outside.*

SHELTERS

- Inuit of the Arctic built ice-houses, or igloos, as temporary shelters.
- The Plains Indians of North America set up camps of skin and pole lodges, called tipis.
- Wigwams were dome-shaped wooden homes built by Native Americans of the Eastern Woodlands.

▼ *Many hotels are designed around a theme. Hotel Excalibur in Las Vegas, USA, offers guests the chance to enjoy an Arthurian experience, complete with knights in armour competing in tournaments, jesters, minstrels and dinner in Sherwood Forest!*

▲ *Knole House in Sevenoaks, England, is one of the biggest privately owned houses in the country, with 365 rooms – one for each day of the year! It was begun in 1456 by Thomas Bourchier, Archbishop of Canterbury.*

➤ Biggest castle-home: Windsor, UK ➤ Most expensive: Hearst Ranch, California, USA, built for £6.5 million (1922–39)

COUNTRIES WITH MOST HOMES	
COUNTRY	**HOMES**
⭐1 China	🏠🏠🏠🏠🏠🏠🏠🏠🏠🏠🏠🏠🏠 277 million
2 India	🏠🏠🏠🏠🏠🏠🏠🏠🏠 195 million
3 USA	🏠🏠🏠🏠🏠 106 million
4 Russia	🏠🏠🏠 52 million
5 Indonesia	🏠🏠 42 million
6 = France	🏠 22 million
6 = UK	🏠 22 million

▲ *In Asian countries such as Thailand and Vietnam, many villages are built beside rivers, the traditional cargo routes. The houses are built on stilts to prevent flooding during the Monsoon rains.*

▼ *High-rise living really means high to residents of Lake Point Tower. With 70 storeys, it is the tallest apartment block in the skyscraper city of Chicago, USA, and the highest all-residential building in the world. There are residential sections in even taller buildings, for those with a head for heights and no fear of lifts!*

▲ *African traditional homes include these small mud and stone houses and grain-stores with cone-shaped roofs, built by the Dogon people of Mali. Homes made from traditional materials are still built in villages across Africa, while city-dwellers live in modern apartments and houses.*

▲ *Windsor Castle in England is the world's biggest castle still used as a home. It is one of the homes of the British royal family. Parts of it date from the 1400s, though an earlier castle was built on the site by William the Conqueror in 1078.*

CRIME AND PUNISHMENT

There have been many famous, or infamous, criminals, such as the outlaws Jesse James and Billy the Kid, highwayman Dick Turpin and Blackbeard the pirate (Edward Teach). World-famous detectives and policemen are fewer – in fact the best-known are fictional heroes such as Sherlock Holmes! The worst murderers in history include a 19th-century Indian bandit or Thug, who was accused of killing more than 900 victims. The biggest robberies have included bank-raids, jewel thefts and train robberies, but the most successful modern criminals get rich through fraud.

ART THEFT

● The shortest art robbery in history was in 1991. Thieves stole 20 paintings valued at about £280 million from the Van Gogh Museum in Amsterdam, Netherlands. The pictures were found in a stolen car 35 minutes after the robbery was discovered.

▼ *The Inquisition was a special court set up by the Roman Catholic Church in 1231 to seek out and punish heretics (people who opposed church teachings).*

CRACK CRIME FIGHTERS AROUND THE WORLD

The Bow Street Runners	**Volunteer police founded in London in 1750**
Scotland Yard	**Headquarters of London's Metropolitan Police since 1829**
The Texas Rangers	**Set up in 1835 to fight Indians and outlaws in Texas, USA**
Federal Bureau of Investigation	**Founded 1935 to combat organized crime in the USA**
Interpol	**International police organization, founded 1923**

▼ *One of the world's most famous prisons was the US Federal prison of Alcatraz, on an island in San Francisco Bay, USA. It housed some of America's most wanted criminals, and was reckoned to be escape-proof. It was closed in 1963.*

Fugitives attempting to escape 'the Rock' had to cross a mile of water running with dangerous currents.

» Biggest crime group: Mafia » First DNA criminal database: 1998 » World's most-used weapon: gun

►► FIVE FAMOUS CRIMINALS

Billy the Kid (Henry McCarty 1859–81): gunman in New Mexico, USA

Jesse James (1847–82): bank and train robber in Missouri, USA

Jack the Ripper (identity unknown, active 1888): serial killer in London

Dick Turpin (1706–39): highwayman, robbed travellers in England

Blackbeard (Edward Teach, d. 1718): pirate in the Caribbean

► *President John F. Kennedy of the USA was shot and killed while riding in a motorcade through Dallas, Texas, in 1963. No one was ever found guilty of the crime. A suspect named Lee Harvey Oswald was arrested, but was murdered by Jack Ruby before he came to trial.*

►► CRIME NEVER PAYS

Most people in jail	2 million, USA
Longest sentence	141,087 years
Most executions	China, 17,000 since 1990
Longest jailbreak	45 years, USA

▼ *Australia's most notorious outlaw was Ned Kelly (1855–80). Kelly was a bushranger, or rustler, and bank robber. He was regarded as a Robin Hood hero-figure by some. But the police caught up with Kelly in 1880, and despite his home-made armour he was shot and later hanged.*

▼ *In 1671 Captain Thomas Blood almost got away with Britain's crown jewels. He gained entrance to the Tower of London vaults dressed as a clergyman, but was arrested with two crowns hidden beneath his coat.*

PETS FOR LIFE

Legend has it that animals have brought up people, as well as people bringing up animals. Romulus and Remus, the twin founders of Rome, were supposedly brought up by a female wolf. DNA tests have shown that a wild wolf was the original ancestor of the domestic dog, the world's number one pet. The second most popular pets are cats, followed by goldfish, rabbits and budgerigars. Many owners claim their pets understand what they say, though scientists doubt that a top-talking budgerigar with a vocabulary of 500 words actually knows what it is saying.

▲ *Few pets grow bigger than a python. But many people think it cruel to keep exotic pets such as snakes and alligators in town houses and apartments. Such animals need special food and care.*

DOG DAYS

● The heaviest dog is the St Bernard, at 75 to 90 kg.
● The tallest dogs are Great Danes and Irish Wolfhounds, both about 100 cm high.

▶ *Horse riding is enjoyed by people all over the world. The tallest horses are over 2 m tall and weigh 1,500 kg, while the smallest are dog-sized and weigh less than 10 kg!*

▲ *Homing pigeons do not always fly home. When 'pigeon fanciers' released more than 6,700 pigeons in northwest England, 5,545 of them were never seen again!*

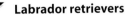

▸▸ MOST POPULAR DOGS	
BREED	
★ **1**	**Labrador retrievers**
2	**German shepherds**
3	**West Highland terriers**
4	**Golden retrievers**
5	**Spaniels**

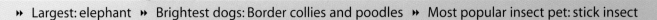
⏩ LONGEST-LIVED PETS

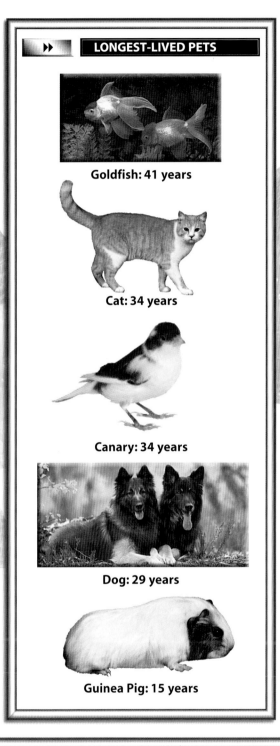

Goldfish: 41 years

Cat: 34 years

Canary: 34 years

Dog: 29 years

Guinea Pig: 15 years

▼ *Love them or hate them, tarantulas are reputed to make good pets. These huge, furry spiders make no noise and can live without food for more than 2.5 years!*

IT'S A FACT
Cats climb trees, but not often mountains. In 1950 a kitten followed a party of climbers to the top of the Matterhorn, 4,478 m high in the Alps!

▶ *People have not always treated mice as pests, even though they can devastate farmers' crops. The fastest-breeding of all pets, they can produce up to 34 young in one litter.*

◀ *A female rabbit can produce 50 babies in a year from 5 or 6 litters. The biggest breed of rabbit is the Flemish Giant rabbit.*

▶ *Cats were worshipped in ancient times. One of the Egyptian gods was represented as a cat. The average house cat (weighing 3 to 7 kg) would look skinny alongside the heaviest cats on record, which weigh in at 20 kg.*

3

4

5

WONDERS OF THE WORLD

The world is filled with amazing sights both natural and man made. The beautiful wildlife havens of Tanzania in Africa are home to many protected animals, while in North America the course of the Colorado River continues to carve its way through the Grand Canyon, the world's biggest gorge.

For centuries man has built great monuments. Some have become lost wonders of ancient times, like the mighty Colossus of Rhodes, a huge bronze statue which towered 37 m high. Some remain, like the puzzling pyramids of Egypt, enormous four-sided structures built as tombs for ancient Egyptian kings. Even today huge structures of incredible height and size are built, like the amazing stainless steel Gateway to the West in the USA. It stands at an incredible 192 m high, and visitors can take a tram to the top.

Explore the biggest and best facts of the *Wonders of the World* and discover some monumental sights. There are the big, serious facts – for reference – and less serious ones, too, for fun. These pages are packed with some of the biggest and best, oddest and strangest, smallest and funniest facts around!

◄ THE NAMIB DESERT, AFRICA

AWESOME PLACES

Climate, wind and water have created and shaped Earth's natural wonders, many of which have existed for millions of years. They have been on Earth far longer than human beings and will still be here in millions of years time. The Great Rift Valley in East Africa, for example, is a 3,000-km-long gash across Earth's surface, containing many great lakes and huge volcanic craters such as Ngorongoro in Tanzania. Shorter than the Rift Valley, but mightily impressive, is the Grand Canyon in the USA. It is the largest gorge in the world, and is being cut from the rock by the Colorado River. Such awesome places fill us with wonder.

▲ The Aboriginal name for Ayers Rock in central Australia is Uluru, which means 'great pebble'! The world's biggest 'pebble' is a lump of sandstone standing 348 m high, more than 2.4 km long and 1.6 km wide. It is more than 480 million years old.

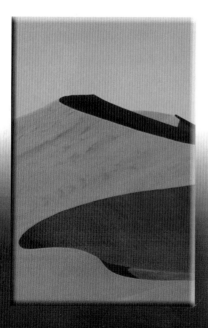

◀ The Namib Desert in southwest Africa is the world's oldest desert. It covers more than 270,000 sq km. Parts of this desolate region have less than 2 cm of rainfall a year. Sand dunes in the Namib Desert can be up to 244 m high.

◀ The Karakorum range on the border of Pakistan and China has some of the world's highest mountains, including the second-highest peak, K2, which towers 8,611 m above sea level. On mountains this high, the snow never melts.

▶ Monument Valley in the American state of Utah (shown here and below) has a stark and beautiful landscape, much loved by the makers of Western films. Towers of red sandstone rock, carved by wind and water, rise from the valley floor.

▲ *One of the most amazing natural wildlife reserves in the world is Tanzania's Ngorongoro Crater, an extinct volcanic crater in the Great Rift Valley of Africa. Within a huge natural bowl live thousands of birds like these flamingoes, along with herds of antelope, zebra and wildebeest.*

DID YOU KNOW?

The rocks of the Grand Canyon in Colorado, USA, appear vividly coloured at sunset, attracting thousands of tourists. The canyon measures 446 km long, 1.5 to 29 km wide and about 1.6 km at its deepest point. The oldest and deepest rocks in the canyon are from 1.7 to 2 billion years old, and have been worn away by the action of the Colorado River.

▶ *The Giant's Causeway is a natural wonder in Northern Ireland. About 40,000 hexagonal pillars of volcanic basalt rock stand by the sea. Legend tells how the giant Finn MacCool piled up the stones to make a bridge to Scotland.*

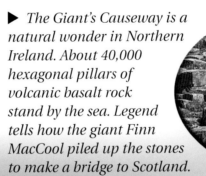

▲ *In Petrified Forest National Park, Arizona, USA, visitors can sit on stone trees 225 million years old. The trees were buried by mud and ash, and over time the minerals hardened into stone, or 'petrified', forming stone tree trunks.*

FIVE COLOURFUL NATURAL WONDERS	
White Sands, New Mexico, USA	Pure white gypsum sands
Laguna Colorado, Bolivia	Tomato-red, algae-filled lagoon
Mato Grosso, Brazil	Vast expanse of green rainforest
Painted Desert, Arizona, USA	Multicoloured sandstone landscape
Wave Rock, Western Australia	Yellow, 15-m high wave-shaped rock

PUZZLING PYRAMIDS

People of the ancient world built astonishing artificial mountain-temples and tombs as far apart as Africa and Mexico, using only their bare hands. Many of these huge structures are still standing. In Iran and Iraq, where they are called ziggurats, and in Mexico and Central America, the pyramids were crowned with temples. But the most famous pyramids were built in Egypt as tombs. For more than 4,000 years visitors have marvelled at the size and construction of these colossal monuments, and wondered how they were built so big, and why.

▲ *The three enormous, four-sided pyramids at Giza in Egypt were built as tombs for Egypt's kings about 4,500 years ago. They were the biggest, and are the only surviving, of the Seven Wonders of the ancient world.*

▼ *The Sphinx is a 73-m-long, 20-m-high stone creature that sits beside the Great Pyramid, the largest of the pyramids at Giza in Egypt. Some historians believe that its base, shaped like the body of a lion, is older than its head, which was added later. The head is thought to represent Khafre, son of the Pharaoh Khufu who reigned from 2900 to 2877 BC.*

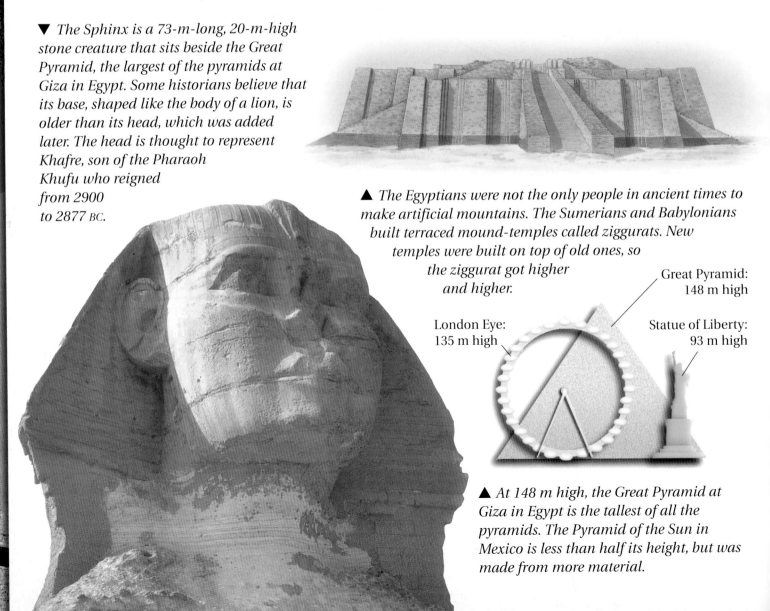

▲ *The Egyptians were not the only people in ancient times to make artificial mountains. The Sumerians and Babylonians built terraced mound-temples called ziggurats. New temples were built on top of old ones, so the ziggurat got higher and higher.*

London Eye: 135 m high

Great Pyramid: 148 m high

Statue of Liberty: 93 m high

▲ *At 148 m high, the Great Pyramid at Giza in Egypt is the tallest of all the pyramids. The Pyramid of the Sun in Mexico is less than half its height, but was made from more material.*

▲ *Without metal tools or the wheel, the Maya people of Mexico and Central America built great pyramids deep in the jungle, like this one at Chichén Itzá in Mexico. The pyramids were used for religious ceremonies, including human sacrifices.*

GIANTS

● The biggest pyramid in Mexico is bigger in volume than the Great Pyramid in Egypt.

● Pyramids in the Americas were made from vast piles of earth covered with stones. Temples were constructed on top.

● Egyptian pyramids were all stone. Tunnels inside led to burial chambers for kings and queens.

▸▸ GREAT PYRAMID FACTS	
Length of base on each side	230 m
Area of base	5 hectares (or 8 soccer pitches)
Number of stones	About 2.3 million
Average weight of each stone	2.5 tonnes
Weight of biggest stone	290 tonnes
Labour force and time taken	100,000 men, about 20 years

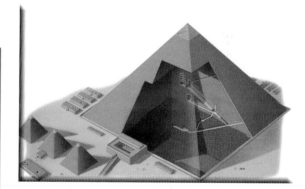

▲ *Inside the Great Pyramid of King Khufu were chambers full of treasure, reached by long passages. These were sealed after the king was buried to keep out robbers.*

▼ *Thousands of workers were used to construct the pyramids. All the work was done by human muscles, hauling the stones on rollers and sledges, and up ramps. The largest pyramid contains more than 2 million stones.*

LOST WONDERS OF THE ANCIENT WORLD

In the 100s BC a Greek writer named Antipater listed seven sights that no tourist in the Greek and Roman world should miss. These fabulous sights were the biggest and most amazing constructions of their time, and became known as the 'Seven Wonders of the World'. Today, only the pyramids of Egypt still stand. Little remains of the other six wonders. The shortest-lived was the Colossus of Rhodes, a giant statue about as high as the Statue of Liberty in New York. It stood for less than 20 years before being toppled by an earthquake.

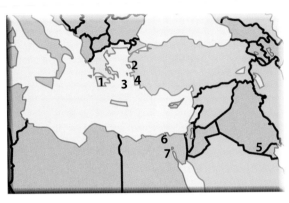

▲ *Locations of the Seven Wonders of the ancient world: 1) Statue of Zeus, Greece. 2) Temple of Artemis, Turkey. 3) Colossus of Rhodes. 4) Mausoleum, Turkey. 5) Hanging Gardens, present-day Iraq. 6) Lighthouse at Alexandria, Egypt. 7) Pyramids, Egypt.*

▲ *At 12 m high, the statue of the Greek god Zeus at Olympia was six times human-size and was made of ivory and gold. People who came to the Olympic Games visited the god's temple to marvel at the statue inside.*

▶ *No remains have ever been found of the Hanging Gardens of Babylon, but historians think they were built somewhere near Baghdad, in Iraq, by King Nebuchadnezzar. The only surviving description of them was written by a priest some 400 years after they were built. The Gardens probably looked like a ziggurat (a brick-pyramid), covered with terraces of trees and plants.*

the Gardens were built for the king's sick wife, who missed her green mountain home

▶ *The Mausoleum, or tomb, of King Mausolus, built about 353 BC, was so impressive that from then on all large tombs were called 'mausoleums'. It was made of marble blocks.*

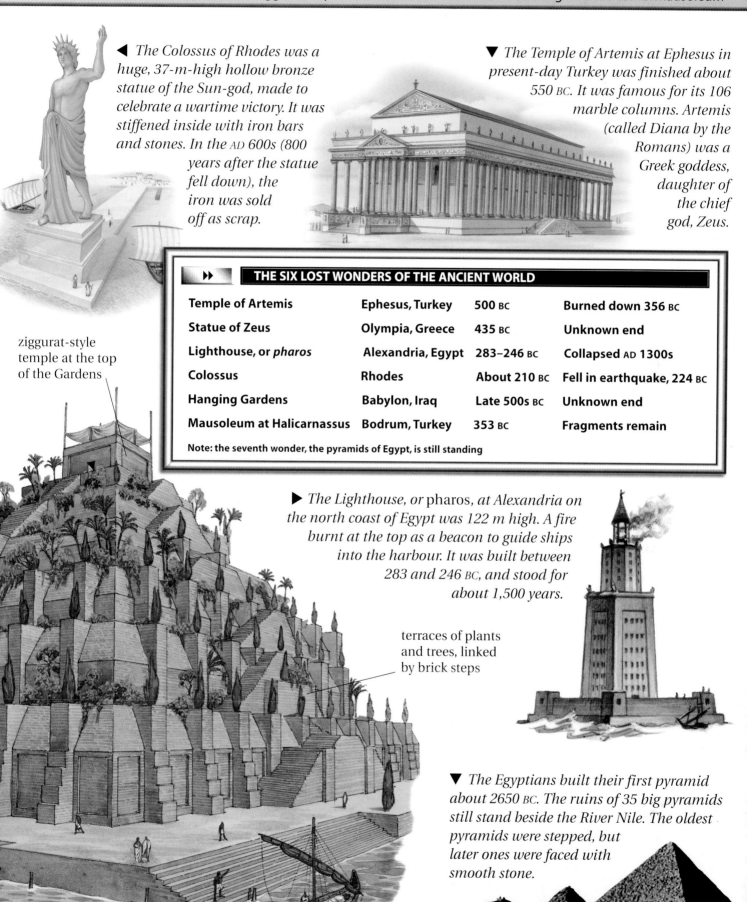

◄ *The Colossus of Rhodes was a huge, 37-m-high hollow bronze statue of the Sun-god, made to celebrate a wartime victory. It was stiffened inside with iron bars and stones. In the* AD *600s (800 years after the statue fell down), the iron was sold off as scrap.*

▼ *The Temple of Artemis at Ephesus in present-day Turkey was finished about 550* BC. *It was famous for its 106 marble columns. Artemis (called Diana by the Romans) was a Greek goddess, daughter of the chief god, Zeus.*

ziggurat-style temple at the top of the Gardens

►► THE SIX LOST WONDERS OF THE ANCIENT WORLD

Temple of Artemis	**Ephesus, Turkey**	**500** BC	**Burned down 356** BC
Statue of Zeus	**Olympia, Greece**	**435** BC	**Unknown end**
Lighthouse, or *pharos*	**Alexandria, Egypt**	**283–246** BC	**Collapsed** AD **1300s**
Colossus	**Rhodes**	**About 210** BC	**Fell in earthquake, 224** BC
Hanging Gardens	**Babylon, Iraq**	**Late 500s** BC	**Unknown end**
Mausoleum at Halicarnassus	**Bodrum, Turkey**	**353** BC	**Fragments remain**

Note: the seventh wonder, the pyramids of Egypt, is still standing

► *The Lighthouse, or* pharos, *at Alexandria on the north coast of Egypt was 122 m high. A fire burnt at the top as a beacon to guide ships into the harbour. It was built between 283 and 246* BC, *and stood for about 1,500 years.*

terraces of plants and trees, linked by brick steps

▼ *The Egyptians built their first pyramid about 2650* BC. *The ruins of 35 big pyramids still stand beside the River Nile. The oldest pyramids were stepped, but later ones were faced with smooth stone.*

MOUNDS, STONES AND CIRCLES

Why did ancient peoples spend so much time and energy building circles of stones and wood, and piling up mounds of earth? Historians believe that some of the stone circles, such as the world-famous Stonehenge in England, were used for religious ceremonies. Standing stones and mounds, or barrows, from the early metalworking period, were often put up on top of high hills, and generally marked the burial site of a powerful person. But the purpose of some prehistoric sites remains a mystery. Some 1,500 years ago in Peru, the Nazca people scraped giant soil-pictures of creatures so big that they can only be seen properly from the air.

▲ At Carnac in northwest France, more than 3,000 granite 'standing stones' make up the biggest group of prehistoric stones in the world. Some are single stones, others are in groups or long lines.

▼ The people of Stone Age Britain constructed Stonehenge, an extraordinary and unique sacred site, over a period of about 1,400 years (2950 to 1600 BC). It started as a ring of ditches, and later giant stones, some from as far as 380 km away, were put up. The biggest upright stones are 9 m long and weigh 50 tonnes. Stonehenge may have been a temple, a meeting place or an astronomical observatory.

▶▶ FAMOUS PREHISTORIC CIRCLES AND MOUNDS

Stonehenge, England	Rings of cut stones	Between 2950 and 1600 BC
Silbury Hill, England	Burial mound 40 m high	About 3000 BC
Carnac, France	3,000 standing stones	Dates vary, about 2000 BC
Avebury, England	Stone circles and earth banks	About 2000 BC

◀ *Silbury Hill in southern England (not far from Stonehenge) is the biggest mound made by prehistoric people in Europe. Over 3,000 years old, the chalk mound is 40 m high and covers an area as big as 3 soccer pitches. In 1970 a burial mound or barrow was discovered inside.*

▶ *What looks like a giant snake coiled in the woodland of Ohio, USA, is actually an earth mound. Called the Great Serpent Mound, it was made more than 2,000 years ago. There are hundreds of similar mounds across North America.*

▼ *In the Nazca Desert of Peru, ground art exists on a huge scale, its purpose a mystery. There are geometric patterns and drawings of fish, birds such as this humming bird, spiders and a monkey. They are visible properly only from the air, but were created long before any known form of air travel!*

▼ *Easter Island in the South Pacific is famous for its 600 mysterious stone faces. The tallest are 12 m high. They were put up more than 1,000 years ago by the original Polynesian settlers. No-one knows why!*

TEMPLES AND TOMBS

The stories surrounding temples and tombs excite the imagination – a lost temple in the jungle, a Greek temple high on a hill, an underground tomb filled with clay soldiers, a marble tomb for an emperor's wife. The ancient Egyptians were the greatest temple and tomb-builders, matched only by the Chinese, who buried an army of terracotta soldiers to guard the emperor Shih Huangdi in the afterlife. This 2,000-year-old tomb was unearthed in 1979. A century before, in the 1860s, a French explorer in Cambodia glimpsed stone towers among the jungle trees. He had rediscovered the enormous Hindu temple of Angkor Wat.

▲ *Kings of Egypt were buried in rock tombs in the Valley of the Kings, near the city of Luxor. So far 62 tombs have been found there, the largest being that of King Seti.*

▲ *Probably the most famous of all Greek temples is the Parthenon in Athens. It was built on the Acropolis Hill between 447 and 432 BC to honour the city's patron-goddess, Athena. In 1687 it was badly damaged by a gunpowder explosion.*

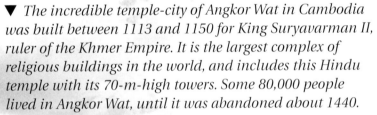

▼ *The incredible temple-city of Angkor Wat in Cambodia was built between 1113 and 1150 for King Suryavarman II, ruler of the Khmer Empire. It is the largest complex of religious buildings in the world, and includes this Hindu temple with its 70-m-high towers. Some 80,000 people lived in Angkor Wat, until it was abandoned about 1440.*

IT'S A FACT

The biggest temple ever built was the Temple of Amun at Karnak in Egypt (about 1250 BC). Its courts and pillared halls were bigger than Angkor Wat, but hardly anyone walked through them. Only priests were allowed inside the enormous sacred building.

▲ *The Taj Mahal was built for Mumtaz Mahal, wife of the Mogul emperor of India, Shah Jahan. When she died in 1629, her husband ordered the most beautiful tomb in the world to be built for her. It took 20,000 people 20 years to complete. The emperor and his wife are buried together under the 60-m-high, white marble dome.*

▼ *The terraced temple of Borobudur in Java, Indonesia, is the biggest Buddhist temple in the world, with pinnacles over 30 m high. Started in the 700s, its three-sphere plan represents the three stages of human life – passion, visible world and spiritual world.*

►► BIGGEST TEMPLES	
NAME	**DATE**
★ 1 Temple of Amun, Egypt	About 1250 BC
2 Temple of Angkor Wat, Cambodia	AD 1113–1150
3 Temple of Borobudur, Indonesia	AD 778–850

► *The awesome rock temples at Petra in Jordan were built in the 1st and 2nd centuries AD, when Petra was a rich trading city under Roman rule. It is known as the 'rose-red city' after the colour of the rock. Petra declined after AD 350, but its Street of Façades, which includes the famous treasury of Khazneh, shown here, is well preserved.*

CHURCHES AND MOSQUES

Some of the world's biggest and most beautiful and inspiring buildings are churches and mosques. Sometimes one mighty building has served two faiths. The great Christian church of Hagia Sophia, for example, built in Constantinople (modern Istanbul), later became a Muslim mosque. Cathedral builders built towers and spires that rose towards the heavens, but sometimes they aimed too high – the main spire of Lincoln Cathedral was the highest in the world (160 m) until 1548, when it collapsed. The world's biggest church is the Basilica in the Ivory Coast, Africa.

▲ *The world's biggest cathedral (though not the biggest church) is the Cathedral of St John the Divine in New York City. Construction of this medieval-style church began in 1892, but was interrupted between 1941 and 1979. The nave is 183 m long.*

▼ *St Peter's Basilica in the Vatican City is the largest Christian church in Europe. It is 218 m long and covers 23,000 sq m (four soccer pitches). St Peter's was built between 1506 and 1614. Many great Renaissance artists contributed to the project, which was designed to amaze the Christian world.*

The huge dome of St Peter's measures 42 m across. Visitors can climb up inside it to the gallery at the top.

From this balcony the Pope blesses pilgrims at the great festivals of Christmas and Easter.

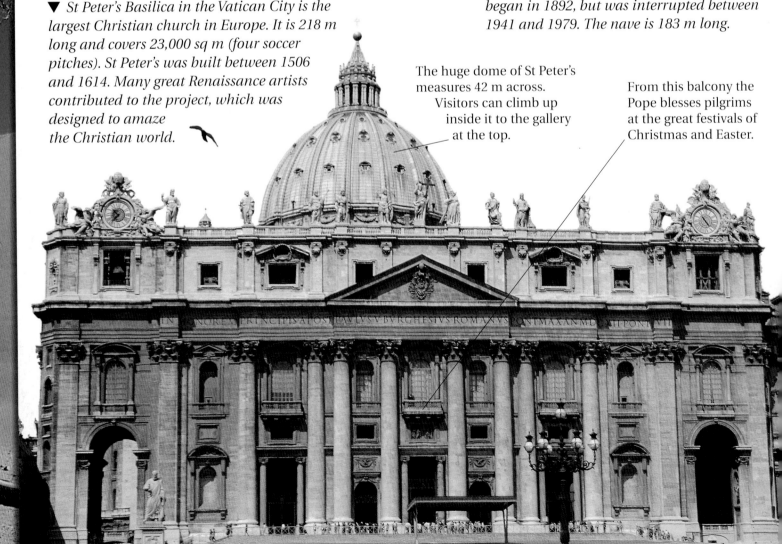

▼ *The Great Hassan II Mosque in Casablanca, Morocco, has the tallest minaret or tower of any Islamic mosque. It is 200 m high. The mosque was completed in 1993. The faithful are called to prayer five times a day by calls that are broadcast from the minaret. When they hear the call to prayer, Muslims generally stop what they are doing and either go into a prayer room, or put down a prayer mat wherever they are, and pray.*

▲ *The world's biggest mosque is the Shah Faisal Mosque on the outskirts of Pakistan's capital city, Islamabad, which means 'place of Islam'. The mosque has space for 300,000 worshippers in its main prayer hall, which is shaped like a giant desert tent, and in its grounds.*

◄ *There are higher crosses on modern church masts, but the tallest cathedral spire, at 161 m high, is that of Ulm Cathedral in Germany. The cathedral was begun in 1377, but the immense stone tower at its western end was not finished until 1890.*

▼ *In Djenne in central Mali, the Great Mosque – made mostly of sun-dried mud – has been a place of religious worship since the 1300s. About this time, the religion of Islam reached this part of north Africa, and Mali became a centre of Islamic scholarship.*

FAMOUS BRITISH CATHEDRALS	
St Paul's Cathedral	Christopher Wren's building (1675–1710) replaced the medieval one, burned down in 1666
Westminster Abbey	Begun by Edward the Confessor in the 1040s
York Minster	England's biggest medieval cathedral with famous stained glass
Canterbury Cathedral	A church was first built on this site in 597; the present cathedral dates from the 1070s
Salisbury Cathedral	Tallest spire in England at 122 m

GLITTERING PALACES

A palace is the home of a king, queen or emperor, though some other buildings later came to be called palaces. In Italy in the 1400s, for example, every prince had a 'palazzo', or palace. The earliest palaces were built for the pharaohs of Egypt and the kings of Babylon and Crete. Palaces were centres of government as well as luxurious homes for the ruler. Some became cities in miniature, like the Imperial Palace within the Forbidden City in Beijing, China. Rulers have gone on building bigger and more splendid palaces, from Versailles outside Paris in the 1600s to today's palaces in Saudi Arabia and Brunei, built from oil revenues.

▲ *The Palace of Versailles in France was built for King Louis XIV in the 1600s. It took 40 years to complete, so rich and elegant were its decorations. Now a museum, the palace has 1,300 rooms, a famous Hall of Mirrors and its own private theatre.*

▲ *Russian emperors, or tsars, enjoyed the splendours of the Baroque-style Winter Palace (built 1754–62) in St Petersburg. It almost burned to the ground in 1837, but was rebuilt two years later and now houses the world-famous Hermitage Museum.*

▼ *The biggest palace ever built for a ruler was the Imperial Palace of the Chinese emperor. It stands within the walls of the Forbidden City, a walled area of China's capital city, Beijing. The only people allowed within the Forbidden City were the imperial family and their officials and servants. Inside the Imperial Palace, the emperor lived in solitary magnificence.*

»	GREAT PALACES OF THE WORLD
Spain	Escorial and Alhambra in Granada; Alcazar in Seville
Italy	Doges' in Venice; Pitti in Florence
UK	Buckingham Palace and St James's in London; Holyrood in Scotland
France	Louvre in Paris; Versailles near Paris
Russia	Winter Palace in St Petersburg

▶ *During the 1400s the Italian city-state of Venice was at the height of its wealth and power, ruled by dukes, or 'doges'. These rulers lived in the Doges' Palace (shown here in the centre of the picture), a treasure-house of art. Next to the palace is Venice's most famous church, the Basilica of St Mark, and the tall bell tower, or Campanile.*

▲ *Not all palaces were homes for kings and queens. Blenheim Palace in England was built between 1705 and 1725 for the Duke of Marlborough, a famous soldier. The huge house was a thank-you from Queen Anne and her government for Marlborough's victories against the French. It became the family home of the Churchill family, and Winston Churchill, Britain's wartime prime minister, was born there in 1874.*

COLOSSAL CASTLES

Enormous amounts of time and effort went into building castles – defensive strongholds for rulers in times of war. Castle-building lasted for over 5,000 years, and was practised all around the world, from South America to New Zealand. Some of the biggest castles were built by Christian and Muslim soldiers during the Crusades, or Holy Wars, of the Middle Ages. The strongest medieval castles had stone walls up to 7 m thick, but cannons brought an end to castles as effective defences in the 1400s, and after that most castles were turned into houses or prisons.

▲ *The most spectacular Iron Age hill fort in Britain is Maiden Castle. Its earth walls and ditches, now grass-covered, presented a maze-like obstacle to any attacking army. Even so, the fort fell to Roman invaders in about AD 43, after a fierce battle.*

▲ *Neuschwanstein Castle in Bavaria, Germany, was never a home to knights, despite its appearance. The fantasy castle was in fact built in the steam-train age, in 1869, by mad King Ludwig II of Bavaria.*

▲ *Krak des Chevaliers in Syria is the biggest surviving Crusader castle. Rock walls dropped sheer on three sides, and the fourth side was protected by a moat. The Crusaders held this castle from 1142 until 1271, when they were tricked into surrendering to the Muslims.*

▼ *Many castles were built in India during the Mogul Empire (1500s to 1700s). The Red Fort in Delhi is surrounded by 30-m-high red sandstone walls, which enclose beautifully decorated pavilions and marble palaces decorated with gold and precious stones.*

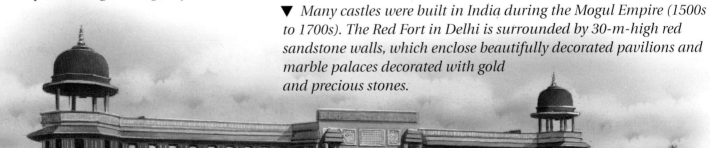

◀ *Chambord is a splendid example of a French 'chateau', a castle in name only. It was built as a large and luxurious home (it has 440 rooms) and not as a defensive stronghold, by the French kings Francis I and Henry I during the 1500s. By this time castles in France had lost their importance in war.*

▸▸ FIVE GREAT CASTLES	
Hradcany	Prague, Czech Rep.
Krak des Chevaliers	Syria
Segovia	Spain
Beaumaris	Wales
Edinburgh	Scotland

▼ *Japanese castles of the 1500s and 1600s, such as Himeji, looked formidable, but had wooden walls filled in with clay and plaster. They were not built to withstand sieges or cannon-fire, since Japanese soldiers preferred fighting on open ground.*

KEEP OUT!
● Slit-like or cross-shaped openings in castle walls were used by archers, who could fire arrows through them without being seen by the enemy.
● In India, castle gateways had unusual defences – iron spikes in the doors to stop war elephants battering them open.
● A moat round a castle made it harder for invaders to reach the castle's walls.

▼ *Conwy Castle was built in north Wales from 1283 to 1287 by the English king, Edward I. It was one of a chain of castles built to help him conquer Wales. The eight strong, round towers were used for defence as well as for accommodation for the soldiers. Round towers had fewer blindspots than the traditional square 'keeps', or main towers.*

▲ *The fortress of Sacsayhuaman in Peru was built of enormous stones like these, some weighing over 100 tonnes, fitted together without cement. It was built by the Incas in 1520, but was pulled down by their Spanish conquerors.*

TREASURES LOST AND FOUND

In their search for gold and silver, treasure-hunters of fact and fiction have gone to extreme lengths. They have made dangerous journeys to far-off places, such as the mythical kingdom of El Dorado, or King Solomon's Mines. They have dug holes, dived into oceans and lakes, and pored over old maps to locate lost treasures – sunken ships, pirates' chests, and gold bars hidden by the Nazis during World War II. Most treasure, however, is found by archaeologists. Their discoveries include the tomb of the Egyptian boy-king Tutankhamun. But just occasionally, metal detectors also strike lucky!

▲ *This gold mask is often said to show Agamemnon, the Greek leader during the Trojan War, but it is probably older (about 1600 BC). It was found in a tomb in 1874 by German archaeologist Heinrich Schliemann.*

◀ *Among the finds in Tutankhamun's tomb was the gold death mask of the young king, found inside the burial chamber.*

▼ *The tomb of the boy-king Tutankhamun, who ruled Egypt from 1347 to 1339 BC, was discovered in Egypt's Valley of the Kings by British archaeologist Howard Carter in 1922. Unlike most Egyptian tombs, it was still mostly intact, though it had been robbed twice.*

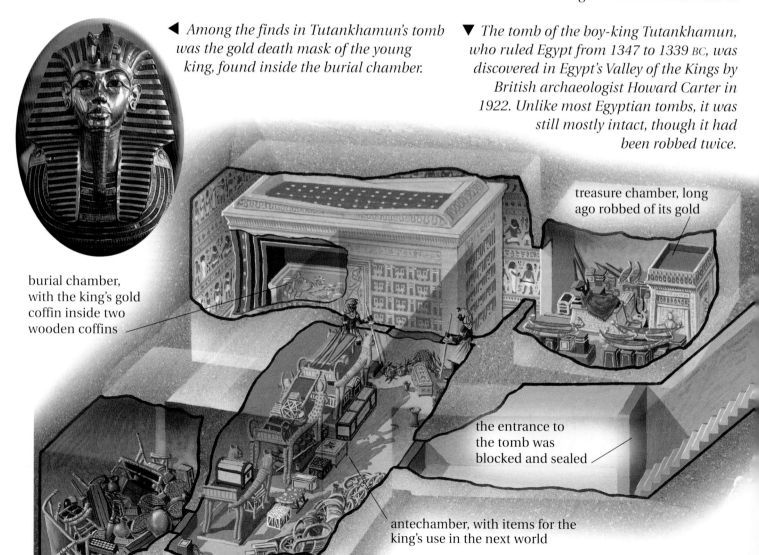

treasure chamber, long ago robbed of its gold

burial chamber, with the king's gold coffin inside two wooden coffins

the entrance to the tomb was blocked and sealed

antechamber, with items for the king's use in the next world

▸ Greediest hunters: Spanish conquistadors ▸ Best place to look: under water ▸ Very unusual find: Chinese jade suits

▸▸ REMARKABLE ROMAN REMAINS

9,213 Roman silver coins found on farmland in Somerset, southwest England	1998
11 Roman ships unearthed under a train station in Italy	1999
43 Roman gold coins found on a building site in London	2000

▼ *In 1939 a long-buried wooden ship was found at Sutton Hoo in eastern England. It was the grave of a great king, probably Redwald of East Anglia, who died about 627. The treasures included this iron helmet.*

◀ *When the Spanish Armada sailed to England in 1588, it carried gold as well as guns. Many Spanish ships were wrecked by storms as they tried to sail home, and ever since treasure-hunters have been searching for the lost Spanish gold.*

▶ *Precious stones such as diamonds, emeralds, rubies and sapphires have been treasured since ancient times. A single diamond can change hands for as much as £10 million, while the famous Kohinoor diamond is literally priceless!*

◀ *The Mildenhall Treasure, a buried hoard of Roman silverware, was dug up in 1942 by a farmer ploughing his field in Suffolk in eastern England. Among the 34 pieces, now in the British Museum, London, was this large decorated dish, probably made in the AD 300s for a rich landowner.*

IT'S A FACT
In 1532 the Spanish conquistador Pizarro demanded a huge ransom to free the captured Inca leader Atahualpa. He wanted one room filled with gold, and another filled twice over with silver. The Incas paid up, but the Spaniards still killed the Inca leader. They then melted down many of the Inca treasures to make gold and silver bars.

GREAT WALLS AND TOWERS

Walls are built to keep people in or out. The world's longest is the Great Wall of China, which extends for 6,400 km. One of the most mysterious walls is the 160-km-long earth bank known as the Eredo in Nigeria, Africa. This huge rampart, 22 m high in places and half-hidden by forest growth, is thought to be about 1,000 years old. Building it involved shifting more earth than was needed to build the Great Pyramid in Egypt. Walls often have watchtowers along their length, built as military lookouts or defensive positions. Other towers were built within medieval cities, many as lookouts, and some, particularly in Italy, as bell-towers beside churches.

▲ *The longest wall built by the Romans was Hadrian's Wall in northern Britain, which was built to control the frontier between Roman Britain and Scotland. It took the army eight years (AD 122–130) to complete. The turf and stone wall is 118 km long and has a 9-m-wide ditch on its northern side.*

▶ *The Leaning Tower of Pisa in Italy was built as a bell-tower. The 55-m high tower began to lean even before it was finished in the 1360s, because the ground was too soft to bear its weight. Modern engineers are trying to prevent it falling over, whilst allowing it to stay leaning, because people like it that way!*

◀ *The Eiffel Tower in Paris was the wonder of the age in the 1880s. Made of 6,000 tonnes of iron and steel, it stands 300 m high. When construction finished in 1889, the tower was the highest structure in the world.*

» Tallest tower: CN Tower, Canada » Longest Roman wall: Hadrian's Wall » Most lopsided: Leaning Tower of Pisa, Italy

» WORLD-FAMOUS WALLS

Great Wall of China	Averages 9 m high, with 12-m-high watchtowers every 60 m
Hadrian's Wall, England	Averages 6 m high, with milecastles, or forts, at intervals
Berlin Wall	Was 5 m high, 45 km long, with electrified fences and watchtowers

◀ *At 553 m high, the CN Tower (1976) in Toronto, Canada, is the world's highest tower – almost twice the height of the Eiffel Tower. Helicopters were used to lift the topmost sections into position.*

◀ *The most infamous wall of the 20th century was the Berlin Wall. Hastily erected by the East German Communists in 1961 to stop refugees fleeing to West Germany, the wall became a symbol of the Cold War. After Communism collapsed in East Germany in 1989, the wall was pulled down amid great rejoicing.*

▶ *The Great Wall of China is the longest structure ever built by humans. Completed in the 200s BC to defend China from northern invaders, the Great Wall winds for over 6,400 km, linking up stretches of old walls with new sections. Thousands of people died while building it, which is why it came to be called the longest cemetery in the world.*

MIGHTY MONUMENTS

Monuments are usually built to mark important events or famous people. The world's tallest monument is an arch, the Gateway to the West, in St Louis, USA, which commemorates the migration of thousands of people to the West in the 1800s. The Romans set up stone arches and columns as monuments. But the highest column in the world is more recent. It commemorates the battle of San Jacinto, fought between Texans and Mexicans in 1836. Another world-famous column is Nelson's Column in Trafalgar Square, London.

◀ The Statue of Liberty is probably the most famous landmark in the USA. It measures 46 m from feet to torch, and stands on a 47-m-high, star-shaped pedestal, on an island at the entrance to New York Harbour. The statue was a gift to the United States from the people of France, and was opened in 1886 as a monument to American independence.

▲ The Washington Monument in Washington, D.C., is the same shape as an Egyptian obelisk, but much bigger. Visitors can go up inside by lift, and descend by 898 steps!

◀ Trajan's Column in Rome is a marble monument set up in AD 113 by Emperor Trajan, whose tomb is in the base. It stands 38 m high and is decorated with a detailed relief picture-strip showing the Roman army on campaign in Dacia (modern Romania).

⏵ Longest Buddha statue: 305 m ⏵ Tallest statue: Motherland Calls, Russia ⏵ Highest column: San Jacinto, USA

FIVE MIGHTY MONUMENTS

	MONUMENT	PLACE	HEIGHT
1	Gateway to the West	St Louis, USA	192 m
2	San Jacinto Monument	Texas, USA	173 m
3	Washington Monument	Washington, D.C.	169 m
4	Motherland Calls statue	Volgograd, Russia	82 m
5	The Monument	London, UK	61 m

a tram takes visitors to an observation room at the top

stainless steel plates reflect the sun

▲ The biggest stone heads in the world loom out from Mount Rushmore in South Dakota, USA. Each head is as big as a five-storey building! The Mount Rushmore National Memorial honours four US Presidents: Washington, Jefferson, Theodore Roosevelt and Lincoln.

◀ Russia's most famous tsar, Peter the Great, is commemorated by a huge statue of himself on horseback in St Petersburg. The entire city is a monument to Peter, who founded it in 1703 as a 'window to the West'.

◀ The Gateway to the West is the world's tallest steel monument. Completed in 1965, this 192-m-high arch honours the pioneers who set out from St Louis, Missouri, to settle in the American West after 1803. The arch is as wide as it is high.

two theatres and a museum are at the base of the arch

GODS AND GODDESSES

Christians, Muslims and Jews believe that there is only one God, a supreme creator of all things. In other religions, especially ancient religions, many gods and goddesses appear. Some of these supernatural beings were thought to live in nature – in rivers, trees or rocks. Others were linked to animals, such as buffaloes, elephants or eagles. In ancient Mesopotamia, there were gods of the sky, water and wind. In Egypt and Central America, the chief god was the Sun-god, while in ancient Greece an entire family of gods was thought to live on top of Mount Olympus. Some of them were helpful to humans, others could be mischievous or violent.

KEY TO THE GREEK GODS

1	Zeus
2	Hera
3	Hermes
4	Poseidon
5	Pan
6	Athena
7	Aphrodite
8	Ares
9	Artemis
10	Hades

▲ *Chief of the Greek gods and goddesses was Zeus, king of the gods, who might hurl a thunderbolt from the skies to show his displeasure. Zeus's brother, Hades, was god of the Underworld and the dead, and Zeus's messenger was the winged Hermes. The Romans adopted these gods, but gave them new names. Zeus, for example, became known as Jupiter.*

▶ *In Christianity, dragons often represent evil, for example in the many pictures of St George killing a dragon. But in China the dragon is a godlike creature with power to do good. The dragon became China's national symbol, and huge paper dragons are paraded in New Year celebrations. In Taoist belief the dragon symbolises the power of nature.*

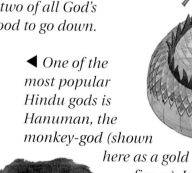

Chinese New Year paper dragon supported on sticks

▲ *The story of how God saved Noah from the Flood, which was God's punishment for people's wickedness, is told in the Old Testament of the Bible. Noah built a great ark, and with his family and two of all God's animals, he waited for the Flood to go down.*

◀ *One of the most popular Hindu gods is Hanuman, the monkey-god (shown here as a gold figure). In the long story called the Ramayana, Hanuman helps to rescue Prince Rama's wife from a demon. Monkeys (left) in India are treated with reverence by Hindus, in honour of Hanuman.*

▶ *The Egyptian Sun-god was Ra, creator of the world and lord of the sky. Egypt's kings called themselves 'sons of Ra', and the god took many forms, including a bird, a snake, and a man with a ram's head.*

» TOP GREEK GODS	
Zeus	**King of the gods**
Poseidon	**God of the sea**
Athena	**Goddess of wisdom and war**
Apollo	**God of music and prophecy**
Hades	**God of the Underworld**

MYTHS AND LEGENDS

Myths and legends are stories that have been told for hundreds of years – stories of gods and goddesses, heroes and monsters with unusual powers, and perilous quests in search of a person, object or truth. Ancient stories in many cultures tell how the world was formed, or explain why the Sun rises and sets each day, or tell of mythical animals that may be friendly or fearsome. No one knows how much truth lies behind such stories, or whether they are based on history or the imagination!

▶ *The Minotaur was a terrifying monster with a bull's head on a human body. It lived in the Labyrinth, a maze of underground tunnels, on the island of Crete, and fed on human victims brought to it as sacrifices. It was finally killed by the hero Theseus.*

▼ *Centaurs were mythological creatures, said by Greek story-tellers to be half-human and half-horse. Most centaurs were wild and dangerous, but the centaur Chiron was wise and taught the Greek hero Achilles how to play music and how to hunt.*

▶▶ MYTHICAL SUPER-HEROES	
Sigurd, dragon slayer	German/Norse
Cuchulainn	Celtic
Hercules	Greek/Roman

▼ *The phoenix was a remarkable magical bird. There was just one, in Arabia, and it lived for 500 years before making a funeral nest that burst into flames. From the cooling ashes, another phoenix emerged. The story may originally have come from Egypt.*

▶▶ MENACING MONSTERS	
The Minotaur	Half-man, half-bull, killed in Labyrinth by Theseus
The Hydra	A many-headed snake, slain by Hercules
Medusa	One of three Gorgons; could turn people to stone

»	**GREEK SUPER-HEROES**
Hercules	Performed 12 astonishing feats of strength and bravery, such as killing lions with his bare hands
Bellerophon	Rode the winged horse Pegasus and slew Chimaera, a monster with lion's head/goat's body
Jason	Led the Argonauts in search of the Golden Fleece
Perseus	Slew Medusa; used his shield as a mirror so her gaze turned herself to stone, and not him

◄ Mermaids were said to sing songs that lured men to them so they could entice them beneath the waves, where they drowned. The legend of the mermaid may be based on sailors' glimpses of sea mammals such as dugongs or seals, which can look half-human in the water.

► St George, England's patron saint, was a legendary hero of Asia Minor (Turkey) in the AD 200s. The story was told that George killed a terrible dragon and saved the local people, who became Christians. Crusaders returning to England in the 1200s brought the story back with them.

▲ The horn of a unicorn was said to have magical medicinal powers. But only a pure maiden could capture the shy, dangerous creature.

▼ According to legend, Rome was founded by twins named Romulus and Remus. Cast adrift on the River Tiber as babies, they were found and suckled by a wolf. In 753 BC, the brothers founded Rome, but later they quarrelled and Remus was killed.

► King Arthur is the best and noblest of all the British legendary heroes, a mixture of possible fact and fantastic fiction. Here the young king is shown drawing the magical sword Excalibur from the stone, a feat that only he was able to do – thus proving himself the rightful king of Britain.

MONSTERS AND SUPERSTITIONS

People are often ready to believe in the unbelievable – mysterious animals, monsters, vampires, werewolves, witches, ghouls and even aliens from space. The truth is we like being scared by spooky stories that cannot be explained! In Scotland, 'Nessie' the Loch Ness Monster, once believed to be a giant reptilian relic from prehistoric times, has evaded all attempts to film or catch it in the murky lake. The world's most famous hairy 'ape-men', the Yeti of the Himalayas and Bigfoot of the North American forests, are also shy of the camera. Could these elusive creatures be real?

▼ *Witches were said to take on animal shapes. This may be the origin of the werewolf legend, in which a person transforms into a wolf and becomes a savage monster, seeking out human victims. In Africa, people were said to turn into leopards.*

THE YETI

● Nicknamed the Abominable Snowman by climbers, the Yeti is said to roam the snowy Himalayas of Asia. Photos of 'Yeti footprints' were taken in 1951, but scraps of skin and droppings have not yet provided enough evidence to prove that this remarkable creature truly exists.

▲ *In 1967 amateur film of a hairy, humanlike creature in the forests of California aroused great excitement. The film, along with photos and footprints, has been used as proof of North America's own Yeti, known as Sasquatch, or Bigfoot, although scientists have not yet been convinced.*

▶▶ COMMON SUPERSTITIONS	
Black cats	Lucky or unlucky!
Spilling salt	Unlucky. To undo the bad luck, throw salt over your left shoulder
Friday	The unluckiest day of the week
Breaking a mirror	Seven years' bad luck
Number 13	Unlucky
Number 7	Lucky

▸ Luckiest food: salt ▸ Most superstitious ruler: Hitler ▸ Worst thing to break: a mirror ▸ Most elusive creature: Yeti

◀ *The blood-sucking vampire of the screen has nothing to do with the vampire bat of South America. The original Dracula was a medieval tyrant named Vlad the Impaler, who stuck his victims on stakes. Comic books and films created all kinds of variations on the vampire theme.*

▶ *Legends abound of giant snakes. One called the Grootslang is said to lurk in a deep cavern in South Africa, guarding a hoard of diamonds. People often exaggerate the size of the snake they have seen out of fear.*

▸▸	SPOOKY BELIEFS
Ghosts	Borley Rectory, England's most haunted house (1863, burned down 1939)
Kraken	Biggest of all sea monsters (as big as an island); found in the sea off Norway
Witches	Salem, Massachusetts, largest witch-hunt in American history (1692); 19 men and women were hanged as witches
Vampires	Fictional pointy-toothed, deathly pale creatures from Transylvania, Romania
Werewolves	Called *loupgarou* in France, where they reputedly dig up corpses

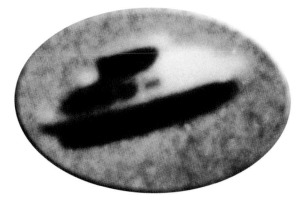

▶ *Cats have been both worshipped and feared by people throughout history. Witches' cats were thought to be demons in disguise. In medieval France, black cats were roasted to make cures for evil spells! But in Britain black cats are generally regarded as lucky.*

▲ *Reports of mysterious Unidentified Flying Objects, or UFOs, including fiery chariots and floating dishes, crop up through history. The 'flying saucer' became front-page news in the 1950s, with a flurry of sightings and photos of alleged visitors from outer space – most of them clearly fakes.*

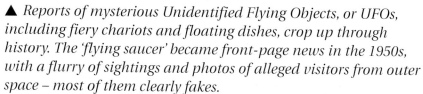

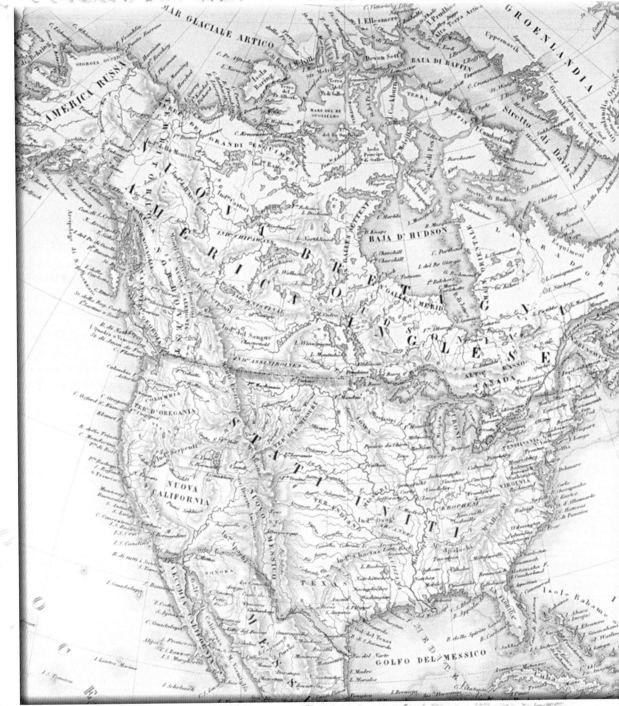

HISTORY

History is constantly changing, year by year, month by month, day by day. Since prehistoric times when man first hunted for food, through to the 21st century, age of complex computers, the written word has been one of the most important ways of passing on information.

We know so much about ancient empires, such as the Romans and Greeks, through writings they left behind. Beautiful architecture and monuments reveal how sophisticated these people were, with ideas ahead of their time. Rome had its own form of central heating 2,000 years ago!

Some facts will never change – the discovery of Australia, the first man on the Moon. Others are more mysterious, like the disappearance of the Princes in the Tower, the ghostly face on the Turin shroud. In fact, as you read this introduction, history is being made all around you.

Explore the biggest and best facts of *History* and and you could become a history maker. There are the big, serious facts – for reference – and less serious ones, too, for fun. Packed into these pages are the biggest and best, oddest and strangest, smallest and funniest facts around!

◄ HISTORICAL MAP OF THE UNITED STATES OF AMERICA

PREHISTORIC PEOPLE

Imagine that all the time since the world began (about 4.5 billion years) was just one year. In this imaginary year, there were no people until about 7.40 in the evening on the last day of the year. Human history is a tiny footnote to Earth's history. The first humans hunted animals and gathered wild plants for food. They made stone and bone tools, and later learned to make fire. About 10,000 years ago humans found out how to grow crops. They settled down in villages, which grew into the first cities. Civilization had begun.

▲ 'Otzi the Iceman' died some 5,300 years ago while crossing the mountains between Austria and Italy. His frozen corpse was found in 1991. Although Otzi had been wearing warm winter clothing made from skins, he was unable to survive the cold when he became trapped by heavy snow.

▼ *This skull belonged to an Australopithecus – someone who lived 3 million years ago and walked upright, like modern humans. In 1974 the almost-complete skeleton of a female* Australopithecus, *nicknamed Lucy, was found in Ethiopia. She was as tall as a 10-year-old girl, but aged about 40.*

▶ *The first humans used rocks as weapons to kill animals for food. They were slower and weaker than many of the animals they hunted, but using their brains and teamwork they became successful hunters.*

First artists: more than 25,000 years ago ▸ First farmers: about 10,000 years ago ▸ First domestic animal: dog

DID YOU KNOW?
The remains of Çatal Hüyük, an 8,000-year-old town, were found in 1958 beneath a grass-covered mound in Turkey. About 5,000 people lived there.

TIMELINE

4 million years ago	*Australopithecus*
2 million years ago	*Homo habilis;* first stone tools
1.5 million years ago	*Homo erectus;* used hand axes and fire
200,000 years ago	*Neanderthal* people; first to bury dead
100,000 years ago	*Homo sapiens;* bigger brains than *H. erectus*
40,000 years ago	*Homo sapiens sapiens* – modern humans
10,000 years ago	Farming begins; many stone tools made
7,000 years ago	First copper tools
5,000 years ago	First bronze tools
3,500 years ago	First iron tools

▲ People who hunted and gathered food never stayed long in one place. But once humans began to plant crops, they stayed to watch them grow and to harvest them. The first crop that farmers grew was wild wheat, about 10,000 years ago.

▲ Fire was the biggest advance made by early prehistoric people. They made fires to keep warm, to give light in the darkness of the night, for cooking meat, and to frighten away wild animals. Stone Age people also made stone tools and used the skins of the animals they hunted to make clothing and tents.

  **STEPS TOWARDS CIVILIZATION**

	HOMINID (HUMAN) SPECIES	WHEN LIVING
★1	*Australopithecus*	4 million years ago
2	*Homo habilis* (handy human)	2 million years ago
3	*Homo erectus* (upright human)	1.5 million years ago
4	*Homo sapiens* (wise human)	100,000 years ago

ANCIENT EMPIRES

Civilization developed close to great rivers, in fertile regions where farmers could plant crops and trade with their neighbours. Villages grew into cities, and people became town-dwellers for the first time. Their leaders became kings, with more power than any leaders before. The strongest kings ruled more than one city, creating the first empires. They led armies into battle, made laws to govern their empires, and were often treated like gods. The first great empire was Egypt, which lasted for almost 3,000 years. But much bigger in area was the Indus Valley civilization. It ended about 1500 BC, either because of floods or invaders.

▲ The Egyptians built mighty monuments in stone, like these giant figures of King Ramesses II (1289–1224 BC), which guard the temple at Abu Simbel.

▶ This clay seal, used to label a merchant's goods, was found in the Indus Valley in present-day Pakistan, where a rich civilization flourished some 4,500 years ago.

GREAT EMPIRES AND RULERS

Egypt

Sumer, Mesopotamia

Indus Valley civilization, Indian sub-continent

Babylonia

Ur, Mesopotamia

Minoan civilization, Crete

China (beginning of Shang power)

Mycenean civilization, Greece and Turkey

Assyria

◀ Ancient empires, such as those of Egypt and Assyria, grew larger and more powerful by conquering neighbouring empires. New weapons, such as the fast, horse-drawn chariot, gave their armies an advantage over the enemy. One man steered the vehicle, while an archer shot at the enemy, who were on foot.

» First writing: cuneiform » Best at maths: Babylonians » First iron users: Hittites » First laws: Hammurabi of Babylon's

▲ *Carved stone heads higher than a person stand as monuments to the Olmecs, a people who lived in Mexico about 2,500 years ago. Their civilization may have been the first great civilization in North America.*

TIMELINE

8000 BC	Farming begins in the Near East; Jericho is built – one of the first cities
6500 BC	Oldest-known woven textiles, from Turkey
5000 BC	Farming in Egypt and China
3500 BC	Sumerians invent writing and the wheel
2000 BC	Start of the Assyrian Empire
1766 BC	Beginning of Shang power in China
1450 BC	Volcano wrecks Minoan palaces on Crete
1250 BC	Greeks capture Troy, according to legend
1200 BC	Rise of Olmec power in Mexico
221 BC	Shih Huangdi is first emperor of all China

3100 to 30 BC	United under King Menes
4000 to 2000 BC	Greatest ruler, Sargon of Akkad
2500 to 1500 BC	No rulers known
1800 to 500 BC	Great kings Hammurabi and Nebuchadnezzar II
2100 BC (strongest)	Under King Ur-Nammu
2000–1100 BC	Named after legendary King Minos
1766 BC	Empire united by Shih Huangdi in 221 BC
1600–1100 BC	Greatest ruler, Agamemnon
800 BC (at its peak)	Last great king, Assurbanipal

▶ *The Sumerians invented writing about 5,500 years ago. Called cuneiform, meaning 'wedge-shaped', it was made by pressing wedge-shaped 'pens' onto soft clay.*

▶ *Babylon in Mesopotamia (modern Iraq) was the capital of the Babylonian Empire. In 605 BC King Nebuchadnezzar II enlarged the city and built a magnificent new entrance, called the Ishtar Gate, in the city's northern wall. The blue-tiled gate stood 15 m tall. Babylonia conquered Assyria in 612 BC, but in 539 BC Babylon fell to Cyrus the Great of Persia.*

▶ *These life-sized clay soldiers, buried in the tomb of the first Chinese emperor, Shih Huangdi, and discovered in 1974, gave historians an accurate picture of the clothes and weapons of the time. The emperor went to the grave with 10,000 model warriors to guard him in the next world.*

» Bloodiest entertainment: Roman Games » Least rights: slaves » Biggest warship: Greek trireme

GREEKS AND ROMANS

Greece and Rome shaped the Western world, through language, art and political ideas. Ancient Greece was not one country, but many quarrelsome city-states. It produced many famous writers, thinkers and scientists. Greek civilization reached its height in the 400s BC. In 146 BC Greece was conquered by the Roman Empire. The Romans, originally farmers from central Italy, adopted many Greek customs and gods. They conquered most of Europe and North Africa, and by AD 100 Rome ruled the biggest empire in the Western world.

▲ *Greek foot-soldiers won many battles by advancing in a formation called a* phalanx. *Each man had a round shield and a long spear, and as the* phalanx *charged, it presented a bristling array of spearpoints.*

◀ *One of the most famous Greek scientists was Archimedes (287–212 BC). His 'bathwater-test' proved a king's crown was not pure gold. The crown displaced more water than a piece of pure gold that weighed the same as the crown.*

▼ *The Greeks were great seafarers. Traders explored the islands and bays of the Mediterranean Sea in cargo boats like this one, founding colonies along the way. The explorer Pytheas even sailed as far north as Britain.*

MOST FAMOUS ANCIENT GREEKS	
Pericles	The wisest ruler of Athens
Alexander the Great	The greatest soldier to come out of Greece
Homer	The most famous poet
Socrates	A philosopher, forced to kill himself
Aristotle	A great scientist and thinker

▶ *The legendary war between Greece and Troy, a city in Turkey, lasted for 10 years. The Greeks finally tricked their way into Troy by hiding soldiers inside a wooden horse, which the Trojans dragged into their city.*

◀ *The Roman Empire at its peak, about* AD *100, ruled Britain to the north of Rome, Spain to the west, Palestine to the east and North Africa to the south.*

▶ *A Roman legionary soldier was a well-disciplined, full-time professional. On the march he wore armour and carried a shield, javelin and sword, tools for making camp, and his kit slung from a pole.*

▼ *The centre of government of the Roman Empire was the Forum in Rome, which was originally a market place. It had imposing temples and public buildings, including the Senate, of which only ruins remain.*

▸▸	MOST FAMOUS ROMANS
Julius Caesar	General, almost became king but was murdered
Augustus	First emperor and winner of civil wars
Mark Antony	Soldier, fell in love with Cleopatra, queen of Egypt
Hadrian	Emperor, famous for his wall in northern Britain
Constantine	First Christian emperor, AD 324–337

▼ *In 218* BC *Hannibal, the Carthaginian general, led an army against Rome. He took his troops, with their war elephants, across the Alps in a daring attack, but in the end he, and Carthage, were defeated.*

TIMELINE	
753 BC	**Traditional date for founding of Rome**
700 BC	**Greek poet Homer composes the *Iliad* and *Odyssey***
509 BC	**Rome becomes a republic, its last king overthrown**
500s BC	**Greeks invent democracy**
490–431 BC	**Greeks defeat Persians; golden age of Athens**
438 BC	**Parthenon temple in Athens completed**
336 BC	**Alexander the Great becomes ruler of Macedon**
200s BC	**Romans defeat Carthage (a rival state in North Africa)**
146 BC	**Greece comes under Roman control**
49 BC	**Julius Caesar rules as dictator in Rome**
27 BC	**End of Roman Republic and start of Roman Empire**
AD 98–117	**Roman Empire at its greatest, under Emperor Trajan**
AD 286	**Empire divided into Eastern and Western parts**
AD 476	**End of Western Empire; Eastern continues as Byzantium**

CONQUERORS

History's great conquerors were men of great ambition and determination. They had the support of well-trained soldiers to back them up – soldiers like the Roman legionary, the Norman knight in chain mail armour, the fast-riding Mongol archer and Napoleon's Imperial Guard, marching in ranks with muskets at the ready. Of all the great conquerors in history, none was more feared than the 12th-century Mongol leader Genghis Khan. His horsemen conquered a vast empire extending across Asia from China as far west as the Danube River in Europe.

▶ *Babur (1483–1530) was the great Muslim leader who conquered India in 1526 by defeating Ibrahim, the Sultan of Delhi, at Panipat. Babur made himself emperor of India.*

▼ *Cyrus the Great was the 6th-century ruler of Persia. He founded an empire extending from the Mediterranean to India, uniting peoples in the region by conquest. Cyrus died in 529 BC and was buried in this huge tomb.*

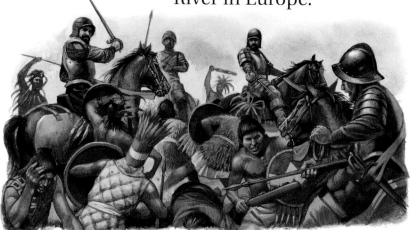

▲ *One thousand Spanish troops, led by Hernando Cortés, conquered the Aztec Empire in Mexico in the three years from 1519 to 1521. Spanish guns, armour and horses, together with Indian allies, proved too strong for the Aztec armies.*

▼ *Napoleon was France's most ambitious general. He dreamt of building an empire bigger than Rome's. In 1812 he reached Moscow, but finding the city on fire he ordered his Grand Army to retreat. The freezing winter came early and devastated his troops. Defeat in Russia marked the beginning of his fall.*

FAMOUS CONQUERORS	
Most ambitious	Alexander the Great (356–323 BC), who dreamed of conquering India
Quickest	Conquest of Aztecs by Hernando Cortés in 3 years (1519–21)
Biggest mistake	Napoleon's decision to invade Russia in 1812
Most feared troops	Mongol cavalry of Genghis Khan (1162–1227), whose speed and ferocity terrified most opponents
Youngest	Akbar the Great, emperor of India, who was only 13 when he succeeded his grandfather Babur in 1556

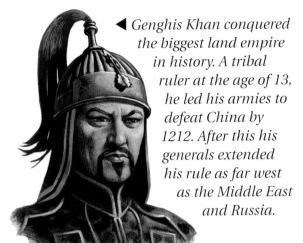

◀ *Genghis Khan conquered the biggest land empire in history. A tribal ruler at the age of 13, he led his armies to defeat China by 1212. After this his generals extended his rule as far west as the Middle East and Russia.*

TIMELINE	
330 BC	Alexander conquers the Persian Empire
44 BC	The Romans invade Britain
AD 715	Muslims from North Africa conquer Spain
800	Charlemagne controls western Europe
1066	The Normans conquer England
1100s	The Khmers conquer Southeast Asia
1200s	Genghis Khan conquers much of Asia
1279	Kublai Khan (grandson of Genghis) conquers China
1397	Tamerlane (Mongol) invades India
1521	Cortés of Spain conquers the Aztecs of Mexico
1526	Babur founds the Mogul Empire in India
1536	Pizarro of Spain conquers the Incas of Peru
1804	Napoleon controls most of Europe

▶ *The best-known conqueror is probably Alexander the Great. In a short but astonishing life, he conquered Persia, Babylon and Egypt, and invaded India. Ferocious energy drove him on, but in India his exhausted troops begged him to return home.*

▶ *Charlemagne, king of the Franks in Gaul (modern France), was crowned western Europe's new Roman emperor in AD 800. His empire covered France, Germany and Italy as far south as Rome. Often called the perfect ruler, his main aim was to spread Christianity.*

LIFE IN THE MIDDLE AGES

The Middle Ages were dangerous, but creative times. Some of Europe's most magnificent cathedrals were built in praise of God, and beautiful hand-painted or 'illuminated' Bibles were made by the monks in Europe's many monasteries. Dangers included disease such as the Black Death, which killed about one quarter of Europe's population. Wars were also frequent, as powerful rulers attempted to extend their territories or assert control. The Crusades, for example, lasted on and off for hundreds of years. Punishments for disobeying the Church were severe, and included being burned at the stake.

▲ *Medieval towns were over-crowded, and drains ran along the narrow, dirty streets. Cooking fires often set light to the wooden houses, and whole towns – such as Rouen in France – sometimes burned down.*

◄ *Most people in medieval times were peasants, who farmed the land for the lord of a manor. They also grew food for themselves. The poorest peasants were not free, but had to obey the lord.*

» PAINFUL PUNISHMENTS FOR LAWBREAKERS
Being burned alive, the usual punishment for witchcraft
Having your ears or hands cut off and your nose slit
Being dragged around town with rotting fish hung round your neck
Sitting in the stocks (a wooden trap) and being pelted with rubbish
Whipping, hanging, beheading – nobles could choose beheading

◄ *Rats were a great menace. They not only ate food stores, but also carried the Black Death, or plague.*

◄ *A tournament was the biggest sporting event in the medieval calendar. Knights, the most important medieval soldiers, charged at one another with lances, testing their skill at knocking their opponent to the ground. From about 1400, the knights wore suits of plate armour.*

» Lowliest workers: peasants » Biggest residences: castles » Greatest engineering feats: cathedrals

▲ *The biggest building projects of the Middle Ages were castles and cathedrals. Some cathedrals took hundreds of years to complete. The craftsmen shown here are making a round cathedral window.*

TIMELINE	
529	First abbey in Europe, at Monte Cassino, Italy
700s	Start of feudal system in western Europe
1066	Normans conquer England
1096	First Crusade or holy war for control of the Holy Land
1249	Britain's first university, Oxford University
1260	Hanseatic League of trading cities founded
1265	First real parliament in England
1270	Last Crusade
1300s	First use of gunpowder and cannon in war
1337–1453	Hundred Years' War between England and France
1348	Black Death reaches England; all Europe is affected

▼ *Some of the biggest medieval abbeys were in France. Cluny Abbey was founded in 910. Its church or basilica, shown here, was the largest in the world until the completion of St Peter's in Rome.*

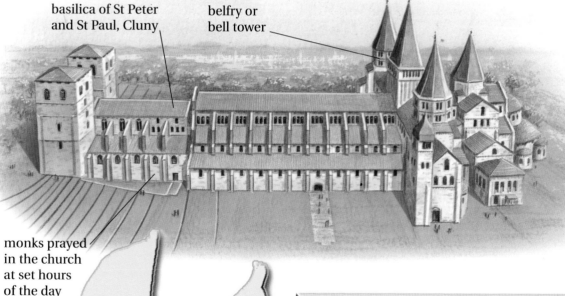

basilica of St Peter and St Paul, Cluny

belfry or bell tower

monks prayed in the church at set hours of the day and night

▼ *Medieval battles were often confused and bloody affairs, fought with bows, swords, spears and spiked clubs. At Bannockburn in 1314, the Scots under Robert Bruce beat Edward II's much larger English army with its formidable knights in armour on their great warhorses.*

PIGS AT LARGE!

● Pigs were a nuisance in medieval towns. Many people kept pigs in their backyards or in alleyways. A law was passed so that any pig found wandering could be 'arrested'. The pig's owner had to pay four pennies to get it back.

NEW IDEAS

The greatest explosion of new ideas in Europe came in the 1400s, a period called the Renaissance, or 'rebirth'. It was a period during which ancient knowledge was rediscovered, and new ideas in art and science were spread by the new invention of printing. By the 1700s this 'age of Enlightenment' had sparked off a revolution in science and technology – the Industrial Revolution – which changed the way people lived and worked. Ideas about politics also changed, bringing new ways of government.

▶ *Michael Faraday (1791–1867) had little schooling, but a brilliant mind. He rose to become a professor of chemistry, and his new ideas led to the invention of the electric motor and electrical generator.*

◀ *Leonardo da Vinci (1452–1519) was a genius far ahead of his time. He drew plans for amazing new machines, such as aircraft similar to this first helicopter, as well as armoured cars and submarines.*

◀ *Andreas Vesalius (1514–64), a Flemish (Belgian) scientist, wrote the first book on anatomy to show detailed drawings of the inside of the human body. He also dissected corpses as a way of teaching medical students – a startling idea in the 1500s.*

▼ *New ideas about machines and making goods in factories brought about the Industrial Revolution of the 1700s and 1800s. With the changes in living and working conditions came new ideas about public health and education.*

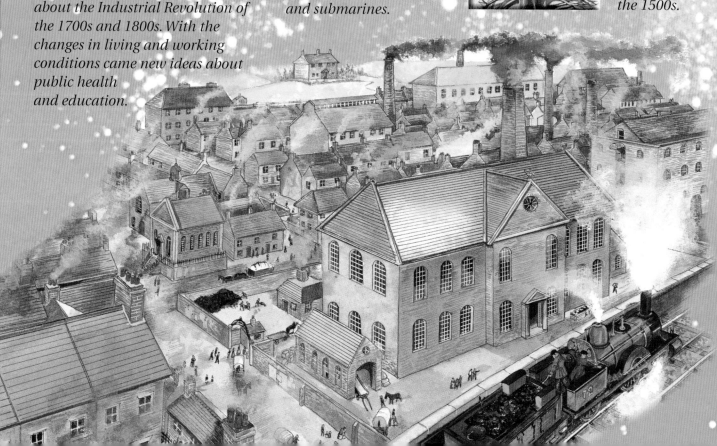

» Greatest Italian scientist: Galileo » Greatest artist–scientist: Leonardo da Vinci » Most famous naturalist: Darwin

▲ *Florence Nightingale, known as the 'lady with the lamp', upset the British army during the Crimean War (1854–56) by voicing new ideas about the way wounded soldiers should be cared for, and demanding changes in nursing practice.*

▼ *One of the biggest new ideas of the 19th century was Charles Darwin's theory of evolution, published in 1859 in his book* Origin of Species. *After visiting the remote Galapagos Islands, Darwin realized that the animals there had 'evolved' over a long period as they competed for food, and that only the fittest survived.*

TIMELINE

1265	Roger Bacon at work on an encyclopedia of knowledge
c.1266	Giotto born – great Renaissance artist of 'lifelike' pictures
1452	Leonardo da Vinci, artist and inventor, is born in Italy
1513	Macchiavelli writes *The Prince*, about the ideal ruler
1543	Copernicus's new idea – that Earth moves around the Sun
1550	Gutenberg invents printing with movable type
1609	Galileo studies the Moon through his telescope
1642	Pascal invents an adding machine
1667	Newton publishes his laws of gravity and motion
1701	Tull invents the first seed drill to help farmers
1709	Darby discovers how to produce iron cheaply
1782	Watt makes the first efficient steam engine

THE GALAPAGOS ISLANDS

▲ *Some ideas are hard to accept, others to understand. Copernicus's idea that Earth moves around the Sun was rejected by the Christian Church in the 15th century. Astronomers today are trying to work out just how old and big the Universe is – a concept most of us will never really grasp!*

►► PEOPLE WHOSE IDEAS CHANGED THE WAY WE SEE THE WORLD

Copernicus	1473–1543	Polish astronomer who upset ancient ideas of how the Universe works
John Locke	1632–1704	English philosopher who declared that all men were free and equal
Sir Isaac Newton	1642–1727	English scientist whose ideas about light, motion and gravity revolutionized science
François Voltaire	1694–1778	French writer who criticised the Church and government
Antoine Lavoisier	1743–94	French scientist and founder of modern chemistry
Charles Darwin	1809–82	English naturalist whose ideas about the evolution of life shocked many people

EXPLORING THE OCEANS

The Egyptians led the way in sea voyaging, followed by the Phoenicians, who sailed out of the Mediterranean and into the Atlantic, navigating by the stars. The Chinese sailed large fleets west across the Indian Ocean to Africa, but they never rounded its tip. Meanwhile the Portuguese worked their way down the west coast of Africa and eventually sailed eastwards all the way to India. For early ocean explorers, calm seas were one of the greatest dangers. With no wind, their ships went nowhere and precious supplies ran out.

◄ *In 1735 John Harrison invented the chronometer, a sea clock that helped sailors navigate safely. Without knowing the time, a sailor could not work out how far a ship had sailed.*

► *Viking longships were seaworthy enough to cross oceans. They sailed from Scandinavia to Iceland, then crossed the Atlantic to Greenland. From there an expedition, led by a Viking named Leif Ericsson, sailed farther west to North America, landing in AD 1000.*

»	GREATEST SEA EXPLORERS
Cook	Sailed farther than anyone had before him
Magellan	Lesser men would have turned back
Dias	Voyage into the unknown lasted over 14 months
Columbus	Made four Atlantic voyages; never gave up
Tasman	Survived fierce storms in the Southern Ocean

► *In 1492 Christopher Columbus sailed from Spain to the Bahamas. By sailing west across the Atlantic Ocean, he had expected to land on the coast of Asia. Instead, he rediscovered North America.*

◄ *During the 1400s the Chinese, led by an admiral named Cheng Ho, sent large fleets of ocean-going junks across the Indian Ocean to trade with Arabia and East Africa. Had they rounded the tip of Africa, they might have met the Portuguese sailing down the west coast in their quest for a route to India.*

TIMELINE

3000 BC	Egyptians explore Mediterranean Sea
400s BC	Hanno of Carthage sails along west coast of Africa
1405–33	Cheng Ho of China sails as far west as the Persian Gulf
1487–88	Bartolomeu Dias of Portugal sails to southern tip of Africa
1492	Christopher Columbus sails from Spain to the Caribbean
1497	Vasco da Gama of Portugal sails around Africa to India
1497	John Cabot sails from England to North America
1499	Amerigo Vespucci sails to America (named after him)
1519–22	Sebastian del Cano sails around the world
1534	Jacques Cartier discovers the St Lawrence River, Canada
1640s	Abel Tasman of Holland sails to Tasmania
1768	James Cook sets out on the first of three Pacific voyages

▶ *Ferdinand Magellan led the first voyage around the world (1519–22). Magellan was killed in the Philippines, but one of his ships completed the return journey back to Spain.*

▼ *Thousands of years before sailors from the West discovered sea routes around the world, the Polynesians had crossed the Pacific Ocean and found numerous small islands. Ancient stories suggest they sailed in large, twin-hulled canoes.*

▲ *One of the greatest sea explorers ever was Captain James Cook. He made three long voyages of scientific discovery in the 1700s. On a visit to Australia, his crew reported seeing creatures they described as 'jumping dogs' – they were kangaroos!*

KEY TO MAP ROUTES
— 1492 Christopher Columbus sails from Spain to the Bahamas
— 1497–98 Vasco da Gama sails from Portugal to India
— 1519–22 Magellan's round-the-world voyage,
▪▪▪▪ completed by del Cano
— 1768–71 James Cook explores the Pacific and lands in Australia

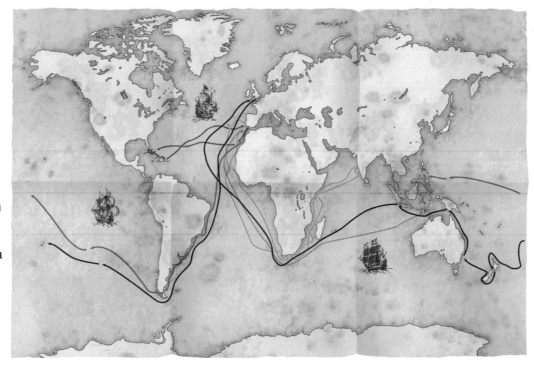

BLOODY BATTLES

In ancient times, armies were small and most battles were settled in an hour or two. Roman soldiers were so well trained that they lost very few battles in more than 500 years. The biggest change in war came in the 1300s, with the first use of cannon and gunpowder. In 1453 the Turks used a monster cannon to fire seven shots a day against the walls of Constantinople. Sixty oxen were needed to drag it! By the 1800s muskets, rifles and machine guns made battles much more destructive. Rapid-firing guns mowed down even the bravest soldiers. The longest war in history was the Hundred Years' War (which actually lasted for 115 years) between Britain and France.

▲ *British infantry under Wellington fired musket volleys at Napoleon's French army during the Battle of Waterloo in 1815. The British and their Prussian allies won.*

▶ *Britain's most famous naval hero is Admiral Horatio Nelson. Despite losing an eye and an arm in earlier battles, he led his fleet to victory against the French and Spanish at Trafalgar in 1805.*

◀ *The best weapon of the Middle Ages was the longbow, used by English and Welsh archers. It was quicker to shoot than the crossbow, and could put an arrow through a wooden shield. Archers helped England win the Battle of Agincourt (1415) against the French.*

▲ *In 1588 the Spanish Armada, a fleet of 130 ships, sailed north to invade England. But not even this mighty fleet could survive cannons, fireships and savage storms – many galleons sank.*

▶▶ GREAT COMMANDERS	
Alexander	Never lost a battle, even against much bigger armies than his own
Napoleon	Expert at using artillery and choosing the right moment to attack
Wellington	Good at choosing when and where to fight, and win
Lee	Led outnumbered Confederate (Southern) armies against Union (Northern) armies in the American Civil War

» First war chariots: Egyptian   » Last battle on British soil: Culloden, 1746   » Biggest loser: King Harold, Hastings, 1066

◄ *Ulysses S Grant (1822–85) was a Union general in the American Civil War, masterminding the defeat of the Confederacy (Southern states). He later became US President (1869–77).*

▲ *Knights seldom charged into battle – they were too heavy – but they usually had a crushing impact on lines of foot-soldiers. At Agincourt, however, in 1415, the French knights were crowded together on boggy ground, which made them easy targets for the English archers.*

▲ *Battles of the American Civil War (1861–65) were fought mainly with cannon and rifles. About 620,000 soldiers were killed during the war – half fell in battles, the rest died from disease.*

TIMELINE		
480 BC	Salamis	Greeks defeat Persians in naval battle
431 BC	Gaugamela	Alexander defeats the Persians
AD 732	Tours	Franks defeat Muslim Saracens
1066	Hastings	Normans beat the English
1346	Crécy	English victorious over the French
1415	Agincourt	English defeat the French
1588	Armada	Spanish invasion fleet destroyed by English
1709	Poltava	Russians beat Swedes
1757	Plassey	British seize control of India
1759	Quebec	British win Canada from the French
1781	Yorktown	Americans beat the British
1805	Trafalgar	British fleet defeats French and Spanish
1815	Waterloo	British and Allies defeat the French
1863	Gettysburg	Union army beats Confederates in American Civil War
1870	Sedan	Germans defeat the French

WORLD AT WAR

World War I (1914–18) was the first truly mechanized war, yet there was very little movement. Pinned down by gunfire, armies became bogged down in defensive trenches, and thousands of soldiers died trying to cross a few metres of muddy ground. World War II (1939–45) was a much bigger war. Few regions of the globe escaped the fighting between the Allies and the German–Japanese Axis forces, and many cities were devastated by bombs.

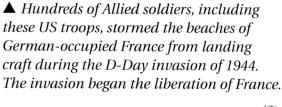

▲ *Hundreds of Allied soldiers, including these US troops, stormed the beaches of German-occupied France from landing craft during the D-Day invasion of 1944. The invasion began the liberation of France.*

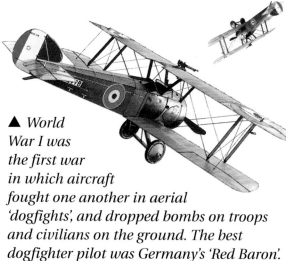

▲ *World War I was the first war in which aircraft fought one another in aerial 'dogfights', and dropped bombs on troops and civilians on the ground. The best dogfighter pilot was Germany's 'Red Baron'.*

▲ *During World War I, German and Allied forces gained ground through trench warfare. In just one battle, the Somme, more than 1 million soldiers were killed going 'over the top' of the trenches into enemy fire.*

▶ *The Vietnam War (1957–75) was the most controversial of modern wars. America used helicopter 'gunships' to back up their ground troops, but despite their superior firepower they failed to win a final victory.*

»» KEY BATTLES OF WORLD WAR II			
Battle of Britain	1940	England	Britain's RAF defeats German air force
Coral Sea	1942	Pacific	US aircraft carriers defeat Japanese fleet
Alamein	1942	North Africa	Allies beat Germans and Italians
Stalingrad	1942–43	Russia	Germans fail to capture Russian city
Normandy	1944	France	Allies invade across English Channel

▲ *The mightiest naval warships of the modern era are the US navy's giant nuclear-powered aircraft carriers. During World War II, aircraft carriers with jets became the most effective naval ships.*

▼ *Tanks such as this one first crawled into battle in 1916, during World War I. The most useless tank was the German 'Mighty Mouse' of 1944, which weighed 190 tonnes. It was very slow and cracked roads as it lumbered along.*

TIMELINE

1914	**World War I begins – Germany invades France**
1916	**Battle of the Somme in France; first use of tanks**
1916	**Naval Battle of Jutland between British and German fleets**
1917	**USA enters World War I**
1918	**Germany is defeated; World War I ends**
1930	**Rise of Nazis in Germany under Adolf Hitler**
1937	**Japan invades China**
1939	**World War II begins – Germany invades Poland**
1940	**France falls to Germany; Battle of Britain**
1941	**Japanese attack Pearl Harbor; USA joins the Allies**
1942	**Germans defeated at El Alamein; Japan captures Singapore**
1943	**Germans defeated at Battle of Stalingrad**
1944	**First German V-2 rockets; D-Day invasion of France by Allies**
1945	**Germany surrenders; USA drops two atomic bombs on Japan; Japan surrenders**

steel armour protected the tank crew from gunfire

BOMBS

- During World War II, new weapons were invented such as flying bombs and V-2 rockets.
- The war ended when the USA dropped two atomic bombs on Hiroshima and Nagasaki in Japan in 1945.

caterpillar tracks enabled tanks to climb over trench walls and crawl through thick mud

PIONEERS AND TRAILBLAZERS

Pioneers were explorers who set out to cross previously unexplored land, sea or air. They led the way, blazing a trail – or marking the way – for others to follow. Sometimes pioneers were in a race with others to reach the goal first. When Captain Scott reached the South Pole in 1912, for example, he found Amundsen's Norwegian flag already there. The modern age of exploration began about 1800. Since then, for the first time people have crossed the United States, explored Africa, climbed the Himalayas, flown across the oceans, and travelled into space. The whole world is now mapped from space, and there are few places where people have not been.

▲ Explorer David Livingstone (1813–73) was the first European to see Victoria Falls in central Africa. He later disappeared, but was found in 1871 by Henry Morton Stanley (shown here) in Uganda.

◀ America's Amelia Earhart was the most famous pioneer aviator, or flier, of the 1930s. She flew the Atlantic solo in 1932, but disappeared in 1937 while crossing the Pacific on a round-the-world flight.

▶▶ AMERICAN TRAILBLAZERS	
Daniel Boone	1769
Meriwether Lewis, William Clark	1804–06
Jedediah Smith	1820s
Jim Bridger	1820s
Kit Carson, Charles Frémont	1840s

▲ The biggest wagon trains rolled west across America from the 1840s. A group of a thousand settlers set out for Oregon in 1843, crossing difficult terrain and Native-American territories. Thousands more pioneers headed for California after gold was found there in 1848.

tobacco

sugar cane

sweet potatoes

pineapple

gold

◀ Pioneers in America often hoped to 'get rich quick' by finding gold. Others settled for selling new products, such as tobacco, or became 'planters', growing pineapples, sugar cane or other crops.

▼ *In 1911–12 two teams of explorers braved icy Antarctica. The team led by Roald Amundsen of Norway (bottom) reached the South Pole first. Robert F Scott's British five-man party (below) arrived a month later, but died from exhaustion while returning.*

LUCKY 13

● Intrepid astronauts had the biggest space escape in April 1970, after the US *Apollo 13* craft was damaged by an explosion on its way to the Moon. Squashed into the tiny Moon lander, with most systems shut down to save power, the astronauts flew round the Moon and back to Earth, and a safe splashdown.

TIMELINE	
1271	Marco Polo sets out for China, returning to Venice in 1295
1500s	Spanish gold-seekers explore Central America
1620	*Mayflower* pilgrims land in America
1788	First British settlers land in Australia
1804–06	Lewis and Clark map the American West; new settlers come
1854–56	Livingstone crosses Africa and sees the Victoria Falls
1860	Burke and Wills cross Australia from south to north
1903	First flight in an aeroplane, by the Wrights
1911	Amundsen reaches the South Pole
1953	Hillary and Tenzing climb Everest
1957–58	First overland crossing of Antarctica
1960	Bathyscaphe *Trieste* dives to bottom of the Pacific Ocean
1961	Gagarin circles Earth in a spacecraft
1969	Armstrong and Aldrin are the first people on the Moon

► *In 1271 Marco Polo, aged 17, left Venice in Italy with his father and uncle to journey to China, following the ancient Silk Road. It took them three years to reach China. Marco Polo worked for Kublai Khan for 18 years before finally returning to Venice, after 24 years away.*

HEROES AND VILLAINS

National heroes are often fighters – people who saved their country from powerful enemies. William Tell gained heroic status in Switzerland for fighting the Austrians, as did Joan of Arc in France for defeating the English. Another kind of hero is someone who risks their own life to save others. Sometimes the distinction between a hero and a villain is blurred. Ned Kelly, for example, was Australia's most notorious outlaw, but he became a folk hero, like the legendary Robin Hood.

▲ *Lenin (left) became leader of Russia's new Communist government in 1917, after the Revolution. When he died in 1924, he was regarded in Russia as a hero. His successor, Josef Stalin (right), ruled until 1953 as a ruthless dictator, sending millions of people to jail, exile or death.*

▲ *Mohandas K Gandhi (1869–1948), known as the Mahatma ('Great Soul'), led India's struggle for independence from British rule. He always urged non-violence, even when being attacked.*

▼ *One of Scotland's national heroes is William Wallace, the 'Braveheart' of legend. He led his men in battles against the English army of King Edward I, but was eventually captured and put to death in 1305.*

▲ *George Washington (1732–99) is a national hero in America for his generalship in the Revolutionary War, and his wisdom as first president of the United States.*

▲ Argentina's Che Guevara was a Communist who helped Fidel Castro's revolution in Cuba (1959). He tried to start revolutions in Africa and South America. Killed in Bolivia in 1967, he was 'immortalized' on posters.

» NATIONAL HEROES	
Joan of Arc	France
George Washington	United States
Simon Bolivar	Bolivia
Giuseppe Garibaldi	Italy
Nelson Mandela	South Africa
Martin Luther King	United States
Mahatma Gandhi	India
Horatio Nelson	Britain
William Tell	Switzerland
William Wallace	Scotland

▲ American gang-boss Al Capone (1898–1947), one of the worst criminals of the 20th century, controlled a violent crime empire from 1925 to 1931. He was 'Public Enemy No.1', accused of at least 300 murders, but never convicted. Capone was finally jailed for eight years, for not paying his taxes.

◄ The 'mad monk' Grigori Rasputin (1871–1916) gained a strange power over Russia's last emperor, Tsar Nicholas II, and Empress Alexandra, who thought him a holy man. But Rasputin led a corrupt life, meddled in politics, and was murdered by Russian noblemen.

► Adolf Hitler (1889–1945) was the worst villain of the 20th century. He ruled Germany from 1933 as leader of the Nazi Party, and planned to take over most of Europe. His schemes led to World War II and the Holocaust – the deaths of over 6 million Jews and other people in concentration camps. Facing defeat, Hitler killed himself in 1945.

▲ An English hero, possibly based on fact, is the outlaw archer Robin Hood of old English stories. With a band of outlaws from Sherwood Forest (including Friar Tuck and Little John, shown here) he helped the poor against King John and his tax collectors.

REFORMERS AND REVOLUTIONARIES

Throughout history, people have fought to change bad laws or to help the weak, sick or underprivileged. Great religious reformers included Martin Luther, a German monk who helped start the Reformation or Protestant movement in the 1500s. In the 1700s and 1800s there were many social reformers who sought to modernize nursing, bring an end to child-labour and make prisons more humane. Some reformers tried to change the structure of society, such as Karl Marx, whose writings inspired the Communist revolutions in Russia, China and Cuba in the 20th century.

▲ *This painting shows American colonial leaders signing the Declaration of Independence on July 4, 1776. The historic document states that all men are created equal. It created a new nation, the United States of America.*

▶ *Fidel Castro, a Cuban lawyer, led a Communist uprising that overthrew the government of Cuba in 1959. Castro turned the island of Cuba into a Communist state, and for the rest of the 20th century he defied all America's attempts to unseat him from power. Castro remained an old-style Communist, surviving even the collapse of communism in Russia, which had backed him for years.*

▲ *From the 1800s, more and more women demanded the same rights as men. In Britain the 'suffragettes' were led by Emmeline Pankhurst (1858–1928) and her daughters. Women chained themselves to railings as part of their campaign for the vote ('suffrage').*

▶▶ FIGHTERS FOR THEIR FAITH

Saint Boniface	about 675–754	English missionary to Germany, killed by pagans
Saint Francis of Assisi	1182–1226	Gave up worldly comforts to preach in poverty
Dietrich Bonhoeffer	1906–45	German churchman who opposed the Nazis and was executed
Martin Luther King Jr	1929–68	American Civil Rights leader who was murdered
Janani Luwum	1922–77	Ugandan churchman, killed for opposing the tyrant Idi Amin
Oscar Romero	1917–80	Archbishop of El Salvador, killed for speaking against the government

19TH-CENTURY REFORMERS

- Johann Pestalozzi and Thomas Barnardo cared for orphaned and homeless children.
- John Howard and Elizabeth Fry improved conditions in prisons.
- Henri Dunant founded the Red Cross in 1864.
- Elizabeth Garret Anderson was Britain's first woman doctor in 1875.
- Harriet Tubman and Booker T Washington fought for black Civil Rights.

▲ *Harriet Tubman (1820–1913), a slave in the American South, guided many black slaves to freedom in the North, and later started schools for black people.*

▼ *The Russian Revolution of 1917 grew out of protests by the Russian people against poverty and backwardness, a weak tsar (emperor) and defeats in World War I. The government collapsed, troops and workers took to the streets, and a Communist group called the Bolsheviks, led by Lenin, seized power. The Communist 'Soviet Union' lasted until 1991.*

▲ *Karl Marx (1818–83) was a German thinker and writer who founded communism. He and his friend Friedrich Engels called on factory workers to seize factories and overthrow the rich.*

▲ *In 1949, led by Mao Zedong, Chinese Communists founded the People's Republic of China. Mao encouraged a violent 'Cultural Revolution' in the 1960s against all things traditional.*

⟫	REMARKABLE REVOLUTIONS
1922	Sultan of Turkey overthrown; Turkey becomes a republic in 1923
1966	'Cultural Revolution' in China; Mao tries to destroy tradition and learning
1979	Islamic revolution in Iran; Ayatollah Khomeini overthrows the *shah* (emperor)
1989	Collapse of communism in Western Europe, with break-up of the USSR in 1991
1990	Nelson Mandela freed from prison; elected president of South Africa in 1994

POWERFUL WOMEN

Queen Hatshepsut of Egypt (about 1500 BC) was probably the earliest really powerful woman ruler. When she took over from her husband and son, she wore royal robes and a false beard, like a male pharaoh (king)! Later, Cleopatra ruled Egypt, but lost it to Rome. Another anti-Roman woman ruler was Boudicca, who led a British revolt against the Romans in AD 60. Some women rulers gained power through marriage, but England's formidable Queen Elizabeth I ruled alone. Catherine the Great, empress of Russia in the 1700s, ruled a huge empire, but Queen Victoria's was bigger, though she had less power.

◄ *Almost all of Egypt's rulers were men. The exception was Queen Hatshepsut. First she ruled with her husband, but after he died she had herself crowned as pharaoh and ruled alone from 1503 to 1482 BC. Hatshepsut famously sent a fleet of ships on an expedition to the Red Sea. The fleet returned with many wonderful gifts and wild animals.*

▼ *Queen Cleopatra of Egypt (69–30 BC) was the lover of Julius Caesar and then Mark Antony. Antony turned his back on Rome to be with her, but was defeated in battle by Augustus. After he killed himself, Cleopatra took poison.*

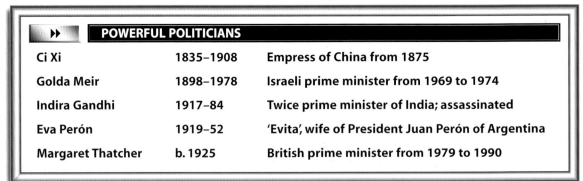

►► POWERFUL POLITICIANS		
Ci Xi	1835–1908	Empress of China from 1875
Golda Meir	1898–1978	Israeli prime minister from 1969 to 1974
Indira Gandhi	1917–84	Twice prime minister of India; assassinated
Eva Perón	1919–52	'Evita', wife of President Juan Perón of Argentina
Margaret Thatcher	b. 1925	British prime minister from 1979 to 1990

▼ *Elizabeth I of England gave her name to the Elizabethan age – the age of playwright William Shakespeare and explorer Sir Francis Drake. During her reign (1558–1603) England became strong and prosperous. Elizabeth never married, for fear of handing control of her country to a man.*

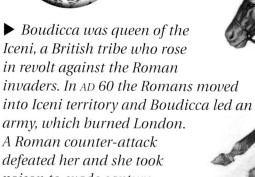

◀ *During the 1900s, Queen Victoria was head of the British Empire, the largest empire in the world at the time. She reigned for over 60 years, and her name was known in almost every country on Earth. She worked closely with her husband, Albert, who died in 1861.*

▶ *Roman Catholic nun Mother Teresa (born Agnes Gonxha Bojaxhiu in Macedonia in 1910) was admired for her tireless medical and missionary work among the poor of Calcutta in India. She died in 1997.*

▶ *Boudicca was queen of the Iceni, a British tribe who rose in revolt against the Roman invaders. In AD 60 the Romans moved into Iceni territory and Boudicca led an army, which burned London. A Roman counter-attack defeated her and she took poison to evade capture.*

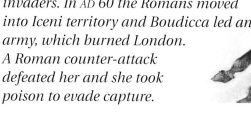

REMARKABLE QUEENS		
Cleopatra of Egypt	69–30 BC	Lover of two famous Romans, Julius Caesar and Mark Antony
Eleanor of Aquitaine	1122–1204	Wife of Henry II of England, mother of kings Richard I and John
Elizabeth I of England	1533–1603	Ruled alone, refusing to marry, and defied the might of Spain
Marie Antoinette of France	1755–93	Wife of King Louis XVI, guillotined during the French Revolution
Victoria of Great Britain	1819–1901	Queen from age 18 until her death in 1901

◀ *Eva Perón (1919–52) was a powerful figure in Argentina, where she became known as 'Evita'. She was the politically active wife of President Juan Perón, elected in 1946, and worked alongside him until her death.*

▶ *Lady Diana Spencer's marriage (1981–96) to the Prince of Wales made her an international celebrity. As the self-styled 'People's Princess', she devoted herself to causes such as AIDS charities and banning landmines. Diana died in a car crash in 1997.*

MYSTERIES FROM HISTORY

Was England's King Richard III really a murderer? Did he order someone to kill his dead brother's two young sons in 1483, so he could take the throne himself? The fate of the 'Princes in the Tower' is just one of many tantalising mysteries from history. We may never know the answers to some of the riddles. But sometimes science solves a puzzle. Ever since the Russian Revolution of 1917, people have wondered whether all the daughters of the last tsar of Russia were murdered in July 1918, or whether one of the princesses escaped. In the 1990s, scientific tests on human remains proved that all were killed, solving just one of many mysteries.

▲ *The Russian royal family was murdered by Bolshevik communists in July 1918. The fate of Tsar Nicholas II, his wife Alexandra, and their children remained shrouded in mystery for years, until their remains were discovered and identified by DNA testing. They were given an official funeral in St Petersburg in 1998.*

◀ *Who reached the North Pole first? Robert Peary claimed to have got there in 1909. His claim was challenged by another American, Frederick Cook, who said he got to the Pole a year earlier. Possibly neither did, because of navigation errors, but modern research suggests Peary got close to the Pole.*

AUSTRALIA

▲ *Australia was unknown to Europeans before 1606, although the Aborigines had lived there for at least 50,000 years. However, sailors may have sighted 'Terra Australis Incognita' (Unknown Southland) 100 years earlier, because a mysterious landmass like it is shown on maps from the 1540s.*

» Most suspected royal murder: 'Princes in the Tower' » Most mysterious prisoner: man in the iron mask

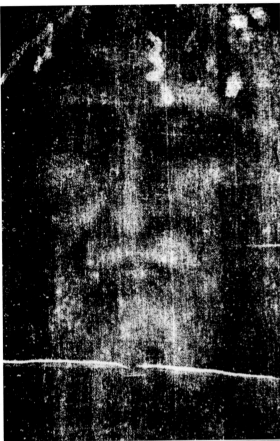

▶ *England's King Richard III (1483–85) is often blamed for the murder of his brother's two sons, but the case has never been proved. The elder boy was next in line to the throne after the death of his father, Edward IV. Richard kept the boys locked in the Tower of London for 'protection'. But neither boy was seen after 1483. Two skeletons were found in 1674.*

▼ *In 1872 the* Mary Celeste *left New York Harbor with ten people on board. A month later, a British ship crossing the Atlantic Ocean found the* Mary Celeste *drifting. When sailors went aboard, they discovered breakfast laid on the table and valuables still in the safe, but nobody there. No-one knows how or why all ten people disappeared.*

▲ *The Turin Shroud is a linen cloth, kept in Turin Cathedral in Italy. It appears to bear an image of a crucified man, seen most clearly in photographs. Some people believe it to be the burial cloth of Jesus. Others say it is a clever forgery. Scientific tests have cast doubt on the cloth's age, suggesting it dates from the 1300s, but the mystery remains unsolved.*

◀ *Atlantis was a legendary ancient island, said to have sunk beneath the ocean. The island of Thera, now called Santorini, in Greece, was destroyed about 3,500 years ago by a volcanic eruption and tidal wave. Maybe Thera, with its rich Minoan (Cretan) civilization, was Atlantis. The Greek philosopher Plato wrote that Atlantis was drowned because its people were wicked.*

INDEX

Entries in bold refer to illustrations

The publishers wish to thank the following artists who have contributed to this book:

Julie Banyard, Andy Beckett, C.M. Buzer/Studio Gallante, Martin Camm, Vanessa Card, Jim Channell, Kuo Kang Chen, Peter Dennis, Nicholas Forder, Mike Foster, John Francis, Terry Gabbey, Luigi Gallante/Studio Gallante, Jeremy Gower, Peter Gregory, Alan Hancocks, Gary Hincks, Richard Hook, Rob Jakeway, John James, Stuart Lafford, Andy Lloyd-Jones, Mick Loates, Alan Male, Kevin Maddison, Janos Marffy, Terry Riley, Eric Robson, Martin Sanders, Peter Sarson, Mike Saunders, Rob Sheffield, Guy Smith, Roger Smith, Roger Stewart, Mike Taylor (SGA), Rudi Vizi, Christian Webb, Mike White/Temple Rogers, John Woodcock

The publishers wish to thank the following sources for the photographs used in this book:

CORBIS: Page 27 (T/R) Roger Ressmeyyer; Page 32 (L); Page 33 (T/L) NASA; Page 49 (B/R) Marc Garanger; Page 49 (R) Shai Ginott; Page 51 (B/R) Ralph A. Clevenger; Page 52 (B/L) Craig Lovell; Page 54 (R) David Muench; Page 58 (T/R) Charles O'Rear; Page 72 (C/L) John Holmes; Frank Lane Picture Agency; Page 79 (T/L) Philip Richardson; Gallo Images; Page 80 (B/L) Philip Richardson; Gallo Images; Page 85 (B/R) Paul A. Souders; Page 90 (B/R) Paul A. Souders; Page 100 (C/L) Bettmann; Page 102 (C) Bettmann; Page 102 (T/R) Owen Franken; Page 105 (T/L) Bettmann; Page 113 (B/R) Yogi, Inc.; Page 113 (C) Dean Conger; Page 115 (C/L) Charles E. Rotkin; Page 115 (B/R) John Dakers; Eye Ubiquitous; Page 116 (C) Darren Maybury; Eye Ubiquitous; Page 117 (B/R) Roger Garwood & Trish Ainslie; Page 119 (B) Wolfgang Kaehler; Page 122 (B) Josef Scaylea; Page 124 (C/R) Papilio; Page 125 (T); Page 127 (C) Underwood & Underwood; Page 127 (C/R) Museum of Flight; Page 127 (B/L) Reuters NewMedia Inc.; Page 130 (B/R) Reuters NewMedia Inc.; Page 131 (C) Kelly-Mooney Photography; Page 131 (B/L) Ali Meyer; Page 132 (B/L) Jerry Cooke; Page 133 (B/L) Christian Liewig; Temp Sport; Page 134 (B/R) Bettmann; Page 135 (B/L) Mike King; Page 136 (T) Raymond Gehman; Page 138 (T/L) Wally McNamee; Page 139 (B/R) Reuters NewMedia Inc.; Page 143 (B) Richard Hamilton Smith; Page 144 (B/R) Reuters NewMedia Inc.; Page 145 (T/L) S.I.N.; Page 145 (B/L) Bettmann; Page 145 (R) Henry Diltz; Page 147 (C/L) Roger Wood; Page 147 (B/L) Reuters NewMedia Inc.; Page 149 (C/L) Roger Ressmeyer; Page 149 (T/R) Bettmann; Page 150 (L) Hulton-Deutsch Collection; Page 150 (B/R) Hulton-Deutsch Collection; Page 150 (T/R) Bettmann; Page 151 (T/L) Barry Lewis; Page 151 (C/L) Earl & Nazima Kowall; Page 151 (C) Laura Dwight; Page 151 (R) Neal Preston; Page 152 (B/L) Bettmann; Page 152 (B/R) Reuters NewMedia Inc.; Page 154 (T/R) Historical Picture Archive; Page 154 (B) Morton Beebe, S.F.; Page 155 (T/L) Pawel Libera; Page 156 (C/L) Franz-Marc Frei; Page 156 (B) Reuters NewMedia Inc.; Page 157 (C/L) Mitchell Gerber; Page 157 (C/R)Bettmann; Page 157 (B/R) AFP; Page 162 (R) Philip Gould; Page 167 (C) The Purcell Team; Page 168 (B) Arvind Garg; Page 173 (T/L) Bettmann; Page 175 (R) Gianni Dagli Orti; Page 176 (C) Angelo Hornak; Page 177 (B) Michael S. Yamashita; Page 178 (L) Vince Streano; Page 179 B/R) Nick Hawkes; Ecoscene; Page 180 (C) Robert Holmes; Page 181 (B/L) Kevin Cozad; Page 182 (B) The Purcell Team; Page 182 (R/C) Martin Jones; Page 183 (B/R) Angelo Hornak; Page 184 Ed Kashi; Page 185 (T/R) Bettmann; Page 185 (T/C) Bettmann; Page 186 Robert Pickett; Page 197 (T/L) Cordaiy Photo Library Ltd; Page 197 (C) Layne Kennedy; Page 211 (B/L) Brian Vikander; Page 236 (B/R) Bettmann; Page 238 (T/R) Bettmann; Page 239 (B/L) Bettmann; Page 245 (B/R) Photo B.D.V; Page 247 (T/L) David Lees

Creative Imprints: Page 138 (B); Klaus G. Hinkelmann: Page 24 (T/R); **www.legomindstorms.com** Page 111 (B/R); Page 137 (B/L)

All other photographs from Miles Kelly Archives and NASA